CONCRETE CITY

IJURR-SUSC Published Titles

CONCRETE CITY

Material Flows and Urbanization in West Africa

ARMELLE CHOPLIN

STUDIES IN URBAN AND SOCIAL CHANGE BOOK SERIES

To the memory of my colleague and friend
Matthieu Giroud
(† Bataclan, Paris, 13.11.2015)

Contents

List of Figures

Series Editors' Preface

IJURR Studies in Urban and Social Change
Book Series

The International Journal of Urban and Regional Research (IJURR) Studies in Urban and Social Change Book Series shares IJURR's commitments to critical, global, and politically relevant analyses of our urban worlds. Books in this series bring forward innovative theoretical approaches and present rigorous empirical work, deepening understandings of urbanization processes, but also advancing critical insights in support of political action and change. The book series editors appreciate the theoretically eclectic nature of the field of urban studies. It is a strength that we embrace and encourage. The editors are particularly interested in the following issues:

- Comparative urbanism
- Diversity, difference, and neighborhood change
- Environmental sustainability
- Financialization and gentrification
- Governance and politics
- International migration
- Inequalities
- Urban and environmental movements

The series is explicitly interdisciplinary; the editors judge books by their contribution to the field of critical urban studies rather than according to disciplinary origin. We are committed to publishing studies with themes and formats that reflect the many different voices and practices in the field of urban studies. Proposals may be submitted to editor-in-chief, Walter Nicholls (wnicholl@uci.edu), and further information about the series can be found at www.ijurr.org.

Walter Nicholls
Manuel Aalbers
Talja Blokland
Dorothee Brantz
Patrick Le Galès
Jenny Robinson

Acknowledgements

In July 2016, I first set foot in Cotonou, Benin, where I had just been accepted as a researcher at the French Institute for Research on Sustainable Development (IRD – Institut de Recherche pour le Développement) for three years. At that time, I did not know Cotonou and I was not very familiar with the Gulf of Guinea, as my research had previously focused on cities located further north, in the Sahara and the Sahel. As I circulated regularly along the Abidjan-Lagos axis, I quickly realized what it meant to be in the heart of one of the largest urban concentrations in the world. I was living in downtown Cotonou, but at the same time in the suburbs of Lagos, 125 km away. Somewhat naively, I set the goal of understanding how the urban takes shape in this corridor and I decided to start with what gives shape, color, and continuity to it: cement transformed into concrete. In order to capture this city-making, I followed for nearly three years the bags of cement and the progression of concrete constructions along the corridor. This journey into the concrete cities was made possible by certain people to whom I am indebted and whom I would like to thank warmly.

In Cotonou, I have benefited from the support of researchers who introduced me to the contemporary urban dynamics of the Gulf of Guinea. I would like to thank the IRD researchers, and in particular Jérôme Lombard, Florent Engelmann, Jean-Philippe Chippaux, and Gauthier Dobigny, as well as the University of Abomey Calavi, which warmly welcomed me in the Department of Geography and the LEDUR (Laboratoire d'Études des Dynamiques Urbaines et Régionales). I would like to thank my Beninese colleagues for their support and valuable insights: Toussaint Vigninou, Benjamin Allagbe, David Baloubi, Messan Lihoussou, Moussa Djibigaye, Antoine Tohozin, and the late Gisèle Glélé.

This research is the fruit of a collective work carried out with a number of collaborators from Benin, Togo, Ghana, and Nigeria who helped me to explore the multiple lives of cement and concrete along the corridor between Accra and Lagos. I would like to express my sincere thanks to Martin Lozivit, geographer and IRD research assistant, who accompanied me in this work producing maps, images, and interviews, and providing constant logistical and scientific support. I would like to thank Sam Agbadonou and Saliou Abdou of OpenStreetMap, Médard Agbayazon of Blolab, and Georges Gnolonfon the chief of the community of Ladji. I am infinitely grateful to all those who helped me to follow the flows of concrete and with whom I learned so much: the students and PhD students – Olivier Ahounto, Hugh Dato, Alice Hertzog, Prince Kpadenou, Nicolas Le Borgne, Ayité Mawussi, Névine Pourcines, Mélanie Rateau, Federico Rogai, Abel Tichidime; the guides and interpreters – Boniface Ahoussovou, Marie-Auxiliatrice Da Silveira, Edmond Hadjagoun, Amandine Yehouetome. I warmly thank all those who agreed to tell me about cement and concrete and whose testimonies feed this text: from the directors of the cement factories to the city dwellers who build their houses, not forgetting the dealers, transporters, and bricklayers. All of them have fueled this research with numerous discussions.

In Benin, Togo, Ghana, and Nigeria, several colleagues guided me in my fieldwork and my readings and invited me to present the results of my research: Moïse Chabi and John Igué at the LARES in Cotonou, Cyprien Aholou, the colleagues from EAMAU and Giorgio Blundo in Lomé, George Owusu at the University of Legon in Accra, Émilie Guitard, Alain Kassanda, Elodie Appard, Ismael Mazaz in Ibadan in Nigeria.

My presence in the field was an opportunity to collaborate with a number of institutions and individuals whom I would like to thank: the Agence Française de Développement; the French Institutes and French Ambassies (SCAC) in Benin, Togo, Nigeria, and Ghana; the Institut Français de Recherche en Afrique (IFRA) in Ibadan; the Swiss Agency for Development and Cooperation (SDC); the Ateliers de Cergy; Marie-Cécile Zinsou and the Fondation Zinsou; Gérard Bassalé and the Centre Ouadada; the Groupe Huit; Urbaplan, UrbaMonde, UrbaSen.

This urban exploration is also nourished by the passionate discussions I have had with colleagues and friends from all over the world. First and foremost, I would like to thank Sylvy Jaglin who guided me with enthusiasm and rigor. She has been encouraging me for years: my debt to her is enormous. I would like to thank also Olivier Pliez with whom I have written so much and whose thoughts have very often nourished mine.

In Paris, I have benefited from many intellectual conversations with my colleagues at the Université Gustave Eiffel, the École d'Urbanisme de Paris, the JEDI group (Justice Environment Discrimination and Inequalities), especially with Matthieu Delage, Martine Drozdz, Claire Hancock, Claire Simonneau, Elsa Vivant, Serge Weber.

At the University of Geneva, I am fortunate indeed for the presence of so many smart and creative colleagues. For their helpful comments, I would like to thank: Sandrine Billeau, André Chapatte, Bernard Debarbieux, Julie De Dardel, Nicola Cantoreggi, Karine Duplan, Irène Hirt, Raphaël Languillon, Laurent Matthey, Didier Péclard, Stéphanie Perazzone, Pascal Peduzzi, Marlyne Sahakian, and Estelle Sohier.

While writing this book, I was immensely lucky to work closely with marvelous PhD and postdoctoral students: Dolorès Bertrais (whom I thank for the fantastic drawings that accompany the text), Hélène Blaszkiewicz, Higor Carvalho, Alice Guilbert, Romain Leclercq, Hervé Roquet, Juliette Reflé, Alexis Sebarenzi. Many chapters and ideas bear the traces of our daily discussions.

I am particularly grateful to colleagues and friends who contributed central elements, thoughtful comments, and questions: Julie Archambaud, Agnès Bastin, Jean-François Bayart, Rémi de Bercegol, Élise Bérodier, Carla Bertin, Monique Bertrand, Bérénice Bon, Delphine Bousquet, Julien Brachet, Sylvie Bredeloup, Victor Brunfaut, Monica Coralli, Saskia Cousin, Doudou Deme, Éric Denis, Marco Di Nunzio, Alain Dubresson, Mathieu Duperrex, Gabriel Fauveaud, Joost Fontein, Thomas Fouquet, Philippe Gervais-Lambony, Cynthia Ghorra-Gobin, Katherine Gough, Robin Gra, Pauline Guinard, Guillaume Habert, Romuald Hazoumé, †Mathieu Hilgers, Ivan Jablonka, Sénamé Koffi Agbodjinou, Jean-Baptiste Lanne, Philippe Lavigne Delville, Céline Lesourd, Michel Lussault, Garth Myers, Benjamin Michelon, Olivier Moles, Marianne Morange, David Morton, Joël Noret, Francesca Pilo', Denise Pumain, Dagna Rams, Marie Redon, Pierre Rosanvallon, Christian Schmid, Camille Schmoll, Philippe Simay, Sara Tassi, Yann-Philippe Tastevin, Amandine Spire, Constance Smith, Odile Vandermeeren, Éric Verdeil, Olivier Walther, Marie-Hélène Zérah.

Because of – or perhaps thanks to – the COVID-19 period, I had the opportunity to give many digital presentations of the French version of the book across Europe and Africa. I benefited enormously from the patience, intelligence, and generosity of many (non) academic audiences. I have received many constructive critical comments and suggestions which helped me to improve the English version.

I am deeply grateful to Jennifer Robinson, Ola Söderström, Laurent Fourchard for their ongoing support. Each of them encouraged me and helped me to publish the book in English. Their multiple comments and valuable advice have largely guided my reflection.

I would like to warmly thank Walter Nicholls, the Chief editor of the IJURR SUSC series and Jacqueline Scott and the board for being very supportive. This English version was made possible thanks to the Director of MētisPresses, Franco Paracchini, and thanks to the financial support of the University of Geneva. The manuscript was first translated by John Crisp, and then edited and proofread by James Christopher Mizes, whom I thank for his suggestions and careful editorial work.

I thank my parents, my brother, my family, and my friends for their great support.

Finally, I deeply thank Riccardo Ciavolella, my partner, colleague, and friend who accompanied me in this journey into the world of concrete. These pages are fueled by our daily discussions and common discoveries. Thanks to you and to our sons, Leo and Romeo, for the beautiful cabins we build with concrete, wood or pure imagination every place we go.

Introduction
Concrete and the City

A Gray Matter

"Those youngsters over there are on strike because they want to be allowed to retake their exams," explained one professor at Benin's largest university, the University of Abomey-Calavi. "They want to start a revolution but they know nothing about life. They do not even know the price of a bag of cement". In 2016, I had just arrived in Benin to begin three years of field research in West Africa, and the social meaning of concrete was already becoming apparent. A few short weeks later, colleagues at the university asked me to contribute to a group gift for the retirement of an eminent professor: "We're offering him two tons of cement," they told me, "it's a mark of prestige and respect".

In West Africa, concrete – a mix of cement, sand, gravel, and water – is increasingly taking hold in physical landscapes, popular consciousness, and everyday conversations across the region. Concrete's presence is first of all physical: roads are lined with an infinite stream of cement warehouses and hardware stores where you can buy bags of cement and breeze blocks, as well as gravel, sand, reinforcing steel, and corrugated iron. Concrete is economically important: its price per ton is chalked up everyday on shop fronts, like prices on a stock exchange (Figure I.1). Concrete is also socially significant: it has come to symbolize success, wealth, and modernity. In the streets of the region's metropolises, lotteries promise prizes of plots of land and tons of cement (Figure I.2). In Lagos, a 12-year-old boy told me that he would like to become rich and famous, but he was unsure if the best way to realize his dreams was to become a Champions League footballer, like Samuel Eto'o, or a cement maker, like Aliko Dangote, the wealthiest African man in the world.

Concrete City: Material Flows and Urbanization in West Africa, First Edition. Armelle Choplin.
© 2023 John Wiley & Sons Ltd. Published 2023 by John Wiley & Sons Ltd.

FIGURE I.1   Price of cement, Cotonou 2018. Source: A. Choplin.

In this part of Africa, a sea of concrete is quickly swallowing up formerly verdant landscapes. The pervasive gray color of concrete is a reminder that cities are permanent building sites and that West African cities, in particular, are constantly under construction. Concrete is ubiquitous: both in the city centers where cranes build modern skyscrapers and in the distant suburbs where poor households incrementally construct their homes. Day and night, building seems to be the dominant activity. It is frenetical. On one plot of land, bags of cement wait, breeze blocks stand drying in the sun. On another plot, steel reinforcing bars point toward the sky, announcing the addition of another story to a growing building already reaching high into the sky. On yet another, men mix cement, water, gravel, and sand to give birth to concrete. The result is a cold and mineral landscape. Yet this landscape is also human and alive. Because behind this inert material, there is life: the lives of powerful decision-makers and lobbyists who have established their careers

FIGURE I.2 Twelve plots and 150 tons of cement to be won, MTN lottery, Cotonou 2017. Source: A. Choplin.

through concrete, as well as the lives of a handful of ultrarich and millions of poor residents. Everyone is linked to this 'stuff' of great banality. Concrete embodies the hopes and dreams of men and women seeking to shelter their loved ones, while it also allows the wealthy to exploit natural landscapes and resources – they dig holes to extract sand, gravel, and limestone to make the concrete needed to build luxurious high-rise towers. People are digging deep and building high, creating a new topography of West Africa's world of concrete – extraction, construction, distribution, destruction, and the flows of material in-between. Excavators, concrete mixers, trucks, cranes, and bulldozers: these are the machines of concrete cities which are merging into each other to create today's urban corridor in West Africa.

Age of Concrete

Age of Concrete

At that time, huts were transformed into villas in a glory of concrete, whereas with the annihilation of economic production came the reign of the city.

                                                            Patrick Chamoiseau (1992), *Texaco*.

In the novel *Texaco*, the Martinican novelist Patrick Chamoiseau (1992) recounts the saga of a poor Creole family in the titular shantytown of Texaco in Fort-de-France (Martinique). Chamoiseau divides the story into four periods which correspond to the various stages of the emergence of the shantytown: Age of Straw, Age of Crate Wood, Age of Asbestos, and Age of Concrete. The novel ends in the 1980s along with the Age of Concrete. But, if the story had continued, would Texaco have another material era after concrete? Forty years later, it seems that the Age of Concrete has not ended but has instead relocated across the Atlantic – today, West Africa has arrived in its own age of concrete.

Archaeologists have summarized human trajectory in terms of material eras, like the Stone Age and the Bronze Age. And scientists have similarly named the planet's present geological era the Anthropocene. But could the world's material era also be defined today as the Concrete Age? How has concrete contributed to this new period of geologic time? As successive waves of concretization have concatenated over time, concrete has come to place a heavy carbon footprint on the contemporary world. Concrete was invented 150 years ago. Or "reinvented" to be more precise, as the material has multiple origins, all linked to the history of cement: at the beginning of the nineteenth century, the English clergyman James Parker invented "Roman cement," a fast-setting hydraulic lime. Following him, in 1824, Joseph Aspdin, a builder in Leeds in England, filed a new patent for a method of making a cement he coined "Portland cement." At the same time in France, Louis Vicat discovered in 1818 the principle of the hydraulicity of lime, the property of hardening with water, which would lead to the development of Portland cements in the 1860s. Since that time, the term *Portland cement* has referred to all hydraulic cements used to make concrete (Simonnet 2005; Courland 2011). One century later, in the 1920s, the Bauhaus School introduced concrete into construction as part of the rationalist and functionalist movements, which subsequently influenced architects like Auguste Perret and Le Corbusier (Forty 2012). Reinforced concrete underpinned the period of reconstruction and mass urbanization following the Second World War, and this turn toward concrete had the further effect of standardizing and simplifying an increasingly global construction industry. The historian Adrian Forty recalls that concrete was, at the time, associated with socialist and communist ideology and was therefore widely considered left-wing (Forty 2012: 150). During the 30 years of economic growth that followed the war, many considered concrete a noble and modern material. Le Corbusier – and the brutalist movement more generally – contributed to the glorification of concrete in the 1960s (Calder 2016), and today starchitects such as Rudy Ricciotti (2020) are advancing similar sentiments. Concrete has the power to transform substances of different kinds – 1 m³ of concrete is the result of clever dosages of water (150 l), sand (700 kg), chippings (1,200 kg), and cement (300 kg) – into a single, highly malleable material, which can be used to model spectacular shapes, buildings, infrastructures, and the city itself in record time. This technological feat has fascinated for decades: it solidifies in 2 hours without any energy input. This metamorphosis of a natural stone into an artificial stone and a quasi-living material appears, as Taussig notes (2004: 162), almost magical:

> You start with stone. You make a powder. And then in the process of building, you add water and end up with a new form of 'stone' in accord with the shape desired. It sounds like magic but we call it technology.

Concrete has become widespread across time and space to become the "world's most common man-made material" (Courland 2011). After water, it is the most widely used substance on earth (Watts 2019). In the space of one century, concrete has become an ordinary, normal, and global product. Ordinary, because nearly everyone uses it or wants to use it to meet a common human need: shelter. Normal, because its use has spread to the point that it is taken for granted, as if it was the only possible construction material for building cities, housing, and infrastructure. Global, because it is now a commodity that is sold and consumed in every country in the world. With its consumption soaring tenfold over the last 65 years (Habert et al. 2020: 559), this material is the earth's most widely manufactured product in terms of volume, ahead of plastics or steel, with 4.5 billion tons produced each year (Van Damme 2018). As a consequence, the consumption of sand and gravel has increased fivefold in the past 10 years. In his essay on concrete, David Harvey (2016) writes about concrete consumption in China, where a third of the national economy depends on construction: since 2003, it has used more concrete in every 3 years than the United States in the whole of the twentieth century. Demand is growing, both in the emerging countries that need to build houses, roads, bridges, and dams to meet the needs of millions of individuals, and in the long-industrialized countries that need to maintain aging infrastructures (Van Damme 2018). And the World Bank views concrete as an irreplaceable material for building fast, high, and cheaply to keep up with the world's demographic and urban growth (The World Bank Group 2016).

However, the consensus that has long existed around concrete is currently being challenged. As one critical commentator put it, concrete is "the most destructive material on Earth" (Watts 2019). The cement industry is the source of an estimated 8% of the world's greenhouse gas emissions (IPCC 2022), 80% of which are caused by the burning of fuel and the release of carbon from limestone in cement plants (Habert et al. 2020: 562). The durability of concrete has also been put into question. In August of 2018, for example, the collapse of the bridge in Genoa (Italy) incited a reassessment of concrete's lifespan which is now recognized as limited to 50–70 years (Forty 2012; Jappe 2020). As a result, concrete has come to seem "both a friend and a traitor to the modern project" (Simonetti and Ingold 2018). Controversies are growing around concrete since it is a core element of "planetary urbanization" (Brenner and Schmid 2015): the city itself has, in many places, become a Concrete City. This book aims to unpack the links between concrete and the city. It examines the centrality of this material in the production of the urban through an analysis of those who build, govern, and inhabit the Concrete City. I focus in particular on West Africa as cement's new urban frontier.

Africa Rising and Cement's New Frontier

In 2022, Knight Frank, the global real estate and property consultancy, published the *Africa Report 2022/2023 – Knight Frank's ultimate guide to the real estate market performance and opportunities in the world's most exciting continent.* (Knight Frank 2022). In this report, Knight Frank highlighted the urban growth hotspots in which to invest (Lagos, Abidjan, Addis-Ababa) and ranked cities according to prime office yield opportunities and backlogs of affordable housing. This mapping of "Real estate investment opportunities" comes 10 years after McKinsey Global Institute (2010) published a report on the economic potential of Africa. The report describes African countries as "lions on the move," a new variation on the older idea of "Asian tigers" (Pitcher 2012). Since then, media and investors have regularly described Africa as both a "rising" and "emerging" continent. From this perspective, African growth is plural: a demographic growth rate of 5% or 1.4 billion individuals; double-digit economic growth and fast rising foreign direct investment; the fastest urban growth in the world with 50% of Africans expected to live in cities by 2030 (OECD/UNECA/AfDB 2022). International financial institutions and experts frequently represent Africa as the "last frontier of capitalism" (Moghalu 2013; Mbembe 2015). Although the rising of Africa is a strongly criticized narrative and has yet to be demonstrated (Beresford 2016), African cities are often perceived as the "last frontier" of capitalist development (Watson 2014). Consequently, Africa's vigorous economic growth is driving a construction boom (Di Nunzio 2019; Mains 2019), and this urban boom is, in turn, rendering the continent as "the last great cement frontier" (White 2015).

Europeans are financing this urban boom, similarly joined by Chinese, Indian, and Turkish investors. New cities are springing out of the earth, and with them new hopes of economic emergence: Eko Atlantic City in Lagos, Konza City in Nairobi, Kilamba in Luanda, or Diamniadio in Dakar (Watson 2014; Van Noorloos and Kloosterboer 2018; Côté-Roy and Moser 2019). Over the course of the COVID-19 pandemic, the construction industry emerged as one of the few sectors that did not collapse and, instead, its growth rates are even positive. Similar findings can be made for the cement industry: In Nigeria, the cement company Dangote saw a 45% year-on-year increase in revenue in the first semester of 2021 as its cement sales volumes rose by 26%. Today, concrete underpins these narratives on "Africa Rising" which celebrate African global capitalism, the financialization of economies, and elite accumulation (Côté-Roy and Moser 2019; Péclard et al. 2020; Choplin 2020a, b; Mizes and Donovan 2022).

The extraordinarily low cost of concrete – it is the cheapest of all building materials–has made possible its massive diffusion in the Global South. In Africa, the rise in cement production and consumption dates to the beginning of the 2000s, with the opening of numerous integrated cement plants (Schmidt et al. 2020). This once-scarce material was formerly imported and was restricted to colonists and local elites. In the 1960s, reinforced concrete structures became showcases of the "architecture of independence" and "African modernism" (Herz et al. 2015; Hoffman 2017). Concrete has been the privileged material of development, and cement consumption is now used as an index of development, often compared to Gross Domestic Product (Byiers et al. 2017). The world per capita average for concrete consumption stands at around 500 kg a year. A country that has reached urban maturity and completed its urban transition would average around 400 kg per capita (White 2015; Byiers et al. 2017). In West Africa, the per capita cement ratio is still low, with an average of 115 kg and marked differences among countries: 121 kg in Nigeria, 180 kg in Benin, 211 kg in Ghana, 83 kg in Cameroon (White 2015). With a spectacular annual increase in consumption of 5% per person, some perceived the growth rate as a sign of development. The concrete market is linked to the emergence of the middle class and the diaspora building homes from abroad (Mercer 2014; Page and Sunjo 2017). But it is also linked with the growing importance of the "Bottom of the Pyramid" (Prahalad and Hammond 2002; Banerjee and Duflo 2011), which represents a mass of poor individuals (2.7 billion people living on less than \$2,5 a day) who have only recently begun to build with concrete. In this sense, concrete is one of the "new technologies of poverty" (Forty 2012: 40), which allowed the democratization of construction to populations with no professional or technical training. Yet it also lends itself well to standardization: the production of prefabricated concrete blocks has become, for the poor, a symbol of wealth on par with the gold bar. In West Africa, the production and commercialization of cement – now considered as a prime commodity like bread or rice–benefits from subsidies, tax incentives, state policy interventions, and agreements between cement companies and governments. Because cement is cheap and widely available, millions of poor people use it to erect walls over which they can place a sheet of corrugated iron and, once all is in place, have a home. At the same time, in Abidjan, Accra, and Lagos, the thousands of (super)rich are also erecting walls, tower blocks and gated communities. Concrete is the common denominator that gives continuity and shape to a new urban form – the Concrete City.

The Lagos-Abidjan Corridor: A Megacity Region under Construction

A gray, monochrome landscape stretches almost a 1,000 km wide. In places, a few palm trees struggle to maintain themselves amidst the thousands of tons of concrete which have been poured in the last few years. Toyota pickup trucks, often carrying at least seven people with heavy luggage, speed past similarly overloaded cargo trucks that, in turn, pass Chinese motorbikes loaded with multiple passengers and baskets full of goods. Roadsides are lined with containers converted into stores selling bags of rice, secondhand clothes, phone cards, as well as cement bags, steel reinforcing bars, piles of gravel, and sand. We are in West Africa, traveling along the thin coastal strip trapped between the sea and the lagoon that links Abidjan (Ivory Coast) to Lagos (Nigeria), running through Accra, Lomé, Cotonou, and Porto-Novo. Everywhere along this corridor, concrete is present: in the blocks on building sites or in the bags of cement sold at any hour, day, or night (Figure I.3). On this 1,000 km strip, concrete highways link cities, together shaping a megacity region of 40 million inhabitants who live, move, and build in concrete (Figures I.4 and I.5). Thirty five million people live on the 500 km strip between Accra and Lagos alone, and demographic forecasts suggest that this population will rise to 55 million by the year 2050 (http://africapolis. org). In its recent report on African urban dynamics, the Organization for

FIGURE I.3   Cement deposit, open 24 hours per day, Cotonou 2018.
Source: A. Choplin.

Economic Co-operation and Development and the Sahel and West Africa
Club (OECD/UNECA/AfDB 2022) goes further in its figures: it identifies
the Lagos-Ibadan-Cotonou area as a compact city cluster[1], with an estimated
current population of 45 million inhabitants – including 33 million urban
dwellers living in 246 cities.

Several geographers have analyzed this huge urban corridor as a neck-
lace of townships (small precolonial villages, former trading posts, large
port cities, and capitals, border post trading towns) (N'Bessa 1997; Dorier-
Apprill and Domingo 2004). They argue it is one of the longest chains of
cities in Africa that, from Port Harcourt to Abidjan, are spaced on average no
more than 50 km apart. The urban areas linked together by this corridor are
significant: there are 5 million inhabitants in Abidjan, 5.4 million in Accra,
2.2 million in Lomé, 2.4 million in Cotonou, 900,000 in Porto-Novo, 5 million in Ibadan, and 23 million in Lagos, sub-Saharan Africa's largest city (see

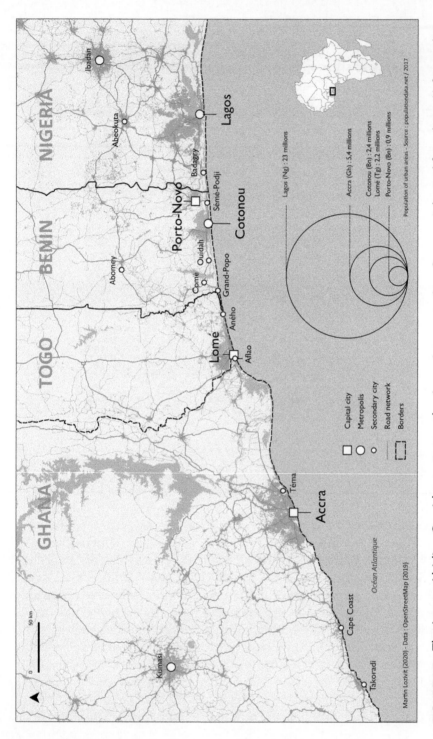

FIGURE I.4 The Lagos-Abidjan Corridor, zoom on the Accra-Lagos section. Source: Adapted from http://africapolis.org; OpenStreetMap; A. Choplin, M. Lozivit 2019.

Trajets

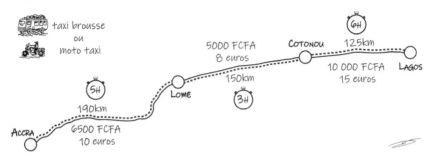

FIGURE I.5 Cities and distances in terms of travel time, cost, and mileage. Source: D. Bertrais.

http://africapolis.org). While some of these cities are growing, a significant and quasi-continuous network of secondary urban hubs is developing: Grand Bassam (pop. 100,000), Sekondi-Takoradi (500,000), Cape Coast (100,000), Tema (350,000), Comé (80,000), Ouidah (100,000), Sèmè-Podji (300,000), Badagry (300,000). On the next rung down on the urban ladder are the border posts of Aflao (pop. 80,000), Aného (30,000), Grand Popo (30,000).

Some cities in this corridor have been studied extensively, in particular Lagos (Sawyer 2016; Lawanson and Agunbiade 2018; Adama 2018; Fourchard 2021) and Accra (Gough and Yankson 2000; Grant 2009; Bertrand 2011; Quayson 2014; Fält 2016, 2019; Dawson 2021), and to a lesser degree Abidjan (Antoine et al. 1987; Dubresson 1989; Steck 2005). The smaller cities of Lomé, Cotonou, and Porto-Novo have received less scholarly attention: e.g. for Lomé (Le Bris 1987; Gervais-Lambony 1994; Gervais-Lambony and Nyassogbo 2007; Spire 2011; Nugent 2021), for Cotonou (N'bessa 1997; Sotindjo 2010; Coralli and Palumbo 2011; Ciavolella and Choplin 2018) and for Porto-Novo (Dorier et al. 2013; Mengin and Godonou 2013). Studies focusing on the corridor itself are recent (Dorier-Apprill and Domingo 2004; Choplin and Hertzog 2020; Hertzog 2020; Nugent 2021). They chart the importance of the road artery as an anchoring point in the multi-centric morphology inherited from the port cities that punctuate this linear stretch and that have long linked the region with the exterior, with colonial cities, and with ports across the Atlantic, first as part of the slave trade and later for trade in raw materials like palm oil (Cooper 1995). The monetary wealth produced in and by these cities today comes from import/export and trade activities (Guyer 2004). This wealth has now been reinjected and stockpiled in land and real estate, with little going into industry. The movement of goods, merchandise, and people has long defined this area and has only recently transformed into a space of agricultural or industrial production. For example, innumerable sheds used as storage warehouses for nearby maritime ports are now beginning to blanket the corridor. The sheds are so extensive that the Beninese-Nigerian scholar John O. Igué has even argued that Benin has become a "warehouse state" (Igué and Soule 1992). According to Igué, "between Accra, Cotonou, and Lagos, people do not sleep" (interview, Cotonou, 2016). They do not sleep because they are in movement, like the goods they carry with them. Yet they are also aiming to build a concrete house where they will one day finally be able to stop and rest.

The Lagos-Abidjan corridor offers an exemplary case study – its urban form, its development trajectory, its modes of governance – through which to reflect on contemporary urbanization. It reveals new population patterns – necklaces and halos – which are far from those of other known mega-regions and megacities (Labbé and Sorensen 2020). As such, they warrant further examination. In this book, I look at these different urban forms in a megapolis like Lagos but also in the small and mid-size "cities of the invisible majority" (Hilgers 2012), as well as the urbanizing satellite and interstitial towns which form part of an often neglected "subaltern urbanization" (Mukhopadhyay et al. 2020). I argue that this part of West Africa offers an excellent case with which to evaluate Henri Lefebvre's (1970) prediction of "planetary urbanization," a thesis recently revisited by Brenner and Schmid (2015). It argues that the world's now dominant modes of production and consumption are tied up with the city. This thesis has been criticized for its sometimes over-theoretical, all-encompassing, and undifferentiated approach to the urban (Storper and Scott 2016). Analyzing the Lagos-Abidjan corridor through the prism of concrete offers an opportunity to discuss this theory by focusing on an African urban reality often overlooked in urban research (Fourchard 2012).

Cement As A Theoretical Binder

What we need to question is bricks, concrete, glass, our table manners, our utensils, our tools, the way we spend our time, our rhythms. To question that which seems to have ceased forever to astonish us.

Georges Perec (1997: 210), *L'Infra-ordinaire* in *Species of Spaces and other pieces*

At Georges Perec's invitation, this book questions concrete, and proposes that we maintain our astonishment at its omnipresence. To do this, the book follows the trajectory of a powder which has the property of binding – cement – and then it similarly follows the trajectory of the material derived from it – concrete – in order to understand the artifact they spawn: the Concrete City. Cement creates a physical binder between water and granulates (sand, gravel, or stone) that, after setting for a few minutes, turn into concrete. Add a steel skeleton, and the result is reinforced concrete. And with it a building, then two, then a neighborhood, then the city. Concrete is thus at the heart of the production of the urban.

Inspired both by critical urban theory and a postcolonial approach, this research aims to explore the production, circulation, and consumption of concrete in West Africa. On the one hand, I mobilize Marxist theory to understand the impacts of the extension of capitalism and neoliberalism in Africa through the lens of this material. On the other hand, I draw on postcolonial urban theory to grasp the local acceptances and adaptations of these urban dynamics. As this research focuses on a socio-technical object, it is also strongly inspired by the Science and Technology Studies (STS) and the material turn in social sciences. I adopt a geographical dimension to analyze these socio-technical relations, seeking to track the flows and circulations of this material in Africa. This book is therefore an invitation to unravel political objectives, economic choices, social practices, and environmental challenges underlying the increasing use of concrete in West Africa. I argue that engaging with concrete serves to examine the recent urban boom in Africa which has received little scholarly attention, notably in relation to its architecture and infrastructure.

(Afri)Capitalism and Neoliberalism

Concrete has become a symbol of economic growth and modernity across the world. It materializes the capitalist production of the city, and it links urbanization, capitalism, the commodification of land, and regimes of wealth accumulation. Concrete is closely associated with capitalist development, to the point that some authors denounce it as a "weapon of mass construction of capitalism" (Jappe 2020). I take concrete as an entry-point from which to analyze the logic of capitalist urban development in West Africa and to examine its impacts on local urban societies.

Using a Marxist framework, cement can be considered as a commodity: it forms part of a chain of production within which it possesses both a utility (use value) and a price (exchange value) determined by the length of human working time needed to produce it. Its use and exchange value are relatively uniform at the world scale: a 50 kg bag of cement costs on average between 5 and 10€ everywhere across the globe. Its price depends on the supply and demand systems of a market. Its value depends on its position in the supply chain and its state: for example, a newly extracted and manufactured powder has a different price than a bag of cement (the object sold) which, in turn, is less expensive than laid concrete (its result). In other words, cement is a commodity whose value is produced not by the factory workers who produce it, but because processing turns it into concrete. An ordinary bag of cement has a potentially greater value than its purchase price because once it is turned into concrete, it has the capacity to convert a plot into a building, land into real estate, and therefore to become capital.

The conversion from cement to concrete, from commodity to capital raises questions about the crucial role of the city as the anchorage point of capital. In *The Urban Revolution*, Henri Lefebvre defined urbanism as "the physical trace on land of human dwelling of stone, cement or metal" (Lefebvre 1970: 151). As a "spatial fix" (Harvey 2001, 2016), concrete gives capital an anchor and enables capitalism to regenerate. The flows of materials are therefore a heuristic entry-point to explore the immaterial flows of capital. With the spread of neoliberalism since the 1980s, cities have become major strategic political and economic spaces for the reproduction of capital (Brenner 2004; Brenner and Theodore 2002). Far from being passive, governments have supported cities' entrepreneurial turns by creating the ideal conditions needed to serve the financial interests of an elite (Harvey 1989: 11). In the context of inter-urban competition, cities have become targets of speculation, in particular through the increasing financialization of real estate (Aalbers 2016; Halbert and Attuyer 2016). Neoliberalism has developed a capacity to transform and adapt "anywhere and everywhere" (Peck and Tickell 2002; Brenner et al. 2010).

This book aims to see whether the neo-Marxist theories developed from observations in the West are also valid for African cities. It contributes to debates on neoliberalism (Pinson and Morel Journel 2017) by introducing a perspective drawn from urban experience in Africa. Recent research has called for an analysis of capitalism in Africa (Wiegratz 2018). Like the experience of Asian cities in the past two decades (Shatkin 2008; Aveline-Dubach 2016; Fauveaud 2020), African cities have also been transformed by rising monetarization and the financialization of land by urban policies. This research complements the existing research on urban spaces, capitalism, finance, and private and real estate investment in Africa (Watson 2014; Steel et al. 2019; Gillespie 2020; Goodfellow 2017, 2020; Mizes and Donovan 2022). It charts how a property development boom across West Africa has allowed capital anchor itself in the urban environment and how this transformation has materialized into the buildings made of concrete and steel today stretching across the skylines of African cities.

In Africa, concrete urbanism is enrolling new forms, channels, actors (Moser et al. 2021), and places – especially cities – where power and capitalism are reconfigured. In 2011, Nigerian billionaire banker Tony Elumelu coined the concept of "Africapitalism" to refer to businesses headed by Africans who describe themselves as entrepreneurs, philanthropists, and liberals. They preach for African capital to be reinvested in the continent, both for the purpose of profit and for its "positive effects" on African populations (Idemudia and Amaeshi 2019). Aliko Dangote – the cement magnate and Africa's richest man – is a prominent and outspoken Africapitalist who is today articulating a new link between concrete and Africa's new capitalism. In this respect, Dangote is re-fashioning Africa's figure of the entrepreneur and the concept of success, illustrating a new approach to making a "fortune" through the business of producing the city's material form.

I argue that the Concrete City has emerged as the new icon of African capitalism. Concrete is completely associated with these narratives on Africapitalism which valorize capitalistic class and elite accumulation (Ouma 2020). I propose to analyze concrete value chain to engage in a critical debate to deconstruct these narratives. To do this, I explore the material intimacies between concrete and power, whether the political power of heads of state or the economic power of private investors and construction entrepreneurs. Several studies have demonstrated the growing role of the state, in its shift from a developmental state to a largely privatized investor state (Hibou 1999) in the quest for emergence and profitable projects to support (Pitcher 2012, 2017; Péclard et al. 2020). Drawing on Marxist theoretical frameworks, this research analyzes the place of political stakeholders and entrepreneurs in urban production and governance. What are their links with the business of the city and its capital flows? What is the political dimension of the Concrete City and its connection with power? How has concrete become a key medium of commodification, accumulation, and even fetishization serving extraverted elite in this part of the world? What can we learn from the construction sector, the limestone quarries, and the cement plants about the circulation of capital and its links with the urban?

Material Matters

This book reflects on a material which is part of a global transformation in the ways of living and consuming in cities across the world. It moves beyond the question of "who makes the city?" to pose the question of "what makes the city?" Following the "material turn" in social sciences, it focuses on the role of commodities and materials in the construction of social reality (Miller 2005; Bennett 2010; Bennett and Joyce 2013; Schorch et al. 2020). Drawing on Arjun Appadurai's (1986) suggestion to follow the social life of things, I follow bags of cement and flows of concrete as an entry-point from which to analyze urban production. In their "treatise on nomadology," Gilles Deleuze and Félix Guattari (1980: 454) explain that knowing materials requires following them – to "follow the matter-flow." In line with Deleuze and Guattari's "matter-flow" approach, Tim Ingold (2012) also proposes to "return to the matter of materials" and to pay attention to the socio-material relation that humans develop with certain "critical" materials of our time, such as concrete or ice (Simonetti and Ingold 2018). These materials reveal things about the evolution of people's relations to their environment. Far from being an inert material, I argue that it is possible to discern life in concrete. Bricklayers, engineers, architects, and ordinary people often say that concrete moves, changes, and evolves with time. Drawing on Science and Technology Studies (STS) and Bruno Latour's Actor-Network Theory (2005), I consider concrete as an "actant": a bag of cement or a block of concrete can interact with many other humans and nonhumans actors. Concrete has agency and makes sense of the world, as other scholars have demonstrated for other non-human things like mushrooms (Tsing 2015), birds (Despret 2016), or spiders (Haraway 2016).

Analyzing concrete as a socio-technic process, this research contributes to STS with a geographical perspective. It follows the spatial spread and flows of material as a method with which to examine social and political relations. Like the seminal works of Appadurai (1986), many studies have recounted the historical, political, and social life of certain globalized commodities, like sugar (Mintz 1986), gold and cocaine (Taussig 2004), metal (Bennett 2010), Chinese products like flip-flops (Knowles 2014), or jeans (Pliez 2007). In Africa, scholars have similarly investigated cotton, shea butter (Chalfin 2004), metal scrap (Rams 2021), wax fabric (Sylvanus 2016), cars (Rosenfeld 2017), and motorcycles (Khan-Mohammad 2016; Blundo 2018). I revisit this STS-inspired framework by tracing the biography of concrete through time and (urban) space. This approach echoes Ola Söderström's proposal to put "cities in relations" and follow the circulation of built forms as a "powerful means to understand changing socio-economic relations across space" (Söderström 2014: 24). In writing this (spatial) biography of concrete, I question its life but also its death. I draw on approaches in Urban Political Ecology (Swyngedouw and Heynen 2003; Keil 2005; Heynen et al. 2006) to analyze relations between nature, politics, (non) humans, and urbanization. I also refer to urban metabolism approach to shed light on the flows and life cycle of matter and energy that are being exchanged between cities and their environment (Barles 2010; Gandy 2014; Lawhon et al. 2014). My work is particularly inspired by Matthew Gandy's (2002) book *Concrete and Clay* that reveals how raw materials have played a major role in the building history of New York. I also draw on his very inspiring work on pipes in the "liquid city" of Mumbai (Gandy 2014). I explore the production of urban metabolic systems by analyzing the widespread but understudied use of concrete – a solid material – in infrastructure and housing. Building materials have been the subject of several metabolic studies, which analyze their production, circulation and recycling (Ravelli 2017; Mongeard 2017; Augiseau and Kim 2021). However, little research has focused on these topics, especially the recycling and discarding of concrete buildings in Africa.

Concrete is emerging as the dominant material in the contemporary urban landscape, particularly in West Africa where it has a considerable influence on political and social relations. Exploring this materiality, and especially the visible flows of building materials, can help us to understand the aspects of African cities that remain elusive, such as city-making, urban governance, or capital flows. This material approach complements the scholarships on urban Africa which has revealed how informality and immateriality shape the lived experience of the African urban environment (De Boeck and Plissart 2004; Simone 2004; Mbembe and Nuttall 2004; Fontein and Smith 2023). It also complements the extensive literature linked to extractivism in Africa (Schubert et al. 2018; Larmer and Laterza 2017). In contrast with other high-value material commodities such as copper (Rubbers 2019; Blaszkiewicz 2021; Dobler and Kesselring 2019), gas, and oil (Soares de Oliveira 2007; Appel et al. 2015; Appel 2019), the limestone, gravel, and sand used to manufacture cement and concrete have received little attention in the social sciences. Scholarly interest in West African sand is quite recent (Dawson 2021), and sand as a problem for global policy-makers has similarly only recently emerged (Beiser 2018; UNEP 2019, 2022). Concrete itself has attracted little research in the social sciences, apart from the works of historians (Simonnet 2005, Forty 2012) and a few noteworthy studies, for example on Mexico (Fry 2013) and Mozambique (Archambault 2018, 2021; Morton 2019). More broadly, little attention has been paid to building materials, such as the steel, scrap metals, reinforcing bars, corrugated iron, tiles, or bricks that are all parts of the "eclectic collection of urban materiality" (McFarlane 2011: 216). This study fills this research gap by analyzing how these material flows position Africa in a vast global market. Like Anna Tsing's *matsutake* mushroom, concrete can be considered "a product with a strong cultural dimension, which is at the same time the object of a globalized commodification" (Tsing 2015: 101). Concrete is a little-known global commodity that creates unexpected connections between spaces of production, distribution, and consumption, that reactivates forms of dependencies, and that contributes to an "inconspicuous globalization" (Choplin and Pliez 2018).

Studying material flows from a geographical and an urban perspective echoes recent work on the "political materialities" which establish links among cities, politics, and human and non-human entities (Pilo' and Jaffe 2020). Concrete gives political and social meanings to the cities, infrastructures, buildings, and roads that are made out of it (Harvey 2010; Harvey and Knox 2015). The large number of recent works on infrastructure (Larkin 2013; Silver 2014; Kanai and Shindler 2019; Furlong 2020; Pollio et al. 2022) tends to overshadow the few studies on the construction sector which is "highly visible, yet at the same time particularly opaque" (Smith 2020). I offer a new angle on the construction industry and the material aspects of city-building by shedding light on both the pervasiveness of concrete and secrecy surrounding its production. Indeed, this material matters: through its flows, concrete metaphorically binds cities, assets, and human lives.

Building, Dwelling, and Inhabiting a Postcolonial World

The philosopher Martin Heidegger (1951) distinguished between the terms "building" and "dwelling" and, in making this distinction, sought to re-situate "being" at the center of philosophical reflection. His ideas ran counter to those of an era marked by the modernist movement, functionalism, and brutalist architecture. According to Heidegger, the notion of building is about spatial planning for roads, bridges, stadiums, and power stations. It is the result of projects and infrastructures initiated by the state, technicians, architects, and planners to produce what Lefebvre would later call "conceived space" (1974: 38–40). Conversely, the notion of dwelling refers to the practices, representations, and symbolisms of the person who inhabits, similar to what Lefebvre would later call "lived space." Heidegger thus distinguishes between two ways of producing the city: top-down (building perspective) and bottom-up (dwelling perspective). This dual path to urban production, which contributed to the thinking of Lefebvre (1970), and later Ingold (2002) and Sennett (2018), shed lights on conflicts between the techno-managerial approach adopted by governments, and the survival strategies of urban inhabitants. Some scholars have sought to decipher the production of African cities from above, with a view of the city as a target of planning practices whose aim is to attract investment and generate competitiveness in the context of neoliberal urbanism (Parnell et al. 2009; Myers 2011; Parnell and Robinson 2012; Watson 2014). Other scholars have focused more on practices of inhabitation, in particular the practices developed by people who build their own houses (Canel et al. 1990; Bertrand 2011; Gastrow 2017). Since the 1970s, works on the socio-economics of construction have shown, in Africa and elsewhere (Turner 1976; Caldeira 2017) that (neo)-urbanites build using their own resources, embark on private construction projects, become self-taught builders, architects, project managers, and building contractors capable of transforming their ordinary dwelling into a unique product (Buire 2014).

In this book, I pay attention to the significance of building and dwelling in the West African context and analyze what is happening between these two processes, by casting light on a world of previously hidden intermediaries involved in making the city. I aim to understand how concrete makes, unmakes, and remakes relations between people and the place they live. To do this, I draw on postcolonial studies that give voice to these inhabitants and analyze the forms of subaltern urban production (Roy 2011). Research in postcolonial urban studies (Robinson 2002, 2006; Roy 2009; Robinson and Roy 2016; Sheppard et al. 2014) has argued for a re-consideration of cities in the Global South as urban spaces in their own right. Inspired by scholars who have called for a new vision of African cities (Myers 2011, 2020; Fourchard 2012, 2021; Parnell and Pieterse 2014), I propose to understand what it means to be urban in West Africa at the beginning of the twenty-first century. I consider this approach to be complementary to the one inherited from Marxist theory, which has sought to universalize the experiences of building and dwelling European and American cities. I engage here with postcolonial theory to understand how subaltern urbanism manifests itself in Lagos, Cotonou, or Lomé. Concrete is a key material to experiment this postcolonial perspective as it is intertwined with colonial and postcolonial relations and power: concrete is both a colonial product (imported by the colonists) and a postcolonial object – African societies have adapted its material form and reinterpreted its immaterial semiotics. It shapes a culture of construction that varies from one place to another. I argue that this affectively charged material gives new values, a new role, and new meanings to the process of southern urbanization substantially different from urbanization in the Global North. I use the concept of "Concrete City" to explore this new urban form taking shape in a postcolonial context, redefining links between architecture, design, and everyday "microbial practices" (De Certeau 1990), such as buying bags of cement, looking for a builder, or drawing the plans of a house. To this end, I conduct a social geography of the Concrete City, giving body and voices to the actors involved in construction, including the ordinary people who build and inhabit this Concrete City. I investigate construction sites as places where relations of power and domination are redefined – the relations between those who produce and those who consume; between those who open the bag of cement, add the water and sand, and those who do the mixing; between the foreman who gives the orders and the apprentice who obeys.

While Heidegger attached the term "thinking" to the "building-dwelling pair," Tim Ingold (2002) prefers the term "Living." In this way, he introduces the role of nonhumans by exploring, "how animals and people make themselves at home in the world." Ingold (2017) analyzes this "Living" through the "mundane surfaces of everyday life." Concrete surfaces form part of domestic life: they offer a way to understand the practices of building, dwelling, and living. As a contribution to Ingold's reflections, I add the term "inhabiting" to the "building-dwelling" pair. Latour (2021) has recently used "habitability" to consider the role of life over the long term and its relations to nature. The relationship between concrete and nature has always been and remains ambiguous: "Concrete is not natural but that is not to say it is unnatural: it has the capacity to resist nature and so gives us power over nature" (Forty 2012: 43). Thus, concreting over nature is a lasting way to tame it, to protect individuals from its hazards. At the same time, however, the generalization of concrete is threatening the very future of our species. By creating a synthesis between building and dwelling, the Concrete City, that grows vertically and sprawls horizontally, raises questions about how humans inhabit the city and more broadly the world. In a context of dwindling resources, in particular the non-renewable fossil resources (limestone, stone, sand) essential to its production, concrete raises the questions of duration, maintenance, repair and, through them, questions about social, economic, and environmental futures in general. The (over)production and (over)consumption of concrete, a marker of the Anthropocene era, could accelerate the end of the planet's habitability.

This book examines the (un)inhabitability of the Concrete City from an Afro-centric perspective by mobilizing the work of African postcolonial philosophers, such as Felwine Sarr (2020) and Achille Mbembe (2020). They argue that Africa is the continent where the future of the planet is being written. Mbembe elaborates the concept of "brutalism," referring to more than an architectural period, which glorified raw concrete. For him, it also refers to our own era of ubiquitous capital, "seized by the pathos of demolition and production," as well as to "wastes of all kinds, residues, the scaffolding of a gigantic demiurgy" (Mbembe 2020: 8). The term brutalism is a reminder that our urbanized societies rely above all on the principle of extractivism, of digging holes to build towers (Bridge 2015; De Boeck and Baloji 2016). In West Africa, producing the Concrete City requires the extraction of limestone in the middle of the savanna, the dredging of vast quantities of sand from the lagoon, the import of clinker from Indonesia and gypsum from Spain, and the release of particles and carbon dioxide into the ozone layer. Thinking with the decolonial and postcolonial perspectives, this book invites us to think about other possible urban worlds: what city and what world can we and do we want to build, dwell, and inhabit? And what can we learn from Africa about this urban future?

Tracking Urban Materiality: A Methodological Approach

Following Bags of Cement and the City under Construction

To understand the significance of new modes of urban production in West Africa, I propose to write a biography of concrete. I follow the trials and tribulations of this gray powder to tell the story of the different stages, spaces, and actors involved in its production, distribution, and consumption. The methodology employed combines two approaches: the material turn which focuses on everyday objects, and a "follow the thing" approach in which an object is tracked all the way up the chain from producer to consumer (Appadurai 1986; Cook 2004; Gregson et al. 2010). This approach borrows from studies on global value chains (GVC) and global commodity chains (GCC) (Gereffi and Korzeniewicz 1994) which analyze how products circulate, as well as the actors and political frameworks that underpin the establishment of a GVC. Like the merchandise it studies, this methodology is both multi-sited (Marcus 1995) and in motion (Blaszkiewicz 2021). It has led me from the quarries from which limestone is extracted to the urban plots where the bags of cement are converted into concrete. In parallel to a physically horizontal approach that analyses concrete's movement across the corridor, I also adopt a socially vertical approach to grasp the diversity of actors involved in every level of the value chain: from the big cement production firms and governments at the top, to the ordinary urban residents building homes on their plots at the bottom, as well as the intermediaries between them: the contractors, the real estate developers, the government agencies and donors, as well as the site foremen, the laborers, the subcontractors, and the craftsmen who all, at their various levels, contribute to (de)regulate the market.

From July of 2016 to December of 2018, I carried out fieldwork across West Africa as a visiting researcher at the French Research Institute for Development (IRD) in Cotonou and at the Department of Geography at University of Abomey-Calavi. During this research, I explored the urban corridor by traveling regularly along the Lagos-Abidjan axis (Figure I.6). Although I was unable to travel by cement truck, I followed their regular routes along the roads where they supply hardware stores, through the city centers that they cross everyday, to the borders where they congregate in convoys waiting often for days for permission to cross, and then onwards into

FIGURE I.6 Circulating along the corridor 2016. Source: A. Choplin.

the urban outskirts where their cargo is sold, as one truck driver put it, "on the sly." My nearly three years of immersion in the field gave me the opportunity to make multiple direct observations, to experience informal interactions with a wide variety of people, to track local situations over time, and to collect data from the daily press. In the field, I recorded personal accounts from the men and the handful of women who have links with concrete: CEOs, senior managers, and sales directors at cement plants agreed to meet me and, in some cases, to give me tours of the region's leading factories. Alongside these meetings, I analyzed the discourses of cement firms, political leaders, and donors through an examination of corporate communication materials and websites.

Beyond cement, I explored the structure of the public works sector and the importance of the Indian, Chinese, and Lebanese diasporas in the production and import of construction materials. I interviewed sand suppliers and visited factories where they make sheet metal and reinforcing steel, as well as the stores of the region's biggest wholesalers. I also examined the emerging real estate sector and interviewed CEOs of international corporations, developers, and realtors (10 of them were interviewed in Cotonou, 3 in Lomé, and 1 in Accra). I followed the implementation of megaprojects, but I was unable to obtain information about the capital invested, or about the agreements between governments and investors. Most of my interlocutors were sensitive to questions about the origin of capital in these sectors and the circulation of this capital in the regional economy, and these questions often provoked evasive responses. Unable to track how capital flows into the Concrete City, I followed the materials that would lead me to the people involved in the construction and the business of the city. I analyzed at length the websites of the international engineering design firms and groups that generate digital images of big urban projects and thereby contribute to urban visions, wondering who were the targets of this city of computer-generated images (Watson 2020). Finally, to further develop my ideas about the possibilities of building differently and with less concrete, I interviewed several architects, contractors, and Non Governemental Organisations developing new techniques and alternative modes of construction.

In addition to motion along the corridor, I developed a more static approach based on the case of Cotonou, where I lived during my field research. In this approach, I followed the city's construction process and observed its day-to-day development. I tracked 10 construction projects over three years in different parts of the cities of Lomé and Cotonou. By tracking these projects, I was able to interview the women and men who make the city, each with their own resources and contributions – from the owner of a self-designed house, to the builders and the European cement manufacturers that dominate the sector. In this way, I met Elinor, François, Sam, Edgard, and Édith who, with 6 or 10 tons of cement, have built or were building their houses in different neighborhoods across the region. By following them over time and space, I analyzed their progress and projects, but also their worries, their setbacks, and their disappointments. I combined these interviews with a collective mapping project undertaken in collaboration with the OpenStreet-Map Benin community. This project geotagged the craft and commercial activities linked with construction, and it conducted a survey with KoBo Toolbox to identify the different cement sellers and hardware stores on the central arteries of the corridor between May and July 2017. Although the locations tagged at that time may no longer exist, they provide a snapshot of the dynamism of this sector at this specific moment. I supplemented these surveys with drone pictures: I took aerial photos of Cotonou, Lomé, Accra, and Lagos to provide a view of the city during the construction process and to tag the survey locations and the names mentioned in the text.

Although the analysis I present in this book is my own, the research on which it is based was the result of a collective effort. My research assistant at IRD, Martin Lozivit, conducted interviews, collected field data, and produced visual tools (photographs, drone images, videos, time-lapse)[2] and maps of Accra, Lomé, Cotonou, and Lagos (Figures I.7–I.10). PhD and master students from University of Abomey-Calavi in Cotonou, from Lomé, France, and Switzerland, similarly assisted in tracking West Africa's gray gold.

Thinking Cities Through West Africa

This research takes West African cities as its starting point, gradually widening the focus and reflection from Cotonou to the Lagos-Abidjan corridor. I focus on cement industry and concrete construction in the least urbanized continent, which is today experiencing rapid urban growth. Africa has long been represented as the continent of wooden and banco huts, of shanty towns made of bamboo, bits of plastic, and corrugated iron. My aim is to tell a different story of Africa, such as Chimamanda Ngozi Adichie has invited us to do in a talk in 2009 entitled "The danger of the single story."[3] Africa can and should be considered a "laboratory of planet-scale changes" (Mbembe 2020: 13) and African cities should similarly be considered as "laboratories of change" as Georges Balandier argued (1985). It is urgent and indispensable to think and rethink the world and its future from this continent, long neglected and denigrated, but which today is home to a quarter of humanity. Inspired by this postcolonial and decolonial perspective, I propose to reverse the starting point and, instead of seeing Africa from the perspective of its rural villages, to take the perspective of urban Africa which is characterized by money, materiality, and verticality (of concrete towers).

My analysis starts from this relatively small space of the Lagos-Abidjan corridor. Home to more than 40 million inhabitants, it is one of Africa's main urban regions and is destined to become its biggest urban concentration. As such, my purpose is to put the observations and stories collected here in conversation with similar experiences in rest of the African continent, as well as in conversation with scholarly reflections on "the urban" in general. This comparative approach is inspired by the method developed by Jennifer Robinson (2016), who proposes "thinking cities through" and "with elsewhere." My approach combines two main traditions of urban research: a close focus on the field drawn from the "micro" tradition of the monograph in the Francophone social sciences, and a theoretical focus drawn from the "macro" tradition in Anglophone urban studies. Without neglecting the complexity of the field sites, I undertake a constant back-and-forth among the cities in the corridor to compare empirical variables. For example, rather than write a monograph on Cotonou, I have linked day-to-day observations of this city with cases across the corridor to establish links among them and to analyze

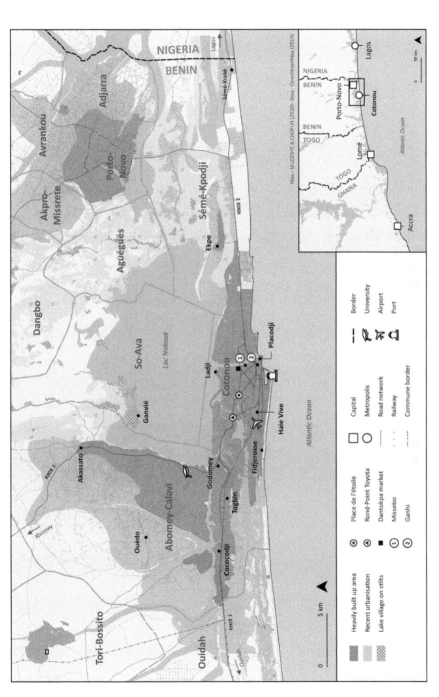

FIGURE I.7 Cotonou. Source: A. Choplin, M. Lozivit 2020.

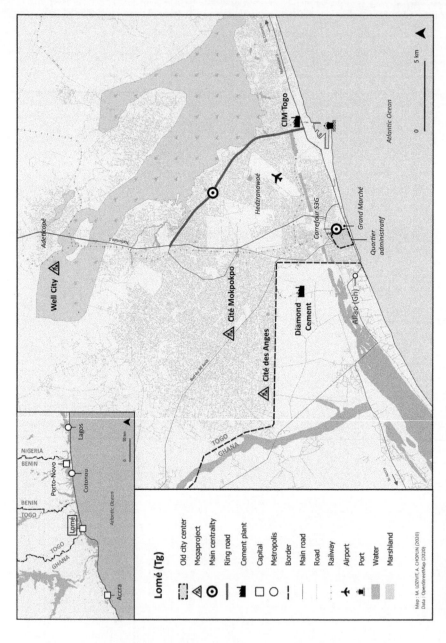

Lomé (Tg)

⬚	Old city center
⚠	Megaproject
⊙	Main centrality
▮	Ring road
▮	Cement plant
□	Capital
○	Metropolis
┼	Border
│	Main road
│	Road
┊	Railway
✈	Airport
⚓	Port
	Water
	Marshland

Map : M. LOZIVIT, A. CHOPLIN (2020)
Data : OpenStreetMap (2020)

FIGURE I.8 Lomé. Source: A. Choplin, M. Lozivit 2020.

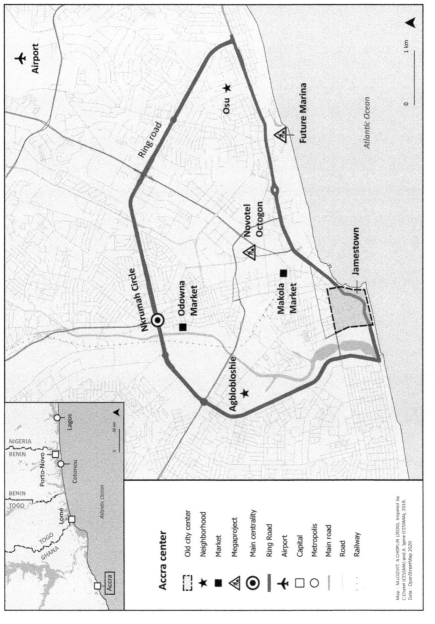

FIGURE I.9 Accra. Source: A. Choplin, M. Lozivit 2020.

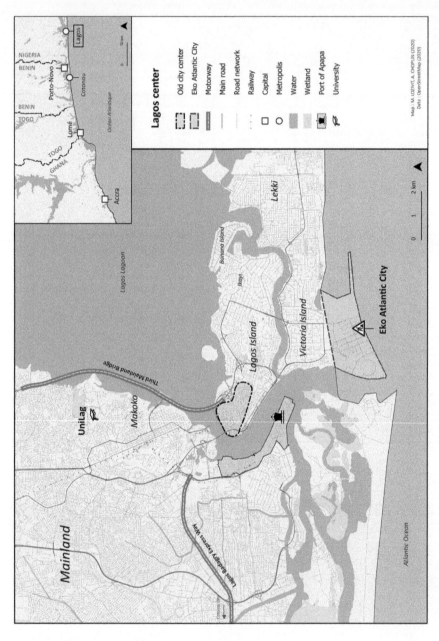

FIGURE I.10 Lagos. Source: A. Choplin, M. Lozivit 2020.

them in light of their specificities. This comparative approach prevents me from over-interpreting the findings: what is true for Cotonou, the main survey location, is not necessarily true of Accra, nor is it necessarily true of Cape Town. Three years of fieldwork gave me the opportunity to familiarize myself with Cotonou, Porto-Novo, Lomé, Lagos, Accra, but also with other cities previously unknown to me, such as Niamey or Ibadan, and to revisit Nouakchott and Dakar, where I have previously conducted research. The (re) discovery of these urban spaces through the prism of concrete contributed to certain ideas about the corridor and, from there, to certain ideas about West Africa and the continent more generally. Though generalization is not always possible, concrete is a crosscutting issue and therefore contributes to thinking beyond the borders of a city and even beyond the borders of a continent.

Concrete is therefore a matter for thought about cities and about the world (Bayart and Warnier 2004); a matter as relevant to the high-rise towers of the city center as to the single-story dwellings of the suburbs and their impoverished but cement-hungry populations; a matter that gives us the power to imagine that, behind form and material, stands an invisible city (De Boeck and Plissart 2004) inhabited by multiple spirits in this region of voodoo culture; a matter that reveals the depth of history of these supposedly "history-less" cities (Ciavolella and Choplin 2018).

This research proposes an exploration of the Concrete City, of its political, economic, social, and environmental implications and meanings in West Africa. It is divided into four chapters, which together outline the concept of Concrete City and the material flows which underpin it. The first chapter focuses on the political economy of concrete. It considers the actors who dominate the construction sector – governments, politicians, cement manufacturers or international donors – to grasp modes of urban production in contemporary Africa. In this part, I chart how concrete symbolizes ongoing economic transformations, from the resource boom in the 1990s and 2000s to the progressive "Africanization" of capital. My analysis of this material critically addresses the links between the marketing expressions of "Africa Rising," "Africapitalism" – a new form of capitalism driven by African entrepreneurs – and the continent's recent construction boom. In the second chapter, I shift focus to the city. I define the Concrete City and examine the different types of cities that emerge from the same material: concrete. I explore how this material is used to build housing projects, large-scale infrastructure, high rise construction, and iconic buildings around the world and across Africa. Yet alongside such elite projects, concrete has also become the most commonly used material in the slums and in precarious areas across West Africa. Thus, this chapter provides an analysis of the real estate and the construction sector, public-private projects, as well as individual and autoconstruction dynamics. The third chapter focuses on the social life of concrete: it describes the extensive use of concrete across all social classes and how this material becomes charged with social norms and affect (Archambault 2018, 2021). Its widespread use is not only due to the cement lobby and state subsidies that consider it as a basic commodity; it is also due to the desires and imaginaries of urban residents who celebrate a local culture of building with the "modern material" of concrete. The fourth and final chapter examines the rise of a global cement industry and its environmental impact as it is today one of the most polluting industries. It sheds light on how scientists, architects, engineers, masons, NGOs, and inhabitants across West Africa are claiming and experimenting with more sustainable ways of building. This book is therefore an invitation to discover the African urban world through concrete, and to reflect on the material limits of the planet's urban future.

Notes

1   Compact city clusters consist of cities with more than 30,000 inhabitants that are within 100 km by road with a total urban population of more than 2.5 million inhabitants (including their own population) (OECD/UNECA/AfDB 2022).
2   See the drone images and the time-lapse images of the city's evolution produced: https://youtu.be/RCuiOwh3dMQ.
3   Ted Talk available at: https://youtu.be/D9Ihs241zeg.

CHAPTER 1

Concrete Politics

In 2017, the CEO of *Nouvelle Cimenterie du Bénin* reluctantly invited me into his large office at the company's headquarters in Cotonou to discuss the future of the region's booming concrete industry. "I'm not going to tell you anything about cement," he warned, "in our business, we do not talk. Cement is secret". But what precisely is there to hide about such a mundane and ubiquitous material? The CEO's secrecy concerning concrete seems all the more strange considering how, across the continent, concrete is far from concealed: it has become the foundational material of contemporary African urbanization. In Africa as elsewhere, concrete allows the regeneration of capitalism and the consolidation of political power (Harvey 2016). In his book *Brutalisme,* Achille Mbembe (2020: 12) notes that "power is, through and through, a method of instrumentalism and of construction. It needs grout, concrete, cement, mortar, beams, gravel, lead, steel. . . ." Following Mbembe, I understand concrete and cement to be crucial elements of the construction of power. But the power of concrete is not a new cultural phenomenon. Consider, for example, V.S. Naipaul's novel *A Bend in the River* (1979). In this novel, the president of a fictional African country in the 1970s, who calls himself "the Big Man", satisfies his thirst for power and development by building tower blocks.

In this first chapter, I investigate the relationships between concrete, politics, and economics in contemporary West Africa. I reveal how the politics and economics of concrete are shaping this urbanization, focusing in particular on how the cement industry and the concrete value chain drive urban development. And I consider how the Concrete City itself is both a motor and a result of these ambiguous relations as it becomes

Concrete City: Material Flows and Urbanization in West Africa, First Edition. Armelle Choplin.
© 2023 John Wiley & Sons Ltd. Published 2023 by John Wiley & Sons Ltd.

increasingly intertwined with economic transformations across the region. To do this, I mobilize the vast literature from history to political science that has analyzed the reconfiguration of African states (Bayart 1993; Hibou 1999) and, in particular, the shift from state-led development to private investment which appeared as governments embraced neoliberal economic policies (Pitcher 2012). Recent research on economic development issues helps to understand the close links between politics, development, and the power of economic elites (Ferguson 2006; Chalfin 2010; Appel 2019; Soares de Oliveira 2021). Anthropologists and political scientists have shown how the analysis of infrastructure and the built environment offers insight into the formation of political ideologies and national identities: the rhetoric of "emergence" – the new watchword of development plans across the continent (Péclard et al. 2020) and the world – relies on infrastructures to provide "a sense of belonging to a broader modernity project" (Larkin 2013). Foucault's (1978) concept of "governmentality" also helps clarify how concrete is linked to power and domination. Concrete has become a key element of governmentality as African states seek to control and to benefit from the private sector, particularly the construction industry, in an effort to consolidate their power over national populations. These states govern through concrete: they legitimize their authority by erecting buildings, bridges, and dams, by laying asphalt roads, intersections, and all sorts of "enchanting" infrastructures (Harvey and Knox 2015) that demand large quantities of concrete.

This first chapter retraces the history of this basic material, formerly associated with the colonists who imported it. This "gray gold" is now an integral part of African aspirations for economic growth – it has catapulted the concrete industry's wealthy CEOs, such as Aliko Dangote, into the public spotlight as models of African corporate success and development. I explore this political economy of concrete through an analysis of state transformation, business competition, price regulation, sweetheart deals, reduced import duties, and subsidies for new cement plants. I pay close attention to the relations between politics and the private sector as they join forces to govern through concrete: ambitious presidents keen to see concrete projects reach fruition quickly, local officials in search of resources, financiers, and cement companies looking for profits, businessmen self-proclaimed philanthropists eager to develop their continent. This array of actors is today constructing what I term the Concrete City, a material form of urbanism which has come to embody new aspirations for the African capitalist economy and a new style of governmentality taking shape through this gray, mundane material.

Africanizing Cement

From Colonial Import to Gray Gold "Made in Africa"

Cement is not new to Africa. Cement's long history in the region began with European colonists who imported cement to build concrete urban settlements in areas often previously settled by Africans in wooden or mud huts. However, unlike other products in wide use across the continent today – such as alcohol or oil (Nyuur and Sobiesuo 2016; Van Beemen 2019; Yates 2012) – the history of cement's arrival in Africa remains a marginally documented aspect of colonization. What accounts do exist reveal that, prior to opening local cement plants, European colonists carried cement with them to construct early colonial towns along the coasts. In 1890, for instance, cement accounted for a quarter of imports into Benin, and by 1930 it became the dominant material used in colonial housing (Lombard 1953: 90). In the 1950s, cement remained an imported material. According to the annual ledger of Benin's commodity board in 1950's, products arriving at the wharfs of Cotonou contained "wheat flour, canned foods, wine and liqueurs, as well as cement" (quoted in N'Bessa 1997: 70). For the European colonists, concrete was understood to be a safe, secure, and modern building material which they contrasted with the flammable and ephemeral qualities of traditional straw huts (see Bigon 2016 for Dakar, Morton 2019 for Maputo). Certain place names in Africa continue to bear traces of this colonial distinction linked to materials. For example, many Mozambican people refer to Maputo as the "Cement City" (*Cidade de cimento*), a legacy of the city's founding by the Portuguese and its early construction in concrete in the eighteenth century. In contrast, the poor, unplanned areas of Maputo are called the "Cane City" (*Cidade de caniço*) (Morton 2019), a reference to the sugar cane that Africans used to construct their own settlements in the same time period. Reflecting these early means of racial segregation, cement continues to embody social inequalities across Africa today.

Yet, in the past century, African urban residents themselves adopted concrete as a preferred – and sometimes legally required – building material which, in many cities, has generalized its usage from the city center and out into the peripheries. Breeze blocks gradually supplanted straw, bamboo, and clay, but also the Afro-Brazilian earth architecture introduced by freed former slaves on their return from Latin America. In the nineteenth century, many Afro-Brazilians (the *Aguda*) came back with new methods of construction (Coralli and Houénoudé 2013; Mengin and Godonou 2013) and left their mark on the old town centers of the Gulf of Guinea. The urban cores of Accra in Ghana, Lomé and Aného in Togo, Ouidah and Porto-Novo in Benin, and Lagos Island in Nigeria all share a rich architectural heritage which emerged in the wake of the Atlantic slave trade. This Afro-Brazilian legacy blended with the concrete architectural styles of the French, German, and British colonists (Sinou and Oloudé 1988; Sinou 2011; Mengin and Godonou 2013; Meuser and Dalbai 2021, see volume 3). As a result, cement slowly diffused throughout local architecture. The mosque of Porto-Novo symbolizes such change: this treasure of Afro-Brazilian architecture is now covered in cement (Figure 1.1).

During colonialism, the French and British were reluctant to invest heavily in costly cement plants and were content to export raw cement to the colonies (Akinyoade and Uche 2016). West Africa's first cement plant, the *Société des Chaux et Ciments du Sénégal*, opened in 1930 in Rufisque, a coastal city not far from the capital of Dakar,[1] and in 1948 became the *Société Coloniale des Ciments,* and subsequently *Société Commerciale du Ciment* (SOCOCIM). This was one of the first integrated cement plants, which differed from the then much more common grinding plants. In an integrated cement plant, cement is produced entirely in situ from local limestone deposits. Once extracted, the limestone is combined with clay respectively in proportions of 80–20%. The substance is then heated in a kiln to 1,450 °C to produce clinker, small nodules that constitute the intermediary product. This solid clinker is then crushed and mixed with

FIGURE 1.1   Mosque of Porto-Novo, 2016. Source: A. Choplin.

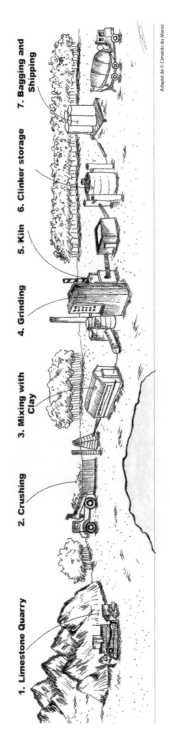

1. Limestone Quarry 2. Crushing 3. Mixing with Clay 4. Grinding 5. Kiln 6. Clinker storage 7. Bagging and Shipping

Adapté de © Ciments du Maroc

FIGURE 1.2 An integrated cement plan. Source: D. Bertrais 2020.

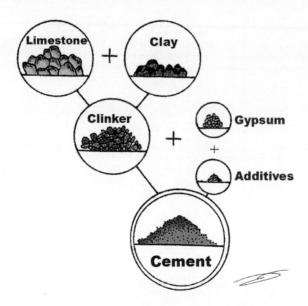

FIGURE 1.3   Cement production. Source: D. Bertrais 2020.

gypsum to make the gray powder we call Portland cement (Figures 1.2 and 1.3). By contrast, grinding plants only perform the second phase: they crush and mix the clinker with gypsum, both of which were imported from Europe or North Africa. Integrated cement plants demanded a great deal of energy and were costly to run, since access to sufficient and uninterrupted power was complicated in this region. Moreover, limestone deposits were rare. In Nigeria, it was not until 1961 that the West African Portland Cement Company Limited (WAPCO) opened the Ewekoro cement plants (now Lafarge Africa WAPCO, a subsidiary of La-fargeHolcim). And it was only in 1978 that the Onigbolo cement plants (SCB-*Société des Ciments du Bénin*, now SCB Lafarge), opened around 100 km away, in Benin. Alongside the opening of this handful of integrated cement plants, grinding units – which were easier to set up – proliferated. Clinker, cement, and gypsum were imported in bulk, hence the location of the grinding units near the ports: *Société des Ciments du Bénin* (SCB) was set up near Cotonou Wharf in 1967, while Cimtogo was built in 1969 next to the port of Lomé. These imports made the industry heavily dependent on foreign countries, which was a problem at a time of fast-growing demand.

The 1980s marked a turning point in the production and distribution of cement in Africa. Serge Theunynck (1994) notes that the price of cement had previously stood at around $40–$60 per ton, i.e., two to three times higher on average than the output from plants in the industrialized world. The reason for this was the much higher cost of energy, the cost of investment (1.5–2.5 times greater) and the overcapacity of the plants relative to demand (which therefore often ran at 30% of capacity). And the European construction market was beset with its own sets of challenges. The global economic crisis of the 1970s led to structural overcapacity and hence to a price collapse of cement. In response, European cement producers sought to expand their external markets and began exporting cement to Africa, a shift also made possible by the fall in maritime freight costs (Theunynck 1994: 343). By the early 2000s, the largest of the European companies began to invest heavily in Africa, opening multiple integrated cement plants supplied from West African limestone deposits. For the first time in history, the old colonial practice of importing cement had largely been replaced by cement produced in situ by integrated factories located on the continent itself.

Patriotic Consumption and National Identity

No fewer than 15 cement plants opened in the 2010s in West Africa, with investment from concrete manufacturing firms like LafargeHolcim and Heidelberg, but especially from Dangote (Figure 1.4). More are due to open soon. Limestone reserves are limited, but of good quality. Similar to the once mineral-rich Copperbelt in Zambia, there is today a "Limestone Belt" emerging in West Africa which is anticipated to shape the future of the region's industry. Limestone is the base mineral of most concrete produced in West Africa. As such, its extraction underpins the growth of cement-based construction and, in turn, the emergence of concrete cities. A large limestone vein crosses West Africa from Togo to Nigeria via Benin, drawing a line that runs through Tabligbo (Togo)/Lokossa–Onigbolo (Benin)/Ibese–Abeokuta–Obajana–Benue (Nigeria). This deposit is tapped by LafargeHolcim in Ewekoro, Dangote in Ibese/Ilaro, SCB Lafarge in Onigbolo and, since 2013, by *Nouvelle Cimenterie du Bénin* (Nocibé–Ciments du Sahel Group). In 2015, the German concrete giant Heidelberg opened an integrated cement plant in Tabligbo, a town near Togo. The plant was a strategic shift for the group, which had previously owned only grinding plants in Cotonou, Ouagadougou, Tema, Takoradi, and Lomé. These new cement plants are set to supply the markets of Togo, Benin, and Nigeria through which the deposit runs, but also those of neighboring countries without significant limestone deposits.

The lack of access to energy – especially electricity – was an obstacle to the installation of integrated cement plants in the region. Heating a kiln to 1,450 °C to produce clinker requires a lot of power. The building of cement plants and the construction of dedicated power plants to serve these factories require huge financial resources. The high cost of electricity explains why the German firm Heidelberg found it more viable to import clinker from China

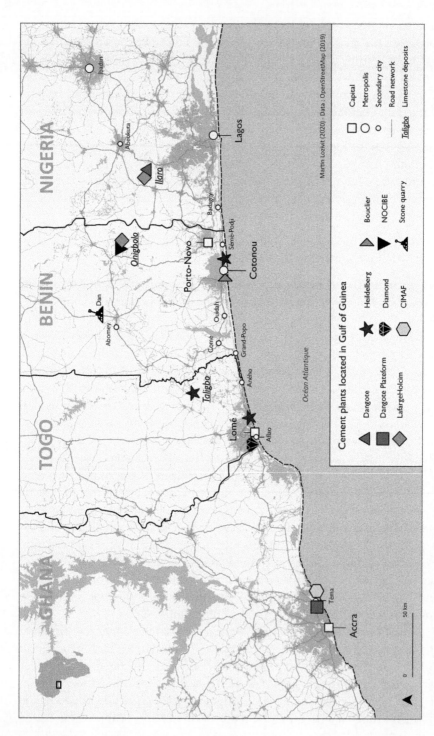

FIGURE 1.4 Cement plants in the Gulf of Guinea. Source: A. Choplin, M. Lozivit 2020.

or Indonesia to supply its grinding plants near the ports of Lomé (Cimtogo) and Cotonou (Cimbénin): according to a former Heidelberg sales manager, one ton of the Chinese product cost $35 as compared with $80 in Africa. As a result, it was not until 2014 that Heidelberg opened an integrated cement plant in Tabligbo. The same was true for Dangote who has begun the challenging work of supplying energy to rural limestone quarries in his push to produce cement locally. Despite these efforts at integration, African cement plants are still highly dependent on external inputs: petcoke for the kiln comes from Venezuela, gypsum for the mixing from Spain. As a result, the cost price of a bag of cement is very sensitive to changes in raw material prices. To mitigate the costs of these imports and limit dependency on overseas production, companies have in recent years invested massively in integrated cement plants.

While there is nothing new about cement in Africa, full local production is a recent phenomenon. Cement, formerly a symbol of colonial domination, has been rapidly incorporated into local material culture to the point that it has now become a foundational building material. After independence, cement plants were nationalized and became a point of national pride in the same way as oil refineries, car assembly plants, breweries, airlines, or flour mills (Dubresson 1989). Almost 60 years later, there is no doubt that cement has been Africanized: many people in the region are proud to buy and use "home-grown" cement, one of the few commodities produced in situ, along with beer, iron, and a some agri-food products. Concrete is a global commodity but strongly linked to local and national identity. At the same time, cement firms develop a rhetoric which argues that consuming locally-produced cement is a patriotic act, as this picture promoting Togolese cement – *le ciment du pays* (the country's cement) – demonstrates (Figure 1.5). As a product that is now perceived as African, cement has become a symbol that accompanies the denunciation of the former colonial domination and, conversely, the affirmation of West-African postcolonial identity. Cement and concrete contribute to a very strong sense of identity, similar to how the concrete industry was glorified during post-war reconstruction in Europe (Forty 2019). In this part of Africa, there are few other industrial empires on which to link visions of development, pride, and modernity, offering concrete a privileged position as a material signifier of the future of African economic growth.

Dangote, a Cement Magnate

Aliko Dangote is the founder and CEO of Dangote Industries Limited. In his biography, *Aliko Mohammad Dangote: The Biography of the Richest Black Person in the World*, Dangote put his professional ethos in simple yet ambitious terms:

FIGURE 1.5   "Let us build the city with the cement of the country." Billboard, Lomé. Source: M. Lozivit 2019.

"to build a successful business, you must start small and dream big" (Fayemiwo and Neal 2013). Dangote's vision of success mirrors his own personal trajectory. According to this biography, Dangote started out by selling three truckloads of cement thanks to his uncle and grandfather, who were shopkeepers. And in the space of two decades, he became Africa's leading cement producer and the richest man in Nigeria, indeed in the whole of Africa, and the world's 25th richest man (Akinyoade and Uche 2016) (Figure 1.6).

Dangote managed to shake up a cement sector largely dominated by big private foreign multinationals that had set up subsidiaries in Africa, such as the French-Swiss LafargeHolcim[2] and the German Heidelberg. Set up in 1977, the company runs more than 10 integrated cement plants, employs around 30,000 people, and operates across 10 countries: Nigeria, Cameroon, Congo, Ethiopia, Ghana, Senegal, Sierra Leone, South Africa, Tanzania, and Zambia

FIGURE 1.6 Dangote, Africa's Richest Man. Source: Saba Dubai /
Wikimedia Commons / CC BY 3.0.

(Akinola 2019). The company is a full-service producer, from quarry to end-user, with a production capacity of 51.55 million tons per year across 10 countries in 2021, and its three cement plants in Nigeria (Obajana, Ibese, and Benue) alone produce 29.3 million tons a year.[3] It controls 65% of Nigeria's cement market, which puts it in a position to set prices.[4] Since April 2020, Dangote has increased his company's earnings by $4 billion thanks to the rising price of cement and to his oil refinery megaproject which has received generous financial support from the National government.[5] In 2021, in just one short year, the Nigerian tycoon has seen his wealth grow by 14.8%. A feat made possible by the boom in housing construction in Nigeria and increased government spending on infrastructure, which increased the price of shares in Dangote Cement stock by 30%.

Aliko Dangote – the African dream. His personal fortune is estimated by Bloomberg to be at $16.7 billion, and by Forbes at $13.9 billion in 2022. By producing and selling cement, Dangote has become the wealthiest individual in Africa and the only African in Bloomberg's list of the "50 most influential people" in the world. His wealth, his family, and his success inspire respect and admiration among many across West Africa. He has developed a globalized business and established an expansive network of contacts. For example, the wedding of his daughter, Fatima, in Lagos in March of 2018 featured some of the world's wealthiest and most recognized figures – Bill Gates even made an appearance – and every guest was given a Rolex watch as a souvenir.

The Nigerian media reported the wedding as the second most important of the year, outranked only by the royal wedding of Harry and Meghan in Great Britain. Beyond dreaming of becoming star football players, young men in the region are now dreaming of becoming cement makers. As for young women, many now desire to appear in VIP Dangote Holland wax fabric, the latest in West African luxury fashion. As one young woman in Benin put it, just wearing a fabric signed "Dangote" is enough to make you a "Very Important Person." However, Dangote is not universally admired. His detractors are quick to point out his predatory business practices and his more than ambiguous links with politics. The provocative Nigerian rapper Burna Boy recently took aim at the cement magnate in his song "Dangote," which criticizes him for making a fortune in one of the world's poorest countries.

Dangote has created a new model of cement production in which the regional industry is now largely owned by Africans, its materials are sourced and processed in West Africa, and some countries have ceased importing cement. Although African cement remains dependent on the import of certain raw materials, Dangote epitomizes the postcolonial transformation of cement, now framed by political stakeholders, international donors, and local manufacturers as a local material "Made in Africa." Dangote's construction of a distinctly African concrete empire marks a shift away from former colonial relations and, in some respects, reverses it: at one point Dangote hinted at plans to buy the famous English football club Arsenal. And in 2019, French President Emmanuel Macron invited Dangote to France as part of *Choose France*, a policy initiative aiming to attract foreign investment.[6] The Nigerian magnate has played a major role in "Africanizing" the construction industry: many West Africans now view the concrete industry, and Dangote himself, as the embodiment of a distinct kind of African entrepreneurial success.

Cement Business

Conquering Africa

A long way in the distance, at the end of a recently laid laterite track, a brand-new cement plant is emerging from the midst of the African savannah (Figure 1.7). I check the time on the pickup dashboard. I'm running late. Although I left at dawn, the ride from Cotonou has taken longer than expected. I'm nervous. The Deputy CEO of *Nouvelle Cimenterie du Bénin* (Nocibé) had warned me: "I do not have much time. I can see you between 8.30 and 9:00." The moment I enter his office, he asks me: "Can you tell me who invented cement?" I'm familiar with the debate over the paternity of cement and, knowing that he

FIGURE 1.7 Nouvelle Cimenterie du Bénin (Nocibé), Massé, Benin, 2018. Source: A. Choplin.

is French, I answer: "Louis Vicat." "And when did he invent it?" the Deputy CEO inquired. I reply: "At the beginning of the eighteenth century, when he was building Souillac Bridge." He seems satisfied with my answers and, with a slight smile, he shows me the Wikipedia page on Louis Vicat, which he has printed in advance. I recognize the photograph of the Souillac Bridge in the South West of France. He invites me to sit down and offers to take me on a tour of his company's recently constructed cement plant, quarry, and living quarters for around 50 families. I left this meeting at 1:00 p.m.

Since the 2010s, cement leader firms, such like LafargeHolcim, HeidelbergCement, and of course Dangote, are competing to conquer West African market, together with other, smaller firms like Senegal's *Ciments du Sahel* (owner of Nocibé in Benin), the Amida group (SCB Bouclier in Benin and *Ciments d'Abidjan*), India's Wacem (West African Cement, owned by the Diamond Cement and Fortia Group), Morocco's CIMAF (*Ciments d'Afrique*), Turkey's Limak, or Burkina Faso's Kanazoé. The opening of new cement plants, whether integrated or grinding units only, has increased production capacities. The companies have had to adapt to the reshaping of this increasingly competitive market. In Benin, for example, the oldest of the cement plants, the Onigbolo plant, was set up in 1978 as a joint venture between Benin and Nigeria. In 1998, the Benin government sold 51% of its shares to

Lafarge while Nigeria sold its 43% holding to Dangote. Benin retained a 6% share in the plant, which changed its name to SCB-Lafarge. LafargeHolcim is also present in Nigeria with its cement plant in Ewekoro (near Ibese), and in Cameroon, Ivory Coast, and Guinea.

Dangote is undoubtedly the most influential cement manufacturer in West Africa. According to its website, the company has had to develop its business quickly to serve a fast-growing market. Without identifying sources, the website explains that by 2050 the population of Africa will exceed 2.4 billion, of which 1.4 billion will live in cities. In Nigeria, Africa's most populous country and the seventh most populous in the world with 210 million inhabitants, the demand for cement grew from 5 to 23 million cubic meters between 2000 and 2014, an increase of 400% (Akinyoade and Uche 2016). To respond to the growing demand, the company owns three cement plants with enormous production capacities: the Obajana plant (Kogi State), opened in 2008, is the biggest cement plants in sub-Saharan Africa with production of 13.25 million tons per year. The Benue plant (Ogun State), the oldest of the Dangote cement plants, opened in 2007 and produces 12 million tons destined for Eastern Nigeria and Cameroon. The Ibese facility (Ogun State), near the Benin border, produces up to 12 million tons of cement a year. Dangote's infrastructural achievements transformed Nigeria into a self-sufficient cement producing country (Akinyoade and Uche 2018), and the country subsequently became Africa's leader in intra-continental cement exports (see Dangote Cement Plc, *Annual Report and Accounts* 2021).

In Ghana, the subsidiary Dangote Cement Ghana Limited began operations in 2010 and now provides jobs, directly or indirectly, for 5,000 people. It has acquired 10 ha of land in Tema, Ghana's main port, located on the outskirts of Accra, to set up a logistics platform for the trucks and bagging operations, from where it re-exports to Burkina Faso, Mali, and Ivory Coast. In 2020, an integrated cement plant has opened in Takoradi. Dangote plans to compete with the Indian facility Diamond Cement Ghana Limited, built in Aflao, a few hundred meters from the Togo border and the city of Lomé.[7] The group is open about its ambitions, which they set out annually in a strategic report. In 2015, the group opened a new plant on the outskirts of Dakar. This new plant is in direct competition with SOCOCIM, now owned by the French Vicat Group, which exports 30% of its output to the subregion, in particular to Gambia and Mali.[8] Another Dangote plant is due to open in Niamey and in Kao, Niger.

Competing with Dangote, HeidelbergCement has also increased its presence and influence in the region by opening a clinker production plant (Scantogo) in 2015 at Tabligbo in Togo (80 km from Lomé).[9] Since then, the Group has supplied clinker to its grinding plants in Lomé (Cimtogo),

Cotonou (Cimbénin), Ouagadougou (Cimburkina), and Tema (Ghacem), which it has owned since 1999 following its takeover of Norway's Scancem, which had itself acquired the previously nationalized firms. In addition, the company owns three cement plants in Burkina Faso: the last one opened near Ouagadougou in 2015, with an annual production of 0.8 million tons, expected to increase soon to 1.7 million tons. In Togo, the Kara plant is in the process of doubling production. In Benin, the plant has doubled in size in recent years and almost 20% of its production is exported to Niger. As well as being the region's third largest cement producer, Heidelberg is the region's leading gravel producer: the Granutogo gravel plant, 72 km from Lomé, produces 1,000 tons of gravel a day.

"The Price of Cement Is like the Stock Market"

"The price of cement is like the stock market, it changes every day," explains Joël, a cement retailer, as he carries out his daily task of chalking up cement's price per ton. In the last five years, with the opening of new plants, shortages have given way to overproduction and lead to a price drop in the region. Yet despite the competition, average cement prices are 183% higher in Africa than in the rest of the world (The World Bank 2016: 41). This figure conceals large differences between countries: in Benin, the cost of a ton fell from 110,000 francs CFA in 2014 to 67,000 (i.e., US $100) in November 2017. By comparison, a ton of cement was worth 90,000 francs CFA in Ivory Coast, 82,000 francs CFA in Togo and Niger, and 72,000 francs CFA in Nigeria (Table 1.1).

In several countries in the region, cement is considered a commodity product in the same way as bread or a bag of rice, and its price is therefore capped. Its production and sale are subject to political regulation. In Benin, the official price per ton was 90,000 francs CFA until 2014,[10] but the retail price could be as much as 110,000 francs CFA. The situation changed with the inauguration of the *Nouvelle Cimenterie du Bénin* (Nocibé), which led

TABLE 1.1 Price of a ton of cement in 2020.

Benin	Nigeria	Ghana	Togo	Niger	Ivory Coast	Senegal
67,000 CFAF	49,000 Nairas	711 Cedis	82,000 CFAF	120,000 CFAF	90,000 CFAF	65,000 CFAF
€102	€120	€110	€125	€183	€137	€100

to a fall in prices, an outcome long sought by governments, financiers, and citizens alike. As Pascal, a shopkeeper in Porto-Novo put it, "before, there was a black market and cement smuggling. People went to Nigeria to buy cement and brought it across the frontier illegally". Smuggling cement between Benin and Nigeria – like the smuggling of adulterated fuels (locally called *payo*) – was previously a common practice, especially as the Nigerian *naira* was weak. But since the opening of the Nocibé plant, cement smuggling has sharply diminished. This is because tax exemptions granted by the Benin government to support the creation of the plant have enabled Nocibé to set a subsidized "ex-factory" price for cement. After the creation of the plant, the price per ton fell immediately, first by 5,000 francs CFA then by 25,000 in the following six months. Competitors had no choice but to reset their prices. They denounced the competition as unfair and are now calling for more government intervention. For example, the sales director of SCB Bouclier has argued in favor of, "the return of the state to regulate the market, because the margins are very tight" and because, in his words, "we are only just breaking even." Similarly, over the past 10 years Lafarge's Onigbolo plant has had to cut its workforce from 500 to 380. According to the plant director, the problem is not one of industrial capacity: "The factory produces around 500,000 tons per year. It could produce more, but there would be overproduction and a risk of price collapse."

The main cement manufacturers are careful not to produce at full capacity, because overproduction would drive prices down. They responded to the competition by closing their sales outlets and forcing the distribution market to reorganize. In Benin, it is not to Dangote's advantage to drive prices down, as he previously purchased the Nigerian state's holdings of SCB Lafarge and now holds a 43%. Moreover, several successive presidents of Benin, Thomas Yayi Boni and Patrice Talon, refused to allow Dangote to distribute its cement in Benin. However, the situation could change. In 2018, there was a rumor in Cotonou that Dangote was preparing to distribute its bags in Benin. Indeed, the Benin government was apparently obliged to let Dangote distribute 100,000 tons a year in the country, if it wanted Nigeria to in return allow Benin businesses to sell their products on the Lagos markets.

In Togo, the price equalization system is still operating, with prices held to a maximum of 82,000 francs CFA per ton. However, nothing prevents the companies from selling more cheaply. This is what Dangote wanted to do in the autumn of 2016 by offering cement at 65,000 francs CFA per ton. When the government refused, there was a heated debate in the National Assembly, with some deputies taking Dangote's side. The Togolese government held firm, saying that it wanted to protect the scarce sectors of local production, such as rice, cereals, and cement. In November 2016, a similar situation arose in Ghana. The Cement Manufacturers Association of Ghana (CMAG), made up of the local producers Ghacem and Diamond Cement, called for a ban on imports of Dangote cement. The director of Dangote Cement Ghana defended the company, arguing that the company had paid its taxes and that its entry into the local market had stabilized cement prices. Moreover, he pointed out that Ghacem and Diamond Cement employed only 3,000 people after 55 years on the Ghanaian market, whereas Dangote already had a workforce of 2,000 after just 6 years of operation.[11]

In Senegal, the price of cement is set by the Senegalese government. However, as a result of growing demand from big projects like a toll expressway from Dakar to the new city of Diamniadio, the price of cement in Senegal exploded to around 3,500 francs CFA per bag, as against the official price of 2,900 francs. The government found itself unable to control the prices, instead anticipating that the market would regulate itself and reduce prices with the opening of the Dangote plant and the subsequent increase in production. However, Dangote company claimed that it was more interested in increasing quality than in lowering prices. The media and the population responded with widespread criticisms of the price increase and effectively forced the government to intervene and block it.[12]

While there is dialogue between the cement manufacturers, notably through the cement producer associations, their relationships are often far from amicable. The companies generally tend to complain about their competitors' unfair commercial practices. For example, the CEO of Cimtogo described with some exasperation his relationship to Dangote: "In order to win markets, Dangote relies on volume effects. The company practices dumping by selling its cement almost at cost price. It makes profits by exporting large quantities. We cannot compete with such an industrial giant, which receives support from every quarter" (interview, Lomé, 2018). In 2022, the war in Ukraine continues to have an impact on cement prices. Whether or not the market is directly linked to the war, the price per ton rises throughout West Africa from 60,000 to 80,000 francs CFA. The constant fluctuation of cement prices fuels tough competition, while it also is the driving force behind the circulation of gray gold across the roads of West Africa.

On the Road: Trucks and Logistics

In September of 2016 at the Togo-Benin border, I count almost 300 Dangote trucks waiting, loaded with cement (Figure 1.8). They are registered in Ghana. I am wondering where they have come from with these loads. A few days later, I come across the same convoy of trucks 60 km further on, at the Ghana-Togo border. They are still carrying full loads. Finally, I meet them

FIGURE 1.8   Dangote trucks waiting at the Benin-Togo border, 2017.
Source: A. Choplin.

again three days later, this time empty, at Tema, the industrial and harbor
zone on the outskirts of Accra (Chalfin 2010).

In May 2016, Aliko Dangote acquired a logistics platform in Tema as a
distribution point for the cement he produces in Nigeria. From here, it is
dispersed to resellers located not just in Ghana, but also in Burkina-Faso,
in Ivory Coast and in Mali, where it fetches a much higher price. To this
end, in July 2016 Dangote bought 1,500 trucks from the Chinese firm SI-
NOTRUK, subsequently creating a joint venture with them to assemble the
trucks directly in Nigeria ready to transport the cement produced there to
Ghana. The factory is in Ibese, less than 100 km from Porto-Novo, the capital
of Benin. In the evenings lines of trucks can be seen filing through the city
center. Every truck carries 50 tons of cement, and every convoy consists of
400 trucks so that, with each one, 20,000 tons of cement batter the 500 km
of asphalt that runs from Ibese in Nigeria to Tema in Ghana. The drivers are
Ghanaian. One driver is responsible for carrying the papers for all the vehicles
and conducting the formalities, which is meant to prevent negotiation and
limit possible corruption with individual drivers.

Dangote's strategy is officially philanthropic: his stated aim is to reduce
prices and distribute cement at affordable prices across the region. Yet it can
also be explained as an effort to make new markets for concrete. Since July

2016, Nigeria has been undergoing an economic crisis. The local currency, the naira, has been devalued, rendering Nigerian cement competitively priced for export. Very quickly, lucrative cement smuggling activities started up on either side of the highly porous Benin-Nigeria border. For Dangote, the Nigerian economic crisis represented an opportunity to expand into the sub-region. Following a series of arguments with the governments of Togo and Benin, Dangote has secured approval to transit through these countries and take over the fast expanding Ghanaian market for cement.

Dangote Industries Limited has a vertically integrated structure that enables it to control production and distribution. The strategy is profoundly spatial: it begins with 3,500 trucks crisscrossing West Africa's roads and then the company establishes a permanent base by taking over production premises and distribution points in remote urban outskirts, where the ratio between the kilo of cement and population numbers is growing most rapidly. Vertical integration allows Dangote to control the whole sector, facilitating the company's expansion across the entire region. As part of this expansion, in 2020, Dangote Company signed a deal with the state to rebuild concrete roads across Nigeria. Vertical integration also frees the company from the potential disruptions caused by transport firms, in particular their propensities for lobbies and strikes. This freedom makes Dangote capable of responding quickly to demand and, beyond securing public contracts, it is also a key supplier of private worksites. In this sense, Dangote is exemplary of the broader transformations taking place in Africa's logistics sector (Blaszkiewicz 2021).

Dangote trucks are not the only ones on West Africa's coastal roads. There are also the 700 "buffalo" trucks – nicknamed for the buffalo logo on their doors – symbol of the German cement producer Heidelberg. These trucks belong to the rich Nigerien businessman Illiassou Moumouni, alias "Alomaro," who has signed an agreement with the giant Heidelberg company to distribute its cement and the clinker it produces in its Tabligbo plant to all the firm's other cement plants in Benin, Togo, Niger, and Burkina-Faso. Some say that Alomaro owns as many as 2,000 trucks, which never travel empty. The German cement manufacturer claims not to be interested in bringing transport in-house. As the Sales Director of Heidelberg Cimbénin put it, "our business is cement, not logistics" (interview, Cotonou, 2018). A point emphasized by the CEO of Cimtogo: "Our core business is to produce cement, concrete, aggregate. Not to do transport" (interview, Lomé, 2018). Heidelberg's bosses prefer to let Alomaro, who manages 20% of Cimtogo transport, negotiate each border crossing. Like Dangote, Alomaro's special connections have allowed him to benefit from economic arrangements (Walther 2015). Alomaro is the son of a second-hand clothes seller, and he started out as a motorcycle taxi driver in Gaya in the 1980s. According to rumors across the region, he was skilled at finding any product and selling it at a good profit. In Cotonou, they say that he used to sleep on his motorbike in front of the cement plant. Between 1985 and 2004, he settled in Malanville, a border post between Benin and Niger, buying and selling all sorts of products, then from 2004 in Gaya, where he sold and transported cement. At the time, he worked with Charfo, one of Niger's biggest cement wholesalers. There is another carrier in Togo also known for his role in the cement industry. This big Togolese trader, who goes by the name of Gado, buys the cargoes carried by Dangote's trucks at the border for 66,000 francs CFA per ton, and then sells them for 88,000 on the local market.

Logistics is fundamental, as Hélène Blaszkiewicz (2021) describes for the cross-border movements of goods in the Copperbelt Region in Central Africa. She explains how roads are no longer a response to problems of isolation but to the imperatives of transport speed and profitability. And cement is a central commodity driving this increase in speed. Although heavy materials are expensive to transport, cement is constantly traveling across borders on flatbed trucks, on dugouts in the lagoon or on the back of motorbikes, and cement companies are always attempting to speed up this circulation. The export figures reflect this intense traffic: cement and clinker are Benin's fifth largest export product, after cotton, cashew nuts, oleaginous fruits and oils, representing 14.4 billion francs CFA per year (INSAE 2020): this national statistical report specifies that the main destinations for these exports are Niger (60%) and Burkina Faso (40%). As a consequence, cement is everywhere, for sale on the edges of the big road arteries, at every street corner, on every building site, in the outskirts, in containers and pickup (Figure 1.9). For example, the Sales Director of Ciment Bouclier underlined that, "getting close to our customers, making sure they can find our cement at anytime, anywhere in Benin. That's our goal" (interview, Cotonou, 2018). The Director of SCB Lafarge agrees: "Distribution has changed. Buyers no longer want to go and fetch the product. The product has to come to them". In Ivory Coast, LafargeHolcim has developed Binastore, a franchise-based local distribution network. The cement manufacturers are careful not to involve too many middlemen, which would cut into their profits, and have instead opted to outsource and develop franchises for sales outlets in response to the general fall in prices and margins. As the director of SCB Lafarge put it: "The current trend is to reduce the number of official outlets and to work through private wholesalers with a licensing system. We are cutting our own outlets and carry out only 15 to 20% of deliveries." (interview, Cotonou, 2018). In this way, cement manufacturers are letting the small retail market develop which has in turn allowed them to argue that they are indispensable to the creation of new jobs in Africa's local economies.

FIGURE 1.9   Cement container in Cotonou, 2017. Source: A. Choplin.

The Rhetoric of Development

African cities are today facing urban sprawl and the increasing needs of urbanization, especially in terms of housing and infrastructure. In Africa as elsewhere (Fry 2013), cement manufacturers claim to be addressing these needs and combating poverty. They argue that they contribute to development, providing the material for houses, opening up national economies by putting asphalt on the roads, and building schools and hospitals for everyone's benefit. West African politicians, for their part, also contribute to this framing and often argue that concrete is a central component of a "rising" Africa today. Hence the enthusiasm and consensus around cement: it is understood to serve the imperatives of economic development, the interests of the wealthy, and to simultaneously benefit the poor by improving their living conditions.

Dangote company, like other cement firms, is presenting itself as a key benefactor of this new industry of urban development. For example, on its website, the company claimed that it is "enriching the life of Africans" through the production of a "vital and irreplaceable" material. LafargeHolcim, for instance, highlights its contribution to the production of an inclusive city through its social housing programmes. The company also funds the 14 Trees program to provide access to so-called "decent" housing, with subsidized materials and micro-credits,[13] as well as the DuraBric* product aimed at poor suburban populations in Malawi.[14] In Kenya, Holcim has delivered Africa's largest 3D-printed affordable housing project, using the 3D-print as a technique that could automate the construction industry. It justifies this program explaining that the need for affordable housing "is most acute in Africa, with countries like Kenya already facing an estimated shortage of two million houses. With 3D printing," the company proclaims, "we are proud of being part of the solution."

The cement manufacturers are keen to describe themselves as essential players in solving local social problems, and Environmental, Social and Governance (ESG) factors have now become an integral part of their business strategies. As one document from the HeidelbergCement Foundation states, "it is strategic, not philanthropic, and linked with our core business." Through their foundations, the corporations launch measures which claim to contribute to the development of the communities where they operate: supply of cement to build schools, health centers and other community infrastructures such as wells and roads. As the head of external relations for Heidelberg Cimbénin described it, these are "charm measures to enhance our local image." To construct this image, the company regularly repairs the roads and roundabouts in the town of Sèmè-Podji where it is located (Figure 1.10). LafargeHolcim takes a similar approach by building schools near the Onigbolo cement plants. For example, the Director of the school at Onigbolo explained that "they bring the cement, their construction crews. Every year, in the annual budget, they include plans for buildings" (interview, Onigbolo, 2017). In its annual sustainable development report, Dangote reports on the work it does on the sustainable development goals with local communities. The company highlights "The Dangote Way" of commitment to local jobs, especially for youth, as well as the development of education, infrastructures, and health centers (Dangote Cement Plc, *Annual Report and Accounts* 2021: 33). For his part, the CEO of Nocibé characterizes his company as "having funded the construction of two modules for Massé College in five years, having built latrines, and provided access to electricity. Two water tankers tour the local villages twice a week distributing water." Nocibé also sponsors the popular *Tour du Bénin* cycle race, with a prize of two tons of cement for the "most competitive" rider. These efforts at social responsibility can be interpreted as "greenwashing" or "social washing": they aim to counterbalance the cement industry's negative impacts on the local environment, and in particular the daily nuisances it creates (e.g., pollution caused by intensive truck traffic and the toxic particles released by the cement plants). Such efforts demonstrate that cement companies are full players in urban affairs.

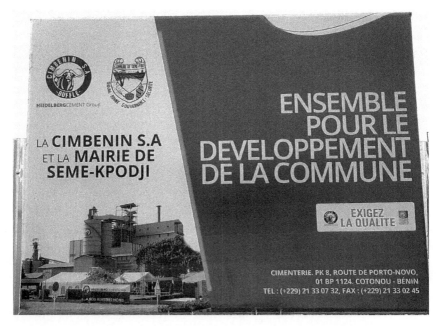

FIGURE 1.10   Billboard "Together for the local development" Heidelberg–Sèmè Podji, 2017. Source: A. Choplin.

Emerging Through Concrete

Promoting Cement and Boosting the Economy

Since the 2000s, development partners and donors have begun to openly support the cement industry as a lever to fight poverty and for "unlocking Africa's potential" (The World Bank 2016). In its 2016 report *Breaking down barriers, unlocking Africa's Potential through Vigorous Competition Policy*, The World Bank argues that cement production is an "effective tool for boosting productivity, innovation, and inclusive growth." The World Bank, as well as the French and German aid agencies (AFD and GIZ), directly support sub-Saharan Africa's labor-intensive cement industry by providing loans to open new plants (Byiers et al. 2017). According to these development banks, competition in the sector forces cement manufacturers to lower prices and the industry's labor-intensive growth will provide income and livelihoods for the continent's poor. For example, the French Development Agency (AFD) via its dedicated private sector investment subsidiary Proparco, invested 20 million euros in the Turkish cement manufacturer Limak to set up on the outskirts of Abidjan, out of a total investment of 68 million. The German Investment Corporation (DEG) – a subsidiary of the German development bank – has also supported the project. Major cement companies similarly justify increasing production by framing it as a way to make cement bags widely affordable. The cement industry is here presented as a source of substantial profit, not only for the big Western companies and investors now present across Africa, but for the construction sector's diversity of stakeholders, including poor African households.

This endorsement of the cement industry among the funding agencies is linked to the idea of cities as drivers of economic development. For example, UN-Habitat (2012: 6) identified megacities, urban corridors, and megacity regions as areas that can contribute significantly to global economic production. The metropolitan scale has gradually come to dominate as the preferred level of intervention in a context of globalized and neoliberal development (Brenner 2004). This observation, originally based on Western cases, is now seen to apply to the Global South as well. At least, this is what may be inferred from the 2009 World Bank report *Reshaping Economic Geography*, which frames cities as opportunities for economic development. The report explains that certain areas, such as metropolitan regions or coastal zones, are necessary anchorages for globalization and competitiveness, and that economic growth and its corollary, urban growth, can act as levers for development in the surrounding regions. These principles were restated in the Sustainable Development Goals (SDG) in September 2015 and at the UN-Habitat III summit in Quito in October 2016, and recently in the report *The State of African Cities 2018*. This UN-Habitat report, subtitled, *The Geography of African Investment,* defines African cities as the best loci for international investment, an endorsement which indirectly supports the concrete industry (Walls et al. 2018).

A wide array of development banks – such as the African Development Bank, the Islamic Development Bank, and the AFD – fund urban, transport, and infrastructure megaprojects across West Africa, all of which require immense amounts of concrete. For example, the Lagos-Badagry Expressway, a section of the Trans-West African Coastal Highway intended to link Lagos to Dakar, is currently under construction and is funded with the support of the African Development Bank. Conceived as a regional asset, this road is the flagship project of ECOWAS.[15] Inspired by the Schengen model, ECOWAS advocates for the free circulation of people and goods between countries in the region to stimulate trade and grow national economies. Big road arteries are the backbones of this project. CORAL (Abidjan-Lagos Corridor), for example, is a road program designed to improve flows and facilitate exchanges along the Abidjan-Lagos axis that accounts for 75% of the zone's economic activities (Banque Africaine de Développement 2016). Indeed, large volumes of cement travel along this corridor, thanks to the support of governments who are prepared to remove import duties as part of the ECOWAS efforts to increase free trade along the regional highway network.

As part of its regional integration plan, the African Union (AU) and ECOWAS, give significant support to Dangote and its strategy. Producing concrete in Africa is consistent with the AU's principles, as the company's aim is to limit West Africa's dependence on the outside world and establish more independent African economies. ECOWAS, for example, helped Dangote make maximum use of the regulatory framework for regional trade. The CEO of Diamond Cement Ghana, a Dangote competitor, explains that the latter receives "a 30% subsidy from Nigeria's Export Expansion Grant Scheme (EEG) to export its cement, and a tax exemption from ECOWAS to export to Ghana" (Akinyoade et al. 2017: 292). Because of this arrangements, thousands of trucks are easily able to cross the Nigerian, Ghanaian, and Nigerian borders which are usually subject to heavy international tariffs. Officially, Dangote completes these tax formalities in advance at the state level, thereby escaping the everyday low-level corruption at customs which is common to this cross-border region (Igué and Soule 1992; Blundo and Olivier de Sardan 2007; Chalfin 2010; Walther 2015; Lihoussou 2017). Unofficially, it is possible that the company negotiates a crossing fee with the politicians. Concrete is a prism through which we can interpret the rearrangements with governments, the interplay of alliances, and the clientelism that influence the capitalist sector and even its product prices. No cement plant can open without strong support from a bank, from sponsors, and from government, because "creating a cement plant means a lot of investment, a lot of risk," as the CEO of the *Nouvelle Cimenterie du Bénin* (Nocibé) once put it (interview, Cotonou, 2017). Government intervention and financial support is needed to encourage foreign companies to invest in this sector which, though profitable, demands the commitment of larger sources of capital than other comparable investments (Akinola 2019).

From Developmental States to Entrepreneurial Presidents

"Build often, destroy sometimes, give service always" – this is the slogan painted on the side of a Cotonou prefecture bulldozer at work in the streets of the capital in January 2017. Patrice Talon, president of the Benin Republic since 2016, wants to "clean" the main roads – a practice he describes as "noble" – by removing street traders. Government officials call this an "operation to liberate the public domain." In contrast, many residents call it an "eviction" (*déguerpissements* in French). Talon is trying to turn the economic capital of Benin into a modern and competitive city, capable of rivaling Africa's other big cities: "Cotonou is in competition with Abidjan and Accra" he tells the press in 2016, and as part of his government action program christened "Benin Revealed," this "builder" president is supporting a litany of urban projects driving the city's construction boom: road infrastructures; a social housing program; a smart city (Sèmè City); a new airport, riverbank, and coastal development projects; and a wide array of other large-scale investments in the urban built environment. In 2018, the government launched the "asphalting project" which José Tonato, minister for the Ministry of Living Environment and Sustainable Development, framed as follows: "The purpose of the asphalting project is to free the public domain. Everyone in Benin knows that if Cotonou is to compete with the other cities in the sub-region, it needs a minimum of development. We need to work to achieve goals of urban quality for our city."[16]

In Benin, as elsewhere, political leaders need to make their own mark as builders and win over voters with roads, pipes, pavements, and tar. In this sense, the head of state resembles an entrepreneur trying to attract long-term investors to invest in "enchanting" infrastructures and megaprojects (Harvey and Knox 2015) (Figures 1.11 and 1.12). The figure of the president-builder marks a recent change in the role of the state in society. In this re-formatted role, states develop new investment opportunities in highly symbolic infrastructure projects (highways, railways, ports, energy) and, in doing so, they break with the budgetary orthodoxy imposed by the Bretton Woods institutions which had frozen a wide array of similar projects for several decades (Péclard et al. 2020). There has been a return to a proactive investment policy, placing the state at the heart of planning and economic development strategies. In this context, the president is known and recognized as a state authority for the projects and infrastructures he undertakes. He finds himself trapped between two different timeframes: the relatively short timeframe of presidential terms and the longer timeframe of project cycles. Many West African citizens judge presidents on the material projects they produce, in particular the number of buildings that rise out of the ground. The creation of "dream cities" (Adeniyi-Ogunyankin 2019) from this constellation of urban construction projects is accompanied by new governance practices and new state structures to manage the implementation of large-scale development projects. In order to avoid administrative delays, governments create new agencies directly under the control of the head of state, but these agencies function similarly to corporations (Blaszkiewicz 2021). In Benin, for example, the president has created agencies for tourism, drinking water, the living environment, and digital technology, and has appointed foreign-educated Beninese to head them. These agencies are often assisted by international consultancy firms which act as project coordinators, and they are

FIGURE 1.11 Poster supporting the Beninese president Talon: "Porto-Novo, the capital-city under construction", 2019. Source: Courtesy of G. Dobigny.

FIGURE 1.12 Campaign poster to "Keep Lagos Clean", 2017. Source: A. Choplin.

capable of signing public-private partnerships by agreement. In other words, their remit – voted directly in the Council of Ministers by presidential order – is opaque. These new agencies play host to well-known private-sector guests and divulge the designs and business plans of future projects in the jargon of management newspeak. As a result, implementing agencies set up in the 1990s at the behest of the World Bank have become obsolete institutions, edged out by these newer more corporate-savvy alternatives. Caroline Melly (2013) came to the same conclusion in her analysis of *Agence nationale de promotion des investissements et des grands projets* (APIX) in Senegal, the national agency in charge of supervising the government's major infrastructure projects, especially the creation of the new satellite city of Diamniadio and the Regional Express Railway project. Located outside the ministerial system, this agency is under the direct executive control of the president, which makes it a "quasi-state office" (Melly 2013). For African citizens, the confusion created by the creation of these parastatal agencies raises issues of not knowing who precisely owns and operates large-scale public infrastructures. Although most infrastructures across the continent are still owned by African states, the rise of parastatal development agencies has also meant that partial ownership of public infrastructures "has changed hands from a public entity (like a state) and shifted to a private entity (like a firm)" (Mizes 2016).

Presidents, like states, have become both entrepreneurs and investors (Pitcher 2012). They legitimate their command of state power through a form of authoritarianism blended with private sector intervention (Péclard et al. 2020). Public-private partnerships are numerous and well known, and they include a diversity of projects ranging from the Cameroonian government's social housing programs to major transport infrastructures in Dakar. For example, the president of Senegal, Macky Sall, has played on the theme of a "fast track" to development in the national "Emerging Senegal Plan." In this plan, everything happens quickly and visibly. And beyond Senegal, "fast urbanism" (Datta and Shaban 2017; Datta 2021) has emerged as a generalized mode of production in the cities of the Global South, today contributing to the rapid spread of concrete.

Builder Businessmen and Other Africapitalists

In a neoliberal context characterized by the development of public-private partnerships, the relationship between the public and private sectors is becoming increasingly important. It is worth remembering that the links between the construction sector and electoral politics are not new. Thirty years on from the era of structural adjustment programs, the state has not simply disappeared, but has instead merged with entrepreneurs and big capital: notably capital in the land, real estate, and construction sector, that many investors perceive as safe havens in which to park their capital. Concrete blocks and big construction and infrastructure projects thus become the shaky foundations on which the often-contested legitimacy of certain financial groups, politicians, and businessmen is built. For example, in Central Africa, the scandals surrounding the Dos Santos family in Angola have recently brought these controversial links back into the spotlight (Soares de Oliveira 2021).

It is worthwhile return to Aliko Dangote, an exemplar of the ambiguous connections between business, politics, and capitalism in Africa. Even though he claims to have no electoral ambitions, he is well known for having strong political connections with the Nigerian government. Since the 1990s, Nigeria's successive presidential administrations have broadly supported the establishment of Dangote's monopoly by giving him access to limestone quarries, reducing taxes, selling him government shares following the privatization of the cement industry, and by facilitating the export of his products (Akinyoade and Uche 2018; Akinola 2019). But not all in the private sector see these agreements as fair. As the CEO of a competing European company complained: "Dangote has wrought havoc in the region. He calls up presidents directly and offers them a cheque to let him sell in their countries. He receives tax incentives for extraction and production, and tax exemptions on the goods he exports. So, it's not hard for him to be competitive" (interview, Lomé, 2018). Speaking on behalf of his company, the CEO went on to express his desire to "be a transparent and responsible player in Africa, a model of responsibility." But in his view, foreign companies like his own "start at a disadvantage compared with certain competitors who have somewhat opaque agreements with highly placed individuals."

Confirmed or not, these complaints corroborate the idea that Dangote receives preferential treatment. Nigerian scholars have pointed out this form of "crony capitalism" (Akinyoade and Uche 2018), reminding us that the former Nigerian president Obasanjo had previously allied with Dangote and promulgated the Backward Integration Programme (BIP) for the local cement industry. Dangote was close to President Obasanjo and contributed significantly to the latter's re-election in 2003 by funding his campaign (Akinyoade and Uche 2016). In 2017, President Buhari personally congratulated Dangote for having transformed the country into an exporter of cement. Other Nigerian scholars have recently criticized Dangote's Environmental, Social and Governance (ESG) practices, revealing how the company manages to convert it into strategic commercial practices that enable it to get around public tendering rules and to win contracts on non-competitive terms (Ezeoha et al. 2020). Drawing on the example of cement roads in Nigeria, these authors demonstrate how, when institutional and regulatory controls are weak, strategic Corporate Social Responsibility can be turned into an instrument of rent extraction and profit maximization.

Dangote is a key figure through which to understand recent transformations in African capitalism. He identifies himself as an Africapitalist, a term coined by Tony Elumelu. These pseudo philanthropic businessmen have today replaced the figure of the highly educated intellectual dominant in the 1980s (Banégas and Warnier 2001). Some of these Africapitalists are rising to become heads of state, similar to the electoral trajectories of Trump in the United States or Berlusconi in Italy. They apply a classical form of "neopatrimonialism" (Médard 1991) characterized by the personification of power, the accumulation of resources, legitimization through redistribution and hence by a high level of clientelism. They follow the trails blazed for them by the entrepreneurs and merchants who made their fortunes in the 1980s, drawing on links inherited from colonization; on traditional and religious, family, and community networks; and on political supporters (Ellis and Fauré 1995). But at the same time, their trajectories are pioneering: they reinvent the relationship to power and money; they consolidate this power by articulating it with new forms of global and offshore capitalism. Some of these businessmen have modest backgrounds and claim to be more discreet than their predecessors by combining business, philanthropy, and charity. Aliko Dangote, for example, describes himself as working for the well-being of the people of Africa: "my secret is that I reinvest my profits in the country instead of hiding the money in Swiss bank accounts, and that I lead a modest lifestyle and stake everything on the domestic market of Africa's most populous country" (cited in Fayemiwo and Neal 2013). Although he claims to privilege investing in Africa, Dangote is also turning to the American market, where he is creating the first African family financial investment office in New York.[17] Thus, Dangote appears much more than a cement manufacturer: he is a member of the world's billionaire class and a symbol of how economic development is changing in Africa today.[18]

Alongside Dangote, other African CEOs are transforming African economy and the construction sector. More and more construction contracts, especially large projects, are being awarded to local firms and not only to foreign companies. Some of the CEOs operating in the construction sector are similarly rumored to be close to African heads of state. This is the case of the Nigerian Abdul Samad Rabiu, also in the cement business (BUA Cement PLC), who is in competition with Dangote for the title of richest man in Africa. Similarly, the Burkinabe entrepreneur Mahamadou Bonkoungou, director of the road construction firm EBOMAF, is another well-known powerful public works contractor. Having enjoyed the favors of Burkina Faso's former president Blaise Compaoré, he is said to be close to a broad array of West African presidents: Faure Gnassingbé (Togo),

Patrice Talon (Benin), George Weah (Liberia), Alassane Ouattara (Ivory Coast), and Umaro Sissoco Embaló (Guinea-Bissau).[19] Burkina Faso's richest man also has close ties with Aliko Dangote. These Africapitalist entrepreneurs are challenging the quasi-monopolies hereto established by European construction companies at a time when the presence of these European firms in Africa is being contested. For instance, French companies such as Bolloré, one of the leaders in logistics, or Bouygues, a construction company, are regularly under fire in the media for corruption and fraudulent contracts. Many African citizens denounce the presence of these European firms as a "neocolonial" presence. But beyond facing domestic criticism, these European firms also face competition from China, which is investing heavily in Africa, with its Belt and Road initiative, announcing to develop African infrastructures to aid trade on the continent. In 2020, China has designated Ghana as one of its preferred countries for FDI and has reinforced links with Nigeria, especially in the banking sector.

The cement industry and the construction sector shed light on the alliances, connections, and affiliations between elected officials and the private sector; informal – not to say corrupt – practices that are well known in the region (Blundo and Olivier de Sardan 2007). These relations are central to what Jean-François Bayart has referred to as the "politics of the belly" (Bayart 1993): the entangled nature of activities in the postcolonial state rely on tight-knit relations between heads of state, central power, resource grabbing, and unequal wealth distribution. It takes place in a context where entrepreneurship is encouraged by the discourses of funding agencies and by political leaders who see it as a means of emergence. The state supports Africapitalists who claim to develop the African continent and, in doing so, take control of the real estate, construction, and infrastructure sectors. Until recently, African entrepreneurs invested mainly in rural agriculture: Ellis and Fauré's (1995) seminal work on entrepreneurs mentions only two occurrences for "real estate" and "land." Today, the change is notable: a recent study showed that 30% of investments by African millionaires and billionaires goes into an urban land and real estate, primarily in their country of residence.[20] The "politics of the belly" has been redirected to the urban sphere and this shift indicates the potential for new forms of urban governmentality and the privatization of the state (Hibou 1999).

Conclusion

Concrete has become a political and geopolitical object of primary importance, in which business and politics are inextricably interwoven. With the recent opening of new cement plants in a now African industry – or at least one that is presented as such – a whole urban political economy of concrete production is driving local economic development and creating the conditions for the production and reproduction of political and entrepreneurial elites, such as in the oil sector (Appel et al. 2015; Appel 2019). The concrete value chain now stretches across unprecedented scales, distances, and itineraries, and it is reshaping the modes of urban production. The cement industry and the construction sector are at the origin of a new geography of extractivism emerging in limestone hotspots across the region. Nevertheless, the existence of the Concrete City highlights the persistent and unequal relationship between the North and the South. Once again, foreign companies are exploiting African resources in search of new markets. As such, cement industry and the construction sector are clearly embedded in neo-colonial relations. But at the same time, they have also allowed the emergence and affirmation of local African figures who are redrawing and even challenging these North–South relations of domination.

Drawing on works in anthropology, geography, history and political sciences that have underlined the ambiguous connections between political and economic elite, this section has demonstrated that the Concrete City in West Africa greatly depends on the strong relations between Africapitalists and the public authorities driving the construction boom. A large array of individuals and political networks depend on this economy of concrete: presidents, statesmen, local governments, municipalities, donors, businessmen, and international and domestic construction companies are all implicated in concrete politics in West Africa today. Dangote in particular illustrates a shift toward neoliberalism: he brings together a new vision of success with the continent's booming concrete construction. The age of concrete is also the age of a new form of capitalism in which Africa now plays a distinct part: the circulation of money is deeply linked to the circulation of the gray gold traveling in massive quantities around the roads of West Africa and ultimately anchoring itself in the region's urban landscapes. It also reveals that the super-rich elites invest in the real estate sector locally but not only. As Ricardo Soares de Oliveira (2021) explains, African elites are now fully part of the "global offshore political economy": a significant proportion of their capital goes abroad. In-depth studies should be carried out to investigate these links between African capital flows, real estate investment, and the offshore economy. A new geopolitical map of concrete is being drawn, while the state is simultaneously being reshaped by the establishment of new types of partnerships with the private sector and by the emergence of actors governing through concrete. And with this new geopolitical map comes a new way of producing and governing a Concrete City.

Notes

1   See the official text published in 1930: http://www.entreprises-coloniales.fr/afrique-occidentale/Chaux_ciments_Senegal.pdf.

2   In 2015, the Swiss company Holcim merged with the world's largest cement company, the French group Lafarge. The new entity was temporarily called LafargeHolcim, before reverting to the name Holcim in 2021. In the text, for simplicity, I use the name LafargeHolcim to refer to the company.

3   Dangote estimates its limestone reserves for the Obajana site at 647 million tons (45 years), for Benue at 133 million tons (30 years), and for Ibese at 1,150 million tons (78 years).

4   Fawehinmi F., 2017, Africa's richest man has a built-in advantage with Nigeria'sNigeria's government. *Quartz* Africa, https://qz.com/africa/1098137/africas-richest-man-has-a-built-in-advantage-with-nigerias-government.

5   See Forbes website: https://www.forbes.com/profile/aliko-dangote/?sh=436971cd22fc.

6   See *Jeune Afrique*, '18.01.2019, « Aliko Dangote, Tony Elumelu et Miriem Bensalah-Chaqroun au sommet « Choose France! »', https://www.jeuneafrique.com/708940/economie/business-aliko-dangote-tony-elumelu-et-miriem-bensalah-chaqroun-au-sommet-choose-france.

7   The Diamond Ghana cement plant is linked to the port of Lomé by a 2.5 km long railway line which carries the clinker. It produces 800,000 tons of cement a year.

8   The new cement plant Dangote opened at Pout in 2015 (54 km from Dakar). It has 100 employees and production capacity of 1.2 million tons per year. Like SOCOCIM in Senegal (Société Vicat), Dangote targets both the domestic and the regional market and produces 3.5 million annual tons, one million of which is exported.

9   The Tabligbo clinker production plant has capacity of 1.5 million tons. If we add production by Wacem (which has its head office in the mining city of Tabligbo), total output in Togo is 2.5 million tons.

10   Up to 2014, with equalization, the price per ton was the same across the whole country. Since then, it has varied depending on the distance from the cement plant: 66,000 in Cotonou, 66,000 in Bohicon, 77,000 in Nattitingou, 80,000 in Tanguietta (February 2018).

11   'Dangote cement defends conduct in Ghana', Global Cement, 1.11.2016, http://www.globalcement.com/news/item/5447-dangote-cement-defends-conduct-in-ghana.

12   See *Jeune Afrique*, "Sénégal: le gouvernement bloque l'augmentation du prix du ciment", 18.03.2019, https://www.jeuneafrique.com/750578/economie/senegal-le-gouvernement-bloque-laugmentation-du-prix-du-ciment.

13   https://www.14trees.com/#anchor-1.

14   www.durabric.com and https://www.holcim.com/largest-3d-printed-affordable-housing-project-africa.

15   The Economic Community of West African States ECOWAS is an intergovernmental organization set up in 1975 With the Aim of Fostering Cooperation and Integration between the 16 Member Countries. It notably facilitates the free circulation of people and goods.

16   See #AskGouvBenin: José Didier Tonato rassure les internautes à propos du projet asphaltage, Bénin Révélé Mag, 19.11.2018 https://www.beninrevele.com/askgouvbenin-jose-didier-tonato-rassure-les-internautes-a-propos-du-projet-asphaltage.

17   See *Jeune Afrique*, 10.01.2020, "Las de l'instabilité des devises africaines, Aliko Dangote veut investir dans la finance à New York », https://www.jeuneafrique.com/879696/economie/las-de-linstabilite-des-devises-africaines-aliko-dangote-veut-investir-dans-la-finance-a-new-york.

18   See the list of billionaires on Forbes Website: https://www.forbes.com/africa-billionaires/list/#tab:overall.

19   See *Jeune Afrique*, 28.10.2020, « Comment l'influent Mahamadou Bonkoungou, magnat du BTP, est devenu l'ami des présidents ». https://www.jeuneafrique.com/1061720/economie/comment-linfluent-mahamadou-bonkoungou-magnat-du-btp-est-devenu-lami-des-presidents.

20   See *Jeune Afrique*, 10.03.2020, « Quels sont les pays africains qui comptent le plus de millionnaires? » https://www.jeuneafrique.com/908229/economie/les-millionnaires-africains-toujours-plus-nombreux-selon-un-classement-de-knight-franck/?utm_source=newsletter-ja-eco&utm_medium=email&utm_campaign=newsletter-ja-eco-10-03-20 See also the website dedicated to African Billionaires: https://billionaires.africa.

CHAPTER 2

Making the City Concrete

In 2018, the McKinsey Group published a podcast on its website entitled "How to win in Africa."[1] The background image is a large concrete tower with two cranes. This picture is similar to one published in December 2011 by the weekly magazine *The Economist* with a headline "Africa Rising," announcing an historic boom in the African economy. The feature opened with a photograph showing, in the foreground, a site foreman with a mobile phone to his ear and, in the background, mechanical diggers working on Eko Atlantic City, a large-scale land reclamation project for the construction of a new residential island on the Lagos coast. In 2012, *Time Magazine* continued the trend, again under the headline "Africa Rising" and a front cover showing a baobab tree blossoming out of a forest of skyscrapers. Through these marketing images, the "Africa Rising" discourse came to be associated with the Africa of cities and glass, steel and concrete towers – icons of capitalist globalization (Sklair 2017; Adeniyi-Ogunyankin 2019). For Côté-Roy and Moser (2019), this narrative represents Africa as a "last development frontier" and a "last piece of cake" for global investment. In this rhetoric, African elites believe that their time has come to have "shiny cities" (Côté-Roy and Moser 2019), cities that are modern and competitive on the world stage, capable of attracting investors and addressing African poverty in the process. In 2022, 10 years after these newspaper covers, and even as the COVID-19 pandemic has slowed down global economic growth, one sector does not seem to be affected: construction. Forbes reports in February 2022 that Africa's richest businessmen–including the concrete king Aliko Dangote–got richer during the pandemic, thanks in part to the high demand for building materials. In West Africa, concrete mixers and arms never stopped mixing cement. Throughout the pandemic, concrete cities continued to grow vertically and horizontally across the landscape to form a new kind of urban sprawl.

Concrete City: Material Flows and Urbanization in West Africa, First Edition. Armelle Choplin.
© 2023 John Wiley & Sons Ltd. Published 2023 by John Wiley & Sons Ltd.

In this second chapter, I define in more detail what I understand as the Concrete City. This concept captures the material, symbolic, and spatial forms of urban transformation at a time when capitalism in Africa is itself undergoing a profound reconfiguration. I demonstrate here that the Concrete City is the outcome and a reflection of this neoliberal shift. To do so, I mobilize Marxist urban theories which have highlighted the relationship between the circulation of capital and urban space (Lefebvre 1968; Harvey 2001). From this perspective, concrete can be seen as a "spatial fix" (Harvey 2001) that anchors capital and enables capitalism to regenerate. In addition to Marxist theories, I build on empirical research in urban studies that has paid attention to the effects of capitalism and globalization on African cities. Following a capitalistic and entrepreneurial turn such as the one observed in Western cities (Harvey 1989), these cities are now managed like private companies. They are presented by investors and governments as smart, sustainable, and/ or green cities by accommodating plans for new or satellite cities. They have become bankable objects, following a business model in which presidential decrees create new megaprojects within showcase-territories auctioned to the highest investment bidders. Images of these futuristic megaprojects, with their iconic architecture–Diamniadio in Dakar, Hope City in Accra, Konza in Nairobi, Eko Atlantic City in Lagos–are now circulating across the world (Watson 2014, 2020; Myers 2015; Van Noorloss and Kloosterboer 2018; Fält 2019; Côté-Roy and Moser 2019). In this chapter, I investigate how these projects have established new links between capital, finance, and real estate. To analyze these new linkages, I draw on the existing research in Africa (Goodfellow 2017, 2020; Migozzi 2020; Mizes and Donovan 2022), Asia (Aveline-Dubach 2016; Fauveaud 2020) and Europe (Aalbers 2016; Halbert and Attuyer 2016; Drozdz et al. 2021) on related trends in economic and urban development. As part of these new trends, Africa's property markets are becoming connected to international financial markets and the global off-shore economy (Soares de Oliveira 2021). Here as elsewhere, the conversion of housing into a commodity is ushering in a "new stage of capitalism" (Aalbers 2016).

To explore the Concrete City's links to capitalism and globalization, and to nuance this Africa Rising rhetoric, I focus on its materiality and follow the flows of materials – especially bags of cement – that shape it. Looking at the intra-urban scale, I note that circuits of capital, actors, temporalities, and spatial forms differ. Though bags of cement are the same everywhere in the city, the money used to buy them, and the people bying them, are diverse. First, I propose a typology of three urban models recurrent in all the cities of the corridor: the megaprojects in city centers and in a few strategic places on the peripheries, what I call the "Premium City"; the social housing programs launched by the state via public-private partnerships, which design what I refer as the "Affordable City"; and the far-away suburban areas resulting of incremental urbanization and everyday practices of autoconstruction, shaping what I defined as the "Low Cost City." What can we learn from these three urban forms about the modes of urban production (capitalist, state-supervised, informal, etc.)? Who are the different stakeholders building these urban spaces? How does capital circulate? What is concealed behind these cranes and these half-built skyscrapers, behind these finance packages and investment strategies, behind these concrete walls, their foundations, and finishes? Second, I explore the city in its innermost materiality to reveal the major role of other actors who contribute actively to the circulation of capital and the making of cities: developers and realtors, banks, donors, diasporas, importers of building materials and public works companies, digital operators, etc. Finally, I offer a tour of the work sites to get information on the construction materials–sand, reinforced steel, tiles–whose unfamiliar but globalized flows are essential to an understanding of urban production. I argue that this multifaceted Concrete City appears as the new symbol of African urban capitalism, materializing new forms of urban governance, circuits of monetary exchange, and regimes of accumulation.

The Multifaceted Concrete City

Premium City–Megaprojects and the Business of the City

In his anticipation novel *Les Furtifs*, Alain Damasio (2019) imagines a city that has been bought up by a large private group. In this city, citizens do not pay taxes, but rather subscribe to a package of segmented urban services: standard, premium, or privilege, the latter being the only package that guarantees free access to all streets and parks. I use this metaphor of packages to analyze the evolution of West African cities in a context of increasing neoliberalization. In these cities, the development of megaprojects leads to the creation of spaces with limited access. Whether located in the city center or in satellite cities, these areas are reserved for those who have "the good package" according to their wealth, status, and class. This way of classifying spaces is very similar to that imagined by Damasio. I propose to use the metaphor "Premium City" to refer to the first face that the Concrete City can take on: a city of private spaces, luxury megaprojects, and infrastructures restricted to the elites.

Megaprojects have been extensively studied in Asia (Shatkin 2008; Goldman 2011), in the Middle East and North Africa (Choplin and

Franck 2010), and across Africa more generally (Watson 2014; Herbert and Murray 2015; Van Noorloos and Kloosterboer 2018; Goodfellow 2017, 2018; Adama 2018; Fält 2019; Terrefe 2020). The negotiations of these megaprojects reveal the city branding efforts of local leaders (Cirolia and Berrisford 2017; Croese 2018) and is accompanied by the demarcation of zones where foreign investors, with the support of the governments, pursue their projects under their own rules. In the wake of opaque land deals, these spaces are generally sold for symbolic sums of money or transferred under long-term leases that leave significant room for maneuvers. They evade local laws and become "exceptional territories" (Roy 2011). In India, Michael Goldman (2011) described this urbanism as "speculative": justified by the strategic need to build global cities, exceptional rules of dispossession come into force, redrawing the boundaries of the relations between the state, urban citizens, rights, and conditions of access. States themselves exploit the process of urbanization to extend their powers. In Asia, they support these projects by both selling and reclaiming land, and by facilitating the privatization of urban planning (Shatkin 2008). Similarly, in Africa, new types of territory fall outside the reach of public institutions. Drawing on the case of two new towns in South Africa (Waterfall City and Lanseria Airport City), Herbert and Murray (2015) show how "privatized urbanism" is implemented in "private enclaves"—where "everything from basic infrastructure (including utilities, sewerage, and the installation and maintenance of roadways), landscaping, security services, the regulation of common spaces, and selling and branding the city are firmly in the hands of private profit-making corporate entities and outside the mandate of public authorities." The creation of these private enclaves and premium spaces requires the clearing of areas. Street vendors, squatters, and other poor inhabitants are usually evicted through the application of decongestion and beautification policies. These evictions (or *déguerpissements* in French) are violent and recurrent in this part of Africa (Gillespie 2016; Mendelsohn 2018; Spire and Choplin 2018; Spire and Pilo' 2021). In many new African cities, these exceptional territories and other premium spaces come into being by exacerbating exclusion, injustice, and segregation (Van Noorloos and Kloosterboer 2018; Fält 2019). These new cities are multiplying across Africa–the International New Town Institute has identified more than 150 new town projects around the world since 1960, the vast majority of which are, since 2010, in Africa.[2]

In Nigeria, kilometers of concrete have been poured to tackle rising sea levels and coastal erosion. The wall is impressive: 8.5 km long, 18 m tall (10 m underwater and 8m above), and 100,000 concrete blocks, all intended to protect Victoria Island's business district.[3] The project is justified as an ecological necessity, but also–and above all–by economic necessities, as suggested by the *Eko Atlantic Milestones* project document, *Shaping the future*.[4] More than 100 million tons of sand have been dredged from the seafloor and spread out to form a polder as the base for the new city of Eko Atlantic, despite widespread objections (Acey 2018; Adama 2018; Mendelsohn 2018). The 10,000,000 m^2 of artificially created land is slated to become home to a "Global City – World Class Design," where "good living meets great business" (Figure 2.1). Access will be controlled and restricted, taking the form of a gated community in the very heart of Lagos. The funding is entirely private, provided by two rich Lebanese-Nigerian businessman, the brothers Ronald and Gilbert Chagoury. The project was supported by Bill Clinton and his foundation, in exchange for funds received from R. Chagoury (Côté-Roy and Moser 2019). In this free zone, the first two towers built (*Eko Pearl towers*) are owned by the Lebanese-Nigerian Elias Saad,[5] who made his fortune in cocoa and stone quarries. His civil engineering and road building company also supplied most of the stone used to build the wall. Yet the funding for the project remains opaque: a visit to the site and the showroom failed to provide any information about the source of the investments and the financial arrangements. I was told only that the licence was allocated for 70 years and that Dutch experts were assisting with the project. There is no height limit on the towers. Nor on the dreams.

A few hundred kilometers away, the capital of Ghana is also under-going multiple changes, following the decision of the former mayor Alfred Vanderpuije to make Accra a "Millennium City"–in other words, a modern and business friendly metropolis (Obeng-Odoom 2015). The coast was cleared to make way for the Marina Drive Project–a huge luxury residential,

FIGURE 2.1   Eko Atlantic City, Lagos, Nigeria. Source: Google, Maxar Technologies, 2023.

business, and commercial zone–under a $1.2 billion public-private partnership (Fält 2016; Gillespie 2020). Nearby, a new Chinese-financed fishing complex is projected to be built in the historic heart of Jamestown which, in May of 2020, resulted in evictions. In the city center, the Octagon project–a luxury residential and shopping complex–has now replaced an informal street market, following bitter resistance of street vendors (Spire and Choplin 2018) (Figure 2.2). Large-scale road development projects have been launched by the government to improve traffic flows, particularly at the Nkrumah Circle interchange which has been rebuilt by Brazilian companies. Several projects are also scheduled in the outskirts of Accra, around Tema and Prampram. For example, the Ghanaian government announced in 2013 its future plans for the Hope City project, Ghana's future technology park but, to date, the project

FIGURE 2.2   Octagon Project, Accra, 2017. Source: A. Choplin.

has yet to break ground. For its part, the Ningo-Prampram Greater Accra urban expansion project is slated to provide homes for 1.5 million people, with the support of UN-Habitat, international consultants, and local leaders, giving an idea of this area's global connections (Grant et al. 2019). A few kilometers to the north, Appolonia City is intended to provide homes for 88,000 people. For the moment, only a few houses have been sold. According to Lena Fält (2019), this project reflects the emergence of a "privatized urbanism" and involves a whole "constellation of actors" including states, property developers, and traditional authorities. Fält underlines the contradiction between this megaproject, targeted at an international elite and driven by profit, and its official presentation as a sustainable and inclusive project.

In Benin, Sèmè City is the smart city slated for construction on the route out of Cotonou, a few kilometers from Nigeria. The Sèmè City Development Agency, which has direct links with the office of the president, is headed by Claude Borna, a Beninese businesswoman who built her career abroad. The future smart city, marketed as "African-made innovation," is meant to counterbalance the "skills desert" in the country and the mismatch between the job market and graduates from the national university: 200,000 jobs and 40,000 "learners" are expected from the project. Among the proposed training courses, an African City Lab has been set up with the swiss school EPFL and offers online MOOCs on urban issues. The project has received a great deal of media coverage in Benin, and even more outside, though local elected officials have not always been kept in the loop, a situation lamented by Charlemagne Honfo, the former mayor of Sèmè-Podji, the city where the future complex is to be located. The chosen area has been taken out of the system of municipal laws and placed under the authority of the presidential agency. The government of Benin commissioned the Singaporean firm Surbana Jurong to draw up the masterplan. Rumor has it that on his first trip to Rwanda, Benin's President Talon asked his Rwandan counterpart for advice on urban management, since Kigali at the time was seen as Africa's best run and cleanest city. It is said that it was President Kagamé who recommended the firm Surbana Jurong, well-known in Africa for drawing up the masterplan for Kigali (Bock 2018). This example illustrates the transfer of models, from Singapore to Cotonou via Kigali, a reminder of the extent to which urban models, ideas, and currents of thought move around the world and across the African continent. It shows the "cities in relation" (Söderström 2014) and the degree to which urbanism is "mobile," through these models designed to modernize the city and make it more competitive, bringing with them so-called good practices and giving support to neoliberal reforms (McCann and Ward 2011; Parnell and Robinson 2012; Peck and Theodore 2015). In this specific case, the links between the political regimes of Benin, Rwanda, and Singapore are transposed into the computer-generated images produced in the Asian city-state. The model of Asian success thus traveled first to Kigali, currently labeled as the model African city and the "Singapore of Africa," then to Cotonou, which Benin's leaders dream of transforming into "Kigali-by-the-sea."

These different projects show that the city is now perceived as a new marketing tool and is becoming a political vehicle and an instrument of capitalism–advertising billboards in the streets showing images of future real estate projects that are as grandiose as they are hypothetical (De Boeck and Baloji 2016). Yet these projects often progress no further than announcements, limited to "fantasy" and computer-generated images produced by international firms with skyscrapers copied-and-pasted from elsewhere into an African urban environment (Watson 2014, 2020; Terrefe 2020). Almost 10 years after the announcement, not a sign of Hope City; in Eko Atlantic, the towers can be counted on the fingers of one hand; and as for Sèmè City, the offices of the agency–decorated with the Singaporeans' 3D images – which were located in an annex of the presidency are supposed to move to Ouidah, the president's home town, designated as the new site of the future smart city. Some of these projects are short-lived or on the back burner, which makes it hard to obtain information and to track the actors involved. "Skeleton cityscapes" (Goodfellow 2017) are emerging and remain vacant because the majority of urban dwellers cannot afford to live in them. In the meantime, whether real or virtual, these projects play a performative role, proposing "Dubaization" as a model for the African city (Choplin and Franck 2010; Di Nunzio 2019: 378). They also provide an opportunity for deal-making, often facilitated by a lack of regulation and relative political stability. The Premium City, with its opaque links to the world of finance, seems to serve the public works and real estate sectors. As one cement plant director put it:

"The only thing that matters for us is the financial flows, and especially that they should not be monitored too closely. Money laundering is undoubtedly what does most to feed the construction market. . . As long as there is no real resistance to corruption and money laundering in Africa, we can consider that the cement industry has a rosy future" (interview, Cotonou, 2017).

Affordable City–Social Housing Programs

In parallel with the big private projects targeting the elites, governments regularly launch social housing programs (*Programmes de logements sociaux* in French-speaking Africa). The production of social housing is part of a long tradition, dating back to the colonial era and decolonization (Biehler et al. 2015). For the new states that came into being following independence in the 1960s, social housing embodied the attainment of a certain modernity.

At this time, domestic construction companies built apartment blocks inspired by the high architectural modernism of the Athens Charter. This type of accommodation (called *Cité* in French-speaking Africa) was designed as a tool to facilitate the birth of a "modern" city-dweller, breaking with the "traditional" ways of life, often perceived to be the preserve of "villagers" (Biehler et al. 2015). These projects were primarily intended to house civil servants. Although the projects we see today are part of this tradition, their objectives, targets, and financial arrangements are distinct. They depend on agreements between the state, the private sector, and banks, as well as international donors seeking to support affordable housing policies. New actors have appeared in this sector, such as FSD Africa, a group specialized in financial markets and development across sub-Saharan Africa, funded by UK aid from the UK government. This group supports, for example, the South Africa-based think tank "Centre for Affordable Housing Finance in Africa," also funded by UK aid, AFD, Cities Alliance, FSD Africa and even the Mastercard Foundation. UEMOA (West African Economic and Monetary Union) and the World Bank also support affordable housing development, which reveals close links between donors, banks, sitting governments, and the local and diaspora elites at which these programs are aimed.

Across East and West Africa, commercial banks have only recently taken an interest in the real estate sector (Gillespie 2020; Goodfellow 2020). These banks essentially lend to big economic players and companies. However, more than that, they tend to play a major role in social housing programs initiated by West African heads of state. In 2013, in Ivory Coast, Alassane Ouattara launched his PPLSE (Presidential Social and Affordable Housing Program) promising 150,000 dwellings; in Benin, Patrice Talon launched his "program for 200,000 social housing units" in 2018; and in 2020, Macky Sall promised the Senegalese 100,000 social homes in the next five years, while Faure Nassigbé has promised 20,000 to the people of Togo. These projects form part of the discourse of emergence and the "redeployment of the state through the politics of social housing" (N'goran et al. 2020). They differ from the social housing programs dating back to the 1960s in that they propose a new kind of financial deal centered around private investment: "the state is no longer the direct contributor, as it was in the 1970s, but more a market regulator" (N'goran et al. 2020). The state guarantee limits the risks and therefore lowers the interest rates. In Togo, two projects are officially presented as social housing programs. The first one, *Résidence Renaissance,* proposes 205 apartments and 394 villas classified in different categories: "Chic, Executive, Luxurious, Privilege," subsidized by the *Caisse Nationale de la Sécurité Sociale* (National Social Security fund). The second one, la Cité Mokpokpo with its slogan, *"À chaque togolais son toit"* (a roof for every Togolese),

FIGURE 2.3 Social Housing Program in Lomé, 2018. Source: A. Choplin.

advertises 540 social dwellings (420 villas and 120 apartments) (Figure 2.3). The program offers 20-year bank loans with interest rates of 7.5%, but they are still too expensive for the majority of the population. As one manager of a real estate agency in Lomé put it, "to start with, you have to be able to borrow 10 million over 15 or 20 years. That's expensive, even for an executive or a civil servant with a decent salary, earning 300,000 a month" (interview with Fabo Immo agency, Lomé, 2017). In other words, even according to key actors in the region's real estate industry, these projects do not meet local demand or needs. For the *Résidence Renaissance* project, the agent continued, "the houses are too expensive. You wonder who is going to be able to buy something like that." Moreover, other agents argued that the standardized design is too rigid: "At Cité Mokpokpo, you cannot change the layout of the house, not even the paintwork," another agent exclaimed, "and that does not go down well with the Togolese" (Interview with SIM 3, Lomé, 2017).

Ten kilometers north of Cotonou in the municipality of Abomey-Calavi, a large social housing development called the Bethel Estate is empty. The site appears abandoned, and weeds have grown in the untrodden alleyways. There are no shops and no people. Yet almost 400 houses have already been sold. A further 200 are still to be built out of the 624 "social and affordable dwellings" originally planned. Launched in 2008 by *Générale du Commerce, de l'Industrie, du Transport et des Travaux* (GCITT), this program has a partnership with the government of Benin. Mr. Smith, General Manager of the estate explained that, "the project is supported by the state, which owns the land and made it available. No taxes or duties" (interview, Ouédo, 2019). This would explain the supposedly "reasonable" price of the houses (between 12 and 40 million francs CFA, i.e., between €18,000 and €61,000). The future owners pay a deposit of 30% and can then choose a plot and the model of house they want. Once the work is finished, they can register their occupancy title, then their land title. Mr. Smith advises us to come back in the holidays to see a bit of life, because 80% of the owners are from the Benin diaspora. He tells us that he has another project: *La Cité de Paix les Cocotiers,* 500 units in Pahou, on the way out of Cotonou on the Ouidah Road, which Mr. Smith suggests is slated to become a "gated community, with a guard post, access control, CCTV, and security alarms."

The same Ouédo district is supposed to be the location of a "program for 20,000 social and affordable dwellings," the 40th and final flagship project launched by the Talon government in 2019. Near Cité Bethel, on a 235-ha site, more than 4,000 buildings and 10,000 dwellings will be constructed, mainly apartments (7,310) and villas (3,539).[6] The promotional video shows plans for the construction of an administrative center combined with shopping and leisure facilities and green spaces. The project is financed by the West African Development Bank (100 billion for 3,035 dwellings), the Islamic Development Bank (43 billion for 2,145 dwellings), the National Social Security Fund (90 billion for 3,099 dwellings), and private partners. A real estate and urban development company (SIMAU, *Société Immobilière d'Aménagement Urbain*) has been created to build the social housing program and the administrative center. The shareholders are mentioned on the website: "The Government of Benin, the West African Development Bank and local banks" as well as the Duval Group, a French asset management and real estate investment company already present in Cameroon, Togo, Senegal, and Ivory Coast. In December 2019, a contract was signed between SIMAU and the Spanish firm PN HG, which created a subsidiary in Benin to build the first 1,735 units over 18 months in 2020. The inhabitants of Cotonou and Calavi remain wary, waiting to see where the project goes. Indeed, social housing gets a bad press, being perceived as uniform, expensive, and poorly finished. The government seems aware of the lack of enthusiasm. President Talon himself brought in two "star" Ivorian architects–Issa Diabate and Guillaume Koffi (Koffi et Diabaté Group)–to demonstrate his personal interest in this program. Some found this choice surprising. As Victor Kidjo, director of the architecture firm *Nature Brique*, noted: "We do not understand why the president brought in an Ivorian architect to design 20,000 social housing units. What's more, it's all concrete. They are good architects, but there are very good architects in Benin" (interview, Cotonou, 2018).

Given the promotional videos, finance packages, and the private actors involved, it is obvious that the only social aspect of these programs is the name. They reflect new methods of urban production in which the private sector has become the dominant force. The presidential building programs give precedence to property developers, investment firms and pension funds, development banks, international banking groups, and private foundations. These projects raise questions about government choices that offer opportunities to the private sector without full regulatory oversight. They also raise questions about the role of public development subsidies whose primary aim is poverty reduction but which, in this specific case, help fund and subsidize homes for financially stable households. These programs and the involvement of these new actors are part of broader neoliberal turn. They also reveal the connection between African real estate markets and global finance. Compared to Asia (Aveline-Dubach 2016; Fauveaud 2020), the financialization of real estate in West Africa is still nascent. However, these examples – both social programs of the Affordable City and the megaprojects of the Premium City – reveal how real estate is in the process of becoming a financial asset. The links between political authorities, banking sectors, and private investors – and more generally the circulation of capital in the Concrete City – need to be analyzed even more closely. Because beyond self-satisfied leaders who congratulate themselves on attracting capital and seeing buildings rise out of the ground, the actual effects of the Affordable City raises questions. With the support of the state, private actors are contributing to the production of a fragmented city with new forms of "premium networked services" (Graham and Marvin 2001). This Affordable City, though not quite a gated enclave like Premium City, is affordable only to the middle and upper classes. Far from its stated ideals of equity and inclusion, the Affordable City is in fact playing a part in the rent capture activities of the private actors commissioned by the state to implement its social housing policies (N'goran et al. 2020).

Low Cost City–Autoconstruction in the Outskirts

Beyond the Premium City and the Affordable City stretch the gray suburbs. Here, as elsewhere, concrete is omnipresent. It travels with the seemingly limitless wave of urbanization. However, in contrast to the private sector driven Premium City, and the state driven Affordable City, construction of the city here relies on the efforts of individual inhabitants with limited resources stacking block upon block of often low-quality concrete–in other words, a Low Cost City. The worksites are self-build projects, directly supervised by their owners. In places, there are still glimpses of corrugated iron and timber, residues of a slum that has only recently been fixed and solidified with cement.

Other spaces lie speculatively fallow: plots have been temporarily allowed to rest until the prices rise. These peripheral areas are land reserves with great potential, places of opportunity and speculation, as well as spaces of desire (Mercer 2020).

This Low Cost City stands at the interface between the city and the rural world, in a space that has attracted much scholarly attention in the Global South. Recent interesting work have been carried out, trying to cast light on the extended processes of urbanization, insisting on plotting urbanism (Karaman et al. 2020), peripheral urbanization (Caldeira 2017), urban periphery (Meth et al. 2021), new African suburbanization (Buire 2014), peripheral urbanism piecemeal and bypass urbanism (Sawyer 2016; Sawyer et al. 2021). Analyzing the Lagos-Abidjan corridor through the prism of material flows offers an excellent discussion case to dialogue with these concepts and the idea of "planetary urbanization" (Lefebvre 1970; Brenner and Schmid 2015). From a certain point of view, this corridor responds to the manifestations of global urbanization as we observe a "concentrated urbanization" and at the same time an "extended urbanization" in rural areas. The pattern corresponds to what Brenner and Schmid (2015: 12) name the "blurring and rearticulation of urban territories" among "expansive catchments of small- and medium-sized towns, and along major transportation corridors such as superhighways and rail lines." The corridor consists essentially of a few big metropolises, spaced at intervals of some 100 km and, between them, a quasi-continuous network of secondary urban hubs. The urban interstices are occupied by big markets that spring to life every day along the road and by a multitude of buildings, houses, stores, and worksites, which resemble urban forms but with no real sign of the presence of a city. Urban forms are there, but not necessarily the attributes of the city. The "unfinished landscapes" identified by Émile Le Bris (1987) and later by Philippe Gervais-Lambony (1994: 65) in the outskirts of Lomé in the 1990s, are still topical today. Stacks of concrete bricks and bags of cement, arranged carelessly in a corner of the plot, are a major feature of "the unfinished," as is freshly poured cement. Among the other markers of urban emergence are the ubiquitous hardware stores selling building materials. The cement giants are well aware of the potential of this permanent peri-urban construction site. Their sales teams criss-cross these suburban areas, with their burgeoning housing estates: "We install containers selling individual cement bags to raise our profile. We are very flexible: we move them into the outskirts where the demand takes us." (interview with SCB Bouclier Group, Cotonou, 2018). In this way, the cement is ready for the city, sitting at the gates of a peripheral construction site.

Alongside the cement depots, other markers characterize this Low Cost City and the advance of city-less urbanization. Sand extraction areas are one

FIGURE 2.4   Sand Extraction, Porto-Novo, 2018. Source: A. Choplin.

of them (Figure 2.4). Spiderwebs–the name given to illegal connections to the power grid – are another, a sign that the official network has not yet reached these interstices (Figure 2.5). The inhabitants lay their cables as if to bring the power companies – and hence the city – to them. It is not unusual to see solar panels alongside these spiderwebs, indicators of the boundaries of the city. On these urban margins, poor households use a solar panel until they have access to the conventional power grid (Rateau and Choplin 2021). Often, these rural areas are devoid of all public utilities and infrastructures–notably access to water, electricity, and education. The presence of private schools is another sign of this gradual urbanization, as well as evangelical churches which settle close to the impoverished populations which constitute their "client base." In these peripheries, thousands of poor people have become familiar with the market economy. Alongside the cement depots and evangel-ical churches, mobile phone operators set up container-outlets, which double as banking facilities (Figure 2.6). These operators, like the now well-known M-Pesa in Kenya, have in recent years turned into mobile banks, setting up in converted containers where people can send and receive money, pay their bills via mobile phone, or buy electricity (Huet and Chakroun 2020; Akindès and Kouamé 2019). Flexible online transactions make it easier to buy a plot of land, to pay a builder or to buy construction materials. Finally, by-the-hour hostels and hotels seek out these periurban areas where electricity has not yet

FIGURE 2.5   Spiderwebs: illegal electrical connections, Cotonou, 2018.
Source: A. Choplin.

FIGURE 2.6   Mobile phone operator in a container, Cotonou, 2018.
Source: A. Choplin.

arrived, where they can offer discrete nocturnal encounters, as suggested by their names ("Top Secret," "From Time to Time," "Direct Line to Happiness"). Still present too are voodoo fetishes, which are traditionally found in villages but have now been caught up in the urbanization process.

To describe this Low Cost City – built up incrementally and resourcefully – I conducted a mapping exercise with the OpenStreetMap (OSM) Bénin community. The aim was to identify all these signs of low-cost urbanization, where urban expansion precedes the city. We first mapped all the cement depots along the city's main arteries: the resulting map (Figure 2.7) give a picture of the omnipresence of this material in the urban landscape. As one member of the OSM team marveled, "It is easier to find bags of cement than bags of rice!" We then chose several neighborhoods on the outskirts of Cotonou to identify the urban markers mentioned above–cement depots, hardware stores, sand extraction, spiderwebs, solar panel sellers, container-outlets for mobile phone operators, private schools, evangelical churches, hostels, and motels – in order to reveal the different stages of urbanization.

In Ouédo, an area where housing construction is ongoing or only recent developed, and that is booming in the wake of the announcement of the big presidential projects, there are large numbers of outlets selling cement, gravel, sand, solar panels – all recently arrived (on average in the last two or three years) signs of sustained urbanization. Other markers of urbanization are also apparent – private schools and dispensaries, evangelical churches, voodoo fetishes, and spiderwebs. A similar exercise conducted in Togbin, an area with a more settled housing fabric (15 years), reveals a predominance of outlets selling materials generally used for finishing such as paint, glass, and tiles. Here, urbanization has advanced further. In Ouédo, people are unwilling to spend a lot on finishing, because of their limited earnings and also because of insecure land tenure and the fear of being evicted at any moment. Conversely, in the areas with older housing developments, such as Togbin, the houses are further advanced, which explains the plethora of stores selling finishing materials.

The type of urbanization observed is unquestionably self-built and low-cost, undertaken with few resources and incrementally. In these areas, the predominance of informal jobs, the absence of regular incomes, the difficulty of long-term planning, the low percentages of bank account holders and, in particular, prohibitive interest rates are all obstacles to property lending. Commercial banks have played relatively little part in individual construction projects. In Benin and in Togo, borrowing rates hover around 12–13%, sometimes rising as high as 25% (compared with an average of 2% currently in Europe). The poorest cannot hope for a bank loan, whereas the rich prefer to pay in cash – both for land and labor – in order to avoid disputes with other

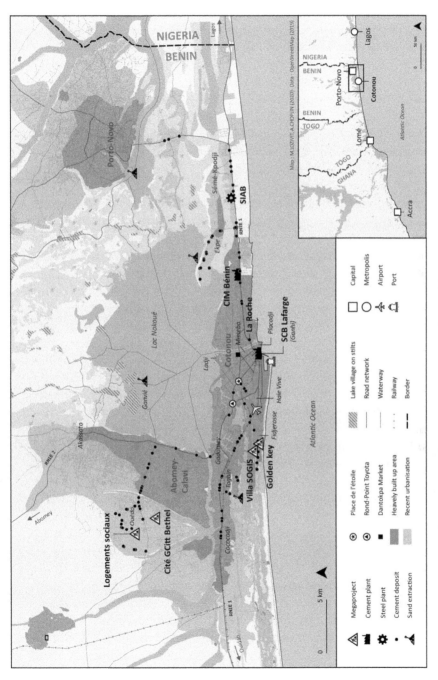

FIGURE 2.7 Cotonou under construction, 2019. Source: Adapted from A.Choplin, M. Lozivit, OSM, personal fieldwork data.

potential buyers. Some companies have developed alternatives to banking services, such as the "Airbag" package offered by one real estate agency:

"It is for people who cannot get bank loans. If a person has 200,000 and wants to buy a plot for 800,000, we lend them the money. The interest rate is 20% a year. As we are not sure that they can afford it, the rate is high. And if they do not pay, we keep the land." (interview with *Global Service Immobilier*, Cotonou, 2016)

This kind of loan provides security (like an airbag) to the real estate company that evicts the individuals and keeps the land in case of non-repayment. This type of funding fits well with incremental urbanization and "plotting urbanism" (Karaman et al. 2020; Sawyer 2016). It can be defined as an "unplanned, plot-by-plot development of land where statutory and customary rights are intertwined in a dual land regime, causing widespread contestations and fraudulent activities over landownership, land divisions and property transfers" (Sawyer et al. 2021: 686). This expression is relevant not only for Lagos, but for all the urban peripheries of the corridor. Often for these district or village chiefs, for mayors and elected officials without resources, the only way to bring in money is to divide up and sell plots, which intensifies the process of speculation and concretization. It echoes what Sawyer et al. point out (2021): "The emergence of heterogeneous but powerful alliances of various state and private actors and the concomitant transformation of regulatory systems are also shaping and defining a process of urbanization that bypasses conventional modes of urban and regional governance." From this perspective, these urban actors "are not following a clear, predefined master plan or overarching strategy," but instead, "a certain logic of capital accumulation and commodification is resulting in a new kind of urbanism that affects people inside and outside the bypass areas" (Sawyer et al. 2021: 677). This process of "bypassing urbanism" is common to the different peripheral urban areas that make up the corridor.

In these peripheries, all the traces of the urban are present (buildings, density), but they cannot precisely be described as city–except perhaps as a Low Cost City without utilities, urban amenities, or an urban center. It produces a price-cut city: in its built forms, constructed incrementally from day to day; in the few services it delivers (often private and unreliable); or in the mediocre quality of life it offers. This low-cost, low-skill, and low-intensity city of capitalism, is continually expanding, as the memory of its rural past disappears under slabs of concrete.[7] As one village chief in the outskirts of Cotonou observed: the "city has overrun us." As has the market economy. As a result, the Concrete City is everywhere, today linked to a diversity of urban actors: states, as well as private companies, but also others, such as urban dwellers. All these actors – with the same bags of cement but in different financial circuits – are stimulating the construction boom.

A Booming Building Sector

"When construction is fine, everything is fine" – the old adage is truer than ever in Africa. This construction boom sustains many urban jobs, which range from the provision of services (real estate agents, developers, architects, bank advisors) to the provision of skills (builders, bricklayers), and also include shopkeepers and deliveries (retailers and wholesalers). A tour around building sites is an opportunity to analyze, from foundations to finishing, this construction sector and these multiple intermediaries at the heart of the urban fabric.

Real Estate Agent: From Broker to Preacher

"Global can find you a plot anywhere in the country. Stop gambling with your money.

Global Serv immo: 7 years, NOT A SINGLE CLIENT has lost their land dispute.

Global builds and renovates, 100% guaranteed, quickly, no cheating, @low price.

10 plots with land title @ Adjagbo, next to highway 40, @500m from the stadium, 7,245,000 F"

On my arrival in Cotonou, in July 2016, I immediately started receiving these text advertisements on my phone. They came from a company called *Global Service Immobilier*, a Beninese real estate agency. The slogan on its homepage reads: "May you be blessed and may God make each of you the happy owner of a beneficial real estate asset." To get to *Global Service Immobilier's* offices, you go past the prayer room on the ground floor and walk up to the first floor. Mr. Ahinon, the sales director, a lawyer by training, ushers me in and explains that the "property sector is suffering" because of the lack of legislation (interview, Cotonou, 2016). When I ask him about the link between religion and property, he answers as if it was the most natural thing in the world: "The Earth is a sacred asset. Everything is linked with *gris-gris*, with witchcraft, with the spirits. We are a Christian business. We have been assigned a mission: to make deals." The founder and managing director of *Global Service Immobilier*, Edgard Guidibi, has an unusual background. The son of the former director of the National Lottery and close to the former president Yayi Boni, he is also a pastor at the *Centre Jésus pour Réussir* (Jesus for Success Center). Guidibi has a page on the EMCI TV (*EnseigneMoi Canal International*) site, a French-language Christian television channel, where he explains that he is "contributing to the growth of the Kingdom of God by means of the resources that his company employs on Benin's property market, where it is by far the leading player." A few months later, I visit Dona Abel Loko, managing director of the Primeco-Bénin real estate agency. A picture of Jesus is stuck to the wall above him, and the walls of the waiting room are dotted with Bible verses that highlight self-confidence and entrepreneurship. He tells me that he is a pastor outside his professional life (interview, Fidjerossé, 2017). Like Jacob Amoussou, director of the *Où va le Monde?* (Where is the world going?) real estate agency. Realtor and evangelical minister are two activities that overlap frequently in my enquiries, which bring into contact with churchmen who preach about building a better world (out of concrete) (Figure 2.8).

These "holy men" offer land tenure security to win the client's trust. They seek to distinguish themselves from vulgar street agents who, according to one pious agent, "are only interested in making money without following the rules of the trade, and do not pay taxes." However, regardless of self-proclaimed piety, these agents use the same network of informal

FIGURE 2.8 Real estate agency "Jesus is back," Cotonou, 2018. Source: A. Choplin.

brokers present everywhere in the town and countryside (Glélé 2015). These agents, who generally take a 10% commission on every deal, work closely with lawyers and bailiffs to avoid any disputes. Disputes are in fact common, as evidenced by the number of houses covered with signs that read "Not 4 Sale" in Ghana and Nigeria, or "This property is not for sale" in Benin and in Togo, indicators of inheritance disputes within families (Bertrand 2011; Tassi 2019). The manager of the AFRI Immo real estate agency brags that his go-to lawyer is the vice dean of the law faculty at University of Abomey-Calavi (interview, Calavi, 2017). For his part, Mr. Lokossou, founder of the *Loked Immobilier Sarl* agency, has just resumed his legal studies in order to refresh his knowledge of the law (interview, Cotonou, 2017). Carole Yaya-Oye, manager of the firm Proximmo, is a lawyer by training. Brokers of a similar kind, halfway between the formal and informal sectors, can be found in the adjacent cities of Accra and Lagos (Obeng-Odoom 2015).

In parallel, structures have been established to give the market a clear legislative framework, to limit bad practices, and thereby improve the image of the real estate agencies. As the manager of Benin Building Service claimed, "we are here to reassure and clean up the market". In Benin, there is an *Ordre des agents Immobiliers* (Order of Realtors) with some 20 member structures, both real estate agencies and construction firms. And in 2017, Mrs. Yaya-Oye created a separate organization, ANAIB (national association of real estate agencies of Benin), to represent "only real estate agencies, because this is a very specific business! My job is making deals, not construction" (interview, Cotonou, 2017). Nonetheless, more and more real estate agencies are involved in construction, delivering turnkey properties with a legal property title. A number of realtors would like to enter this development business, but lack the resources. In Lomé, the manager of *Société Immobilière du 3eme Millénium* (SIM 3) says that he has "several real estate projects ready to go. The problem is uncertainty. The banks do not want to lend, they lack confidence in the market." The manager of the Fabo Immo agency corroborates this view, explaining that he already owns land but lacks the funds to start construction (interview, Lomé, 2018). Mr. Lokossou at *Groupe Loked Immobilier Sarl* works with his son, a civil engineering graduate, who covers the construction side. Yet others, such as Benin Building Service, are preparing the ground for vertically integrated expansion. As Mr. Ahouanjenou, the company's manager explained, "we want to build, and to do that we have acquired a sand quarry and two gravel quarries, and we have an agreement with a cement plant." Pointing to the picture of a religious figure hanging behind him, he added confidently: "That's Saint Benoit. The patron saint of builders. He will help us."

Property Developers and the Diaspora

In July 2019, at the Élysée Palace in France, President Macron welcomed his Ghanaian counterpart Akufo-Addo and almost 400 guests for an event titled, "Let us talk about Africa: discussions with the African diasporas." In their short speeches, the two presidents encouraged the diasporas to invest in Africa, they offered to support entrepreneurial initiatives to develop the continent and, in the longer term, to improve North–South relations. The real estate sector was mentioned several times as one of the possible vehicles for attracting capital.

Private property development is booming in Africa, as recent studies have shown (Obeng-Odoom 2015; Goodfellow 2017; Gillespie 2020; Terrefe 2020). It reflects growing demand for detached houses built to international quality and standards. This is what the aspiring middle and upper classes want, as well as the diaspora and recent "returnees," as they are called in anglophone Africa, or *repats* (returning expats) in French. Indeed, many in the African diaspora invest in property (Page and Mercer 2012) because it is one of the easiest and least risky investments to make from abroad.[8] In contrast, housing construction requires significant time and energy and, of course, being present to monitor the work. This is difficult for members of the diaspora which leads them to buy ready-made houses delivered by developers in order to avoid disputes over land and nasty surprises such as stopping the construction, disappearance of the family member with the money, or the purchase of bad materials. Many West Africans are even unwilling to trust family members to carry out projects on their behalf. As the manager of *Proximmo*, a real estate agency in Cotonou noted, "the diaspora wants to have a pied-à-terre in the country. But it does not want to send money to the family. It does not trust its brothers" (interview, Cotonou, 2017). Instead, the diaspora appears to prefer security and guarantees, which explains why it accounts for between 60% and 75% of the clientele of the property developers I interviewed. As part of their broader international business and marketing strategy, these developers establish contacts with them at property fairs in European cities. When members of the diaspora do decide to construct housing, they similarly require architects they can trust at a distance. Romarick Atoké, a Beninese architect, uses new technologies to build such trust with his international clients (Figure 2.9):

> I supervise the work by drone and send them regular pictures by WhatsApp so that they can see the progress in real time. People in the diaspora are wary. There have been many stories about scams where local brokers send supposed photographs of construction sites to owners in Europe. Then they come back a year later and find that the pictures were of a neighboring

FIGURE 2.9   Drone supervision of a construction site, Cotonou, 2019.
Source: M. Lozivit.

site, that theirs had not progressed and that the broker had swallowed up all the money and done a runner. The diaspora prefers to delegate the work to a competent architect

(interview, Cotonou, 2017).

Property developers use new technologies to attract this market, with sites specializing in project oversight, like the Paris-based company Wizodia in Cameroon, in Togo and soon in Ivory Coast, or *Global Services Immobilier* in Benin. For its part, the firm *GANDA Immobilier et Construction* runs a website designed like a blog, which provides advice "with a smile" to the diaspora on investment projects. LafargeHolcim, through its 14Trees program, backs the SmartDiaspora digital platform for people wanting to build a house in Malawi, and soon in Ivory Coast and Kenya.

The structure of the property development network reveals significant differences between the countries in the corridor. In Ghana and Nigeria, developers are major players in the public works sector and sell products for the diaspora–luxurious, often private dwellings, in the form of compounds, condominiums, or gated communities (Grant 2009; Gillespie 2020). In Ghana, GREDA (Ghana Real Estate Developer Association), an organization set up in 1988 to support property developers, has 380 members. In Abidjan, the sector is organizing, notably motivated by numerous presidential projects that offer opportunities for local private players (N'goran et al. 2020). In Benin and in Togo the sector is still taking shape, with smaller scale projects. In Lomé, several real estate projects have seen gated communities spring up on the outskirts of the city. One of them, WellCity, proposes a new town with 5,000 dwellings for 35,000 inhabitants, where the main activities will be housing and medical tourism, and which is clearly aimed at middle and senior managers, as well as Togolese living abroad. In Cotonou, the Golden Key project has put 56 luxurious villas up for sale on the seafront. It is a modest private project, built by the developer THI, a subsidiary of the Chinese group TIANHE, but has nevertheless received wide media coverage since it was launched in person in 2016 by President Talon himself. The company emphasizes the "safety" offered by this new gated estate on the waterside, as well as its supposedly "reasonable" prices. The deluxe villas, called Azur and Riviera, are sold by the West Coast Property real estate agency, which specializes in "prestige" properties. *Société de Gestion Immobilière et de Services* (SOGIS SA) also sells plots with pre-installed security and utilities, and villas designed and built by AGETIP-Bénin (a public interest construction agency in Benin). Its *les villas de l'Atlantique* [Atlantic Villas] is a gated residential community of 120 villas in Fidjerossé. The brochure advertises: "*Les villas de l'Atlantique,* an ideal, high standard environment, suitable for all! Foreigners, residents, and Beninese diaspora." The prices are given in euros.

Architects and Building Permits

In West Africa, the reliance on property developers or access to a social housing programme remains a privilege open only to the wealthiest or to civil servants. The same is true for architects, who are employed for major projects or by wealthy clients, and contribute to the growth of urban inequalities by reinforcing the status and wealth of their clients through their buildings (Di Nunzio 2019). Most individuals lack the resources to employ architects and, out of distrust, prefer to monitor the construction of their dream house themselves. They therefore build without an architect, and indeed without a permit or land title. In Benin, any hard construction officially requires a building permit, and the law stipulates that any application for a building permit must be submitted by an architect (Article 21 of Decree no. 2014–205 of 13 March 2014). The law stipulates that each municipality is responsible for verifying this. But in practice, no building inspections are carried out and no penalties are imposed for construction without a permit. As a district chief in Togbin admitted, "Since my arrival, I have heard people talk about building permits, but I have never seen one. The few who apply for a permit are civil servants who want to build big houses and employ architects" (interview, Abomey-Calavi, 2017). Mr. Anise, a building technician who oversees several projects, agrees:

"Normally, you are supposed to wait to have your building permit approved by the planning departments before starting construction, and therefore to have submitted an application with land surveys, the land title. In our case, we do not have any of that, it's expensive. So, if there is an inspection, they may ask us to stop the work. But often for private dwellings, there are no inspections." (interview, Fidjérossé, 2019).

These accounts reveal that there is not much oversight of the construction sector. For the owners, monitoring often consists simply in making sure that no building materials disappear. In most projects, owners draw up the plans on their own, or in collaboration with the builder, and they do so to avoid paying the high costs of employing a trained architect. As François, a night guard in a residential neighborhood, explained: "Employing an architect costs millions. I prefer to use that money to build the foundations of my house."

Through the orders of architects, professional architects in the region have organized for broader recognition of their role, utility, and legitimacy in West African societies. Jean-Paul Houndeffo, member of the Council of the National Order of Architects and Urbanists of Benin (ONAB), which has 200 members, explains that "people starting a project do not know where to find us or think that we are too expensive. The government does nothing to promote us and often brings in foreign architects" (interview, Cotonou, 2018). According to Houndeffo, households are not aware that architects can save them money: "It is a pity that private individuals do not use architects, because while it is true that this increases the cost of construction, they recover that money later because the running and maintenance costs are lower." The order is trying to change bad practices and, in particular, to prevent the use of poor-quality materials. Several architects in the national order have proposed collaborating with wholesalers and retailers to encourage the use of high quality, local materials.[9] They are also trying to put pressure on the property developers to improve building practices. As one Beninese architect clarified, "we are not really their friends. We would like to force them to build well, to obey the rules, with good material. We annoy them."

Ignorance of the laws, non-use of architects, high deposits, and rents, exploding land prices–these are all signs of the instability and lack of regulation in the real estate sector in the sub-region. There are initiatives that seek to counter this instability, such as BenBen Ghana, a Ghanaian start-up that supplies an app that checks the status of a piece of land before the transaction and ensures that it is possible to acquire a land title. West African governments want to facilitate the formalities associated with land deals and to make them more secure. The Benin government, for example, has developed an online app called *E-notaire* that people can use to carry out land-use changes, to access the online land registry, and to lodge complaints in land disputes.

Co-ownership is another tricky issue, as the manager of *Proximmo* explained: "The idea of co-ownership is not accepted. People here want to own the land; they do not want to share or divide it" (interview, Cotonou, 2017). This reluctance over co-ownership–which additionally has no corresponding legal land title – prevents individuals from pooling money into larger projects. This explains, in part, the scarcity of tall buildings and the prevalence of urban sprawl: most people prefer to move to the outskirts to have their own place and avoid having to share a land title which may not even be recognized. They prefer to build for themselves and obtain their own supplies from wholesalers and retailers, who are mainly Lebanese.

Wholesalers and Retailers: Lebanese, Indian, and Chinese Connections

Miziara is a small Lebanese town with a population of not more than 5,000. Nonetheless, it is known for the strange shapes of its 300 "bling-bling" villas: Boeing 747, Greek temple, pyramid, 30-room palace.[10] It is said that the money comes from Nigeria. Two of the villagers, born in Lagos, are none other than Gilbert and Ronald Chagoury, the richest Lebanese in Nigeria, who have promised to build – in the middle of Lagos – a gigantic, modern, and luxurious city by the sea envisioned as the new African Dubai: Eko Atlantic.

In West Africa, the Chagoury Group is also known for its subsidiaries in telecommunications, hotels, and public works. In Benin, the group is based on the alliance of four brothers, the first of whom is thought to have arrived in 1967. It employs almost 450 people and owns 11 companies in the industrial, real estate, and catering sector. It owns two commercial firms both set up in 1982: Chaftel for telecommunications and *La Roche* for the distribution of construction materials. Other family members head *La Roche* stores in Lomé, Lagos, Abuja, and Port-Harcourt.

The Lebanese have been present in the region since the 1920s and today play a central role in the telecommunications, restaurant, import and construction sector (Dubresson 1989; Arsan 2014). They are represented at all levels: at the head of material manufacturing plants, large construction, and real estate development firms, but also large hardware concerns. There are many success stories in the community, like the Chagoury or the Fakry family in Ghana, which specializes in the production of pipes and plastics (Interplast Group); or the steel producing group Hage, created by the Burkinabe of Lebanese origin, Joseph Hage. They took advantage of the economy opening up in the 1990s. Yet these success stories should not hide a reality that is often more difficult for most Lebanese who live and work in Africa. The lack of trade agreements between the local and Lebanese authorities have meant that some barely make a living and face serious economic insecurity. For example, many Lebanese, notably those working in second-hand car imports (Rosenfeld 2017), left Benin following the Nigerian economic crisis of 2015. According to figures from the Lebanese consulate in Benin, the number of Lebanese residing in Benin fell from 7,000 to 1,500. Some may have returned to Lebanon, while others moved elsewhere in the region – the Lebanese diaspora spans several West African countries, allowing them to move from one to another in the event of crisis or conflict.

The Indian Diaspora is also significant in the region, operating between Togo, Benin, Nigeria, and Ghana. A rich Indian importer, born in Ghana and settled in Benin for more than 30 years told me:

"I do not get involved in construction materials or second-hand cars. The Lebanese are already not too fond of me, so I prefer not to step on their toes. I have a brewery that produces beer, a plastics factory, and a lot of land. I'm planning to open a supermarket to sell all the low-cost products I import" (interview, Cotonou, 2017).

The list of products he imports is seemingly infinite: Maxam toothpaste from China, Biskrem biscuits from Turkey, Gino tomato concentrate from India made with Chinese tomatoes, Don Simon sangria from Spain, and an array of similarly eclectic goods from across the world. In West Africa, Indians are also a big presence in the selling of fabrics and in public works, and the production of materials, especially steel (Rams 2021). In Togo, two Indians, Prasad Motaparti Siva Rama Vara and Manubhai Jethabhai Patel, made their fortune in construction and cement. In 1994, they took over the former National Steel Company–set up in 1978 and privatized in 1985– which they renamed Amexfield Togo Steel (ATS). This company produces reinforcing steel and sheet metal, like the Ghanaian company Tema Steel Company (TCS) which they also own. In 1996, they diversified and took over the former Cimao (Cement of West Africa) company to create Wacem (West African Cement). The names of these two "Indians from Africa" were made widely known across the world as part of the Panama Papers scandal in which they were accused of evading their tax obligations in Togo.[11]

In addition to the Indians and Lebanese, the Chinese have become more present in recent years on the African markets for consumer goods, textiles, and construction materials (Kernen and Khan-Mohammad 2014). Lagos' "China-town," a gated showcase village with some 20 stores, remains almost entirely empty, but the Chinese are nevertheless leaders in many sectors of Nigeria's national economy. In November 2016, Cotonou hosted the China-Benin summit in the Chinese Economic and Trade Development Center located in the city's oldest neighborhood. The merchants came from Ningbo, a big port city on China's eastern coast. One of them told me in French that he was "on a tour . . . attending trade fairs in Lagos, in Cotonou, and in Lomé for two weeks." All sorts of products are on show: hair extensions, decorations, and synthetic Christmas trees, a variety of small sundry goods, but also and in particular solar panels, generators, and home security equipment (alarms, electric gates).

The active role of these diasporas shows the growing importance of the region in the world economy, in particular, in the construction sector. In cities across West Africa's urban corridor, large hardware stores owned by Lebanese and Indians occupy the former warehouses of the trading firms that conducted import – export business in colonial times. In Lomé, the Watt store occupies the former *Société Générale du Golfe de Guinée* building, which gave its name to the S3G intersection, a hardware Mecca for the Togolese. Joseph Azar acquired the building in 1984 to house his import firm, SOC-ODIM (*Société Commerciale d'Importation*). In 1993, it adopted a new name, ETS Aja Le Watt, now Sté Le Watt SARL, owned by an Indian family which sells bathroom equipment, tiles, plumbing supplies, and electrical products. Watt's Lebanese competitor, CCT Batimat (formerly *Comptoir Commercial du Togo*), with its 2,500 m² of exhibition space, has been similarly present in the country since 1988. Batimat also exists in Cotonou and Dakar. In Dakar, the two main firms specializing in the import of construction materials – *Comptoir Commercial du Sénégal* (CCS) and Batimat, also owned by Lebanese –are located in the old center, between the Medina and the Plateau, near Sandaga market and Peterson Avenue.

The Lebanese dominate the wholesale sector for the distribution of construction materials: *La Roche*, ROUHIMAS, CTPS, SONIMEX, SOREMAC, to cite only the best known in Cotonou. They prefer contracts with big companies or those associated with large state projects (roads, social housing, maternity clinics, hospitals, etc.). Drawing on his experience and history, Mr. Jihad, manager of SOREMAC since its creation 25 years ago, explains that he has a network that enables him to obtain very competitive prices: "We buy our products from wholesale importers here who themselves buy in China or elsewhere" (interview, Cotonou, 2017). The firm *La Roche*, the main distributor of construction materials, has just moved into property development with the creation of *La Roche Immobilier* to build and sell villas on a turnkey basis. On the website, the company claims to "supply building professionals with the materials best suited to achieving their objectives, (and to be) rightly able to credit *La Roche* with the development of architecture in Benin." The entry of this firm into the construction sector is not surprising given that it belongs to the Chagoury Group, one of the powerful Lebanese business groups which produced the first private villa developments along the Benin coast (the Censad, Maison rouge, Marina, Fadoul districts) and, more recently, the four-star Golden Tulip Hotel.

Alongside the wholesalers, retail outlets for cement and construction materials are proliferating, often unlicensed, which can be found everywhere in the city, but particularly in the outskirts where demand is high. In the 2013 population census, 4,329 people reported that they worked as "retailers of construction materials." Three quarters of them are registered in the Cotonou and Porto-Novo agglomeration. In 2017, the mapping exercise conducted with OpenStreetMap in Cotonou identified and counted more than 50 retail outlets for construction materials on the main road that runs through Cotonou from east to west. Among the small-scale cement outlets, some are official resellers and can obtain supplies directly from SCB or Nocibé. Most, however, get their supplies from wholesalers. Profit margins are tight. The small retailers and wholesalers establish close and trusting trade relations and, as a result, they have developed a system of credit: the resellers only pay once they have sold their stock, which means that they do not need to pay in advance. The small retailers do not always get a good press. They are sometimes accused of reducing the quantity of cement packaged at the factory by opening and resealing the bags, and of calibrating the weighing machines to falsify the real weight. Whether true or (peri)urban legends, these rumors primarily reveal that the construction sector and construction sites are places of mistrust, conflict, and struggle. They also show the vitality of this small-scale market economy, an economy situated at the intersection between subsistence and entrepreneurship.

Materials: From Foundations to Finishing

Dakar, 23 April 2019, fieldnotes:

"Let's Build (in) Africa" is the slogan adopted by the West African International Construction, Finishing and Infrastructure Salon (SEN-CON 2019), which was held in Dakar in Senegal from 23 to 26 April 2019 (Figure 2.10). On the flyer are pictures of cranes working and a building under construction. Contractors, individuals, sightseers, and big company representatives all come together to celebrate the revival of construction in Africa. Turks and Indians have come to sell power plants and concrete pumps. Moroccans boast of new mortars and façade coatings. A few Italians present tiles and marble, materials much prized by the African elite.

Alongside the cement traveling the roads of Africa are many other construction materials. Reinforcing steel, sand, and gravel (freshly extracted from the lagoon), and added to cement to make slab, timber for formwork,

FIGURE 2.10   "Let's Build (in) Africa", Advertisement, Dakar, 2019.
Source: A. Choplin.

sheet metal for roofs, trellises for ventilation, and also tiles, doors, windows, and pots of paint for finishing. An analysis of these flows of materials reveals the globalized and unequal commercial relations which connect fragments of West African cities to Europe but also Lebanon, India, and China. The Lebanese, Indian, and Chinese diasporas in Africa–like the West Africans in Europe, the Middle East, and Asia–dispatch, carry, and receive these goods and, through this labor, they reshape international trade routes.

A Matter of Sand

Women casually carry baskets of sand on their heads to the trucks, which, once loaded, plunge into the congested suburbs of Cotonou, Accra, and Lomé. Sand extraction punctuates the life of the lagoon, which is now perforated at every point, profoundly amputated to allow the concrete to rise to the surface.

As Katherine Dawson has said of Accra, sand is the "city's material skeleton" (Dawson 2021: 999). As an essential but non-renewable resource, sand is at the heart of the process of urbanization in the Gulf of Guinea, but also of global economic and geopolitical relations, as the UNEP and the Global Sand Observatory points it out (UNEP 2019, 2022). As in other coastal cities, many individuals are engaged in the extraction of fluvio-lagoon sand in search of new sources of income after the fishing industry declined as a result of pollution and eutrophication. In Porto-Novo lagoon, for example, the non-mechanized Djassin Ko quarry provides the sand for the building of the political capital. On a visit to the quarry, Mr. Hounguè explains how the "holiday job" of his youth, done by all the schoolchildren in the neighborhood, over the years became his main "breadwinner" (interview, Porto-Novo, 2017). Today, he has 120 employees and his business is officially recognized and registered with the Chamber of Commerce and Industry. He describes the changes that have recently taken place: "Our grandparents already did this kind of work, but they took gravel sand to make concrete, for slabs. It was after it became illegal to take sea sand that we began to take fine sand." This activity has indeed grown since the extraction of marine sand was banned in 2007 in order to limit coastal erosion, which was causing environmental problems in the lake environment. Mr. Hounguè explains that there are several kinds of sand, distinguished by their color, used for different parts of the construction process: large-grained sand, dark or black in color, is used for foundations (a 10-wheeler truckload costs 18,000 francs CFA); the finest and lightest colored sand is used for finishing; white and clay sand is used to make bricks (a 10-wheeler truckload costs 30,000 francs CFA). For lack of funds, most people opt for the cheapest. Indeed, many are content with the cheaper sand collected in the street, used for foundations or for subsidiary structures like septic tanks or wells. Hundreds of people sweep and collect this sand on the main roads and sell bags of it by the roadside.

Sand extraction is a very profitable business which employs large numbers of individuals, especially young people and women (Figure 2.11). The activity is very hierarchical. In the quarry, on land, or in the water, everyone has their role: there are the people who dive and dig, the ones who collect, the ones

FIGURE 2.11   Sand extraction in the lagoon, Cotonou, 2019.
Source: A. Choplin.

who load the dugout and unload it into the truck, and the ones who drive the truck. The price per truckload varies from 80,000 to 100,000 francs CFA. The quarry operator takes a cut of 15,000 to 20,000 francs CFA per truckload. He can expect to earn five times more than a fisherman in the area. A female sand collector can earn 10,000 CFAF per boatful. The diver earns the most, between 12,000 and 15,000 francs CFA per boatful. Mr. Hounguè describes the difficulties of this activity: "Divers spend three or four minutes under water. They will have problems with their ears, with their eyes, and breathing problems. They swallow dirt and bacteria in the water. There are a lot of deaths".

Mr. Hounguè complains about the competition: "These days, there are quarries everywhere. And then there are the big players who come with machines to extract the sand." In fact, several sand dredging companies have moved into the lagoon depths of Porto-Novo and Cotonou (Dragon SA, STPA Sarl, Minex Bénin Sarl, BMR, Ola Douchou, Afritec). Each of these companies load around 120–200 tractor-trailers with a capacity of 10 m³ per vehicle per day, as one truckdriver tells us. My own investigations confirmed these figures: on the Togbin-Cotonou Road, my research team counted up to 55 trucks of sand leaving the quarries per hour.

In principle, a tax of 1,000 francs CFA per truck is paid to Calavi municipality and 200 francs CFA to the district chief. In greater Accra, between 700–1,000 truckloads of sand leave the extraction zones every day, according to the official Minerals Commission figures for 2018, cited by Katherine Dawson (2021).

In Lomé, similar dynamics can be observed since the 2011 ban on the extraction of marine sand. In 2015, the Togolese geographer Nayondjoa Konlani counted 79 sand quarries in the capital's lagoon zone, only two of them official and 57 very active unlicensed quarries. The state is trying to close these wild quarries and, as with cement, to regulate sand prices to prevent speculation, especially in the rainy season when it becomes difficult to transport (Konlani 2015).

The sand economy is also linked to the economy of gravel and stone. In Benin, gravel extraction takes place in the Mono and Couffo region, near the town of Lokossa. Stone for crushing is extracted in the region of Dan, near Dassa. Among the firms that operate the granite quarries, there is the public works company Adeoty, the German firm Heidelberg (GranuBénin since 2014), Minex Bénin, and SERM (mining extraction and resource company). However, these quarries are a long way from the centers of consumption in the coastal cities and it is often too expensive to transport the stone. It is easier to use cement, which is more widespread, and granite is mainly reserved for particular buildings. For road surfaces, the companies use cement cobbles, which are very common in West African cities and allow drainage during heavy rain.

The issue of water is as tricky as the question of sand and gravel. There are several possible sources of water for making concrete: sink a borehole, use water from a well if there is one, or use the mains water supply if the plot is connected. Another solution is to bring water from the lagoon if that is close by, "where it is free," as one construction manager explained (interview, Fidjerossé, 2018). To extract this free water, a truck goes to the lagoon to fill large blue tanks which are then delivered to the worksite. Yet the cost of transporting water by truck needs to be calculated to see if it is worthwhile – ultimately, the most important thing is to avoid connecting to someone else's main supply, adding another owner to the loop and potentially further complicating the water supply. "It costs more," the manager explained, "and you are less autonomous." Sinking a borehole from the start is the best way to obtain water for making bricks, laying the slab, building the foundations, and the borehole can then be used to supply the finished property.

For many people "sand is life," as Katherine Dawson (2021) reports, quoting the words of an official at the Minerals Commission in Accra: "One out of every 10 people needs sand everyday. They're thinking of how to build." In this way, sand has become an essential commodity and a key input for the production of the similarly essential – together, sand and cement have become the foundation of the Concrete City.

Reinforcing Steel and Corrugated Iron

While a large share of construction materials is imported into West Africa, creating dependency on foreign countries, sand, cement, and also reinforcing steel and sheet metal are an exception, since a percentage of them is produced locally. In the 1970s, more than 90% of iron and steel rebars came from France, and sheet metal from Japan (76%) (N'Bessa 1997: 35). Today, some are imported from China, but they are also produced in situ from imported iron ore and steel recovered locally then melted down. As Dagna Rams shown from Accra steel market (2021), this business is global, and the factories located along the corridor are connected with or belong to big international firms.

"African Industries" is one of the global steel giants, with 8,000 employees and a presence in 10 countries. This Indian company owns 17 manufacturing plants in Nigeria (making windows, pure water, and construction blocks), including three steelworks. It sells high quality reinforcing steel–mainly used by the big construction companies (like Julius Berger) – which are aiming to achieve construction standards similar to those in Europe. African Industries exports to the sub-region. It is also present in Ghana with warehouses in Tema. Jean, an employee of African Industries in Lagos, has worked in the sector since 1971. According to Jean, "apart from a few plants like ours, nothing is monitored. There is no regulation, no certification. People use imported products and materials, which are banned everywhere else. And people are surprised to see frequent accidents. A year ago, there were 14 deaths on a work site in Porto-Novo caused by bad reinforcing steel. Everything collapsed. There's only one solution: standards need to rise" (interview, Cotonou, 2018).

A competitor of African Industries, *Société Industrielle d'Acier du Bénin* (SIAB), located in the suburbs of Cotonou, is the other big rebar and sheet metal supplier in the region. SIAB has been a subsidiary of the Hage Industries Group since 2001. Having started out importing materials into Africa in the 1970s, Joseph Hage, a Burkinabe of Lebanese origin, opened steel production plants in Burkina Faso, Togo, and Benin in the 1990s (sheet metal, false ceilings, doors, rebars). In 1992, he bought *Société Togolaise de Tôles* (SOTOTOLES), owned by the state of Burkina Faso, then in 2001, *Société Industrielle d'Acier du Bénin* (SIAB). Today, the Hage Group is a big player, with 1,400 employees divided among Burkina Faso, Togo, and Benin, and total investment volumes of some 20 billion francs CFA. It has a few rivals, in particular Indian firms like Steel Cube and ATS in Togo and TCS in Ghana. In Benin, SIAB is the leading player in the production, processing, and sale of steel products (with more than 300 employees). The raw material – reels or rolls of steel – is imported from Ukraine and Turkey and is then processed in the SIAB plant. As with African Industries, quality is the priority, as Mohamed Ayoub from SIAB's sales department explained:

"We avoid importing from China. We have done a lot of work to educate the public to understand the importance of product quality. There have been numerous building collapses recently. Each time, it was observed that the steel was not up to standard" (interview, Sèmè-Podji, 2018).

Fatal collapses are frequent in African cities, as evidenced by press articles and academic studies (Boateng 2021; Smith 2020). The issue of standards on project sites and the quality of materials is often raised. That is why SIAB has chosen to talk publicly about the standards needed for safe buildings. In response to competition with rebar from Nigeria or Chinese steel, SIAB broadcast a video on the national television channel (ORTB) on good construction practices, in partnership with the Benin Order of Architects. As with cement, SIAB products are distributed and sold through wholesalers, distributors, or simple retailers spread across the country, with whom the company maintains special relations. Apart from sales for the individual construction market, SIAB supplies public projects. Mr. Ayoub regrets that the contract for the future Glo Djigbe airport was given to the Chinese who "will undoubtedly want to bring their own materials."

SIAB and its sister factory SOTOTOLES in Togo, which both belong to the Hage Group, export 50% of their output to Niger (4% exports of tubes and 7% of rebar, according to INSAE figures), to Burkina-Faso and to Chad. As Mr. Ayoub explained, "over there, there are no factories, while the needs are huge. Those countries are building at a tremendous rate. Rebar, sheet metal, they are becoming essential products." Invoices and payments are sent via WhatsApp. Under its Social and Environmental Responsibility policy, SIAB is involved in the development and planning of infrastructures for the municipality of Sèmè-Podji where it is located. "Every 2–3 months," Mr. Ayoub noted, "we resurface the road in front of the factory."

When I ask him what the company does with the waste it produces, Mr. Ayoub replies that it is sold to a company, though he does not know what happens to it afterwards: "On one occasion we tried to follow the van to see where it went, but we lost it." Like the others in the region, this factory is connected, discreetly, to the unexpected pathways of the steel market, which extend beyond the frontiers of West African States. In Nigeria, the steelworks operate with iron that is recovered locally and melted down. The same is supposed to be true in Ghana, where the laws prohibit iron and steel from leaving the country, so that they are reused locally, but in reality, they are part of a whole parallel market (Rams 2021). According to investigations we conducted locally, steel from Ghana and Togo arrives in Cotonou and is then re-exported to India. The iron is not melted down locally, but weighed by an Indian company then discreetly re-exported. Equally discreet are the containers of construction materials headed for China: my field research led me to a Chinese entrepreneur, nicknamed The Boss, who recovers zinc, bronze, and copper – and to a lesser degree lead – in Benin, and then sends it on to China. Learning by word-of-mouth, the city's semi-wholesalers began to sell their stock to The Boss rather than to the Indians or Lebanese in the sector. He claims to work with scrap merchants from Nigeria: "Guys come across the border with their loads to sell them to me in Cotonou," he underlined, "they know that we pay better here." The Boss has a plan to build a waste processing plant in the Sèmè-Podji free zone, which will employ 700 people.

Whereas the price of cement is more or less harmonized across the world, the price of rebar, which depends on steel prices, varies greatly from one region or country to another. It is very high on the African continent (Rams 2021). There are big price differences between steel manufactured locally, steel manufactured in Nigeria and steel imported from China. Regardless of these differences, building in Africa costs more than elsewhere.

Tiling from Floor-to-Ceiling

Dakar, Senegal, 27 April 2019, fieldnotes:

"Touba Carreaux distribution," "Prestige céramique, Carreaux et sanitaire," "Digital Céramique". . . *Parcelles Assainies* road is a more than surprising sight: tons of tiles are displayed for sale. A strange feeling to stroll through an immense open-air bathroom.

Near the *Patte d'Oie*, Dakar's main interchange, the *Parcelles Assainies* neighborhood has specialized in selling tiles for the last 20 years or so.[12] The buildings on the plots here are now largely complete, and their main feature is that they are covered in tiles. The competition between sellers is tough. Dozens of stores sell tiles from all over the world: Italy, Spain, Portugal, and of course China, at all prices and all qualities.

Tiles form a second skin on buildings. Like cement, they are a signal of wealth and social distinction. In this part of the world, clay, ceramic, and porcelain tiles are not only used in bathrooms. It is fashionable for well-off households that can afford it to pay for the external façades of their houses to be covered entirely in tiles. "For people, when you have used tiles to build your house, it means that you have moved up socially. So, when you cover your house in tiles, you are the boss of the neighborhood!" explains Daniel, head of the JAFCO tiling firm in Cotonou. This practice is very common in Senegal but also in Nigeria and Ghana–countries with high growth rates and many migrants with plenty of purchasing power. Rich Lebanese are said to have originated this practice, which was then imitated by the Senegalese and Nigerian diasporas settled in Italy, who brought back tiles and sanitary appliances (Tall 2009: 203). Industrial plaster and tiles then replaced shells and paint. Full external tiling is in no way sustainable in tropical zones: tiles prevent air flow and allow humidity to collect between tile and brick. After a few years, it is common to see the tiles begin to drop off. In Benin and Togo, tiles are also used in cemeteries to cover the graves of important people (Brivio 2012).

Like the tile sellers in Dakar's *Parcelles Assainies*, the sellers in Alaba Market–an immense tiling realm located in the western suburbs of Lagos–are directly linked to the ceramic factories in the Foshan district, on the Pearl River, near Canton, in China. "The Chinese helped us out. They brought down the prices of tiles," explained Pascal, a Beninese who has worked and lived in Nigeria for a long time. The manager of a tile store told me that she buys her merchandize in China – "I do not speak Chinese, but I speak calculator. That's enough to get Chinese tiles sent here" – as she watches the unloading of boxes of tiles with Chinese writing on them, where the word "Parma" is visible, in reference to the Italian city. Italy is the other big national supplier of ceramics. Africa offers a huge market, according to the Confindustria Ceramica Association, which represents the main Italian ceramics producers located between Sassuolo and Faenza (Emilia-Romagna region). At the Cersaie, the international salon for architectural and bathroom tiles held every year in Italy, Africans are now present as both buyers and as a target market. The world's biggest brands have dispatched representatives to prospect Africa.

The tiling firm JAFCO is a good example of the industry's linkages outside Africa. Created in 1988 by Daniel Jalis, a Lebanese who arrived in Benin in 1977, JAFCO today has 120 employees, 4 sales rooms in Cotonou, and 7 warehouses, and the group is present in all Benin's cities, as well as in Niger. Fifty percent of its products come from Europe, especially Italy and Spain, and 50% from China, where his father established contacts in the 1990s. Daniel visits his suppliers from time to time to look at the products, in Spain or in China, but undertakes most of his transactions remotely, online. He is not interested in Nigerian products, which he considers "too downmarket." He would like to incorporate more standards and quality into people's consumption habits: "We start by training the architects, to familiarize them with the ranges, the differences in quality and the use of each tile when undertaking projects." In addition to the private sector, JAFCO also responds to calls for bids on public state or internationally funded projects: "We have ranges coming from Europe that meet the standards required by the donors." One of his priorities is also to improve JAFCO's social media presence. He is thinking of setting up an online sales platform for construction materials aimed at the Beninese diaspora.

Digital Banking or How to Buy your Cement Online

In December of 2019, the headline of an advertorial in the magazine *Jeune Afrique* read: "Digital technology, the 'accelerator' of LafargeHolcim's development in West Africa." Given that distribution is one of their big challenges, cement manufacturers in the region are turning to digital technology (Figure 2.12). Since the development of the M-Pesa system by Vodafone in Kenya, digital banking has spread to the point that it is now a part of life for

FIGURE 2.12   Advertisement "The joy of ordering cement online," 2020. Source: SCB Bouclier – MTN.

many Africans (Akindès and Kouamé 2019). Jean-Michel Huet and Farid Chakroun (2020), in a report on digital banking, note that 70% of adults still have no bank account, but that the telecommunications operators offer a wide range of mobile banking services: cash in and cash out, bill payment, bank to mobile transfers. Today, there are around 346 million Mobile Money accounts registered in Africa, compared with 120 million bank accounts. These studies are a reminder that the international financial institutions, such as the World Bank and the IMF, back the digitalization of economies, in part, because digital technology is perceived as a driver of financial inclusion (Akindès and Kouamé 2019).

Certain cement manufacturers have well understood this shift to mobile banking and are developing online sales apps in the hope of reaching a new clientele. In Cameroon, in 2019, LafargeHolcim launched its digital platform MyCimencam, as well as the free application Sabitou Construction, which offers "everything you need to know about building," in partnership with the National Order of Architects of Cameroon (ONAC) and the National Order of Civil Engineers of Cameroon (ONIGC). The app offers support for building projects. It presents the different categories and features of cement, but also tutorials on various construction techniques for slabs and foundations. The application also has a calculator to estimate material quantities and a directory of professionals (architects, civil engineers, and technicians). In the same vein, new applications have recently appeared for monitoring the progress of construction projects and assessing costs and budgets ("Site Diary" or "BatiScript").

In Ivory Coast, LafargeHolcim has joined forces with the Jumia e-commerce platform to develop the eBélier online cement buying app. Since June 2019, in this virtual store, customers have been able to pay by bank card or Mobile Money for quantities of 10 bags of cement or more. The promotional video explains how to "order with a click": the order is recorded by Jumia and sent to the LafargeHolcim platform, which organizes delivery to the Binastore outlet (its distribution subsidiary) closest to the place requested by the customer. In Guinea, in August of 2019, LafargeHolcim launched the Easy Pay payment system in partnership with Orange Money, to enable people to buy cement. A code makes buying cement as easy as buying phone credit.

Digital technology is expected to expand possibilities for reaching new customers, distributing new products, and offering new services. According to Xavier Saint-Martin-Tillet, Managing Director of LafargeHolcim Ivory Coast, customers enjoy "the absence of middlemen and the transparency: they can buy their cement and receive delivery quickly without having to travel. Payment is secure with mobile money and they can track their order in real time. We simplify their lives!" A whole network of services, of particular interest to the diaspora, is being established to enable people to track the progress of their building work remotely: online land purchase, real estate agencies that deal with the legal aspects to avoid land disputes, and progress tracking by drone camera. The first results have proved positive. In Cameroon, the company reported more than 800 orders after the MyCimencam platform had been in operation for two months. For its part, the Sabitou app had more than 1,200 users after less than a year. In Ivory Coast, 70% of orders by companies are now made via eBélier. And in Guinea, the group is developing phase 2 of the Easy Pay project, which will allow other materials to be bought on the platform (bricks, reinforcing steel).

However, behind the enthusiasm and the media hype over digital technology, these new methods also raise new concerns. They are a source of new inequalities linked with both the lack of skills and financial constraints. Acquiring a smartphone, buying credit to make calls, or paying by funds transfer, are activities that remain very expensive in this part of Africa. This type of service is aimed at the emerging urban professional class and the diaspora, which both drive and demand this Concrete City. These observations require further research into the links between digitalization, bank use, and the financialization of the construction and real estate sector. They show that digital technology and internet banking play a full part in urban production. This type of digital application is also a good example of "leapfrog technology": users skip stages of the development path as they have direct access to digital banking services without ever having had a bank account. Following these evolutions, cement companies could indirectly become housing financiers.

Conclusion

Capital flows and regenerates urban spaces by producing, consuming, destroying, (re)building, and landfilling (cf. Harvey 2001). This capitalistic logic is strongly interwoven with the material flows underpinning the creation of the Concrete City. In this second chapter, I have exposed the neoliberal forms of urban production that rely on the highly capitalistic cement industry. This analysis confirms that the West African city has become a Concrete City and an avatar of our capitalistic system. I have sought to define precisely what the Concrete City is, by typologizing its different faces, timeframes, and forms. Multiple and heterogeneous actors shape it: states, foreign investors, but also small landowners, property developers, and the middle classes who speculate in land. Other intermediaries, standing between the leaders and the inhabitants, such as architects, urban engineering experts, contractors, materials wholesalers, and retailers, are also responsible for the consumption of tons of concrete and kilometers of cables and pipes. Yet others, such as domestic or foreign design offices, produce the computer-generated images of what this city is supposed to become (Watson 2020). Meanwhile, poor, and not-so-poor inhabitants raise walls of concrete at arm's length.

This multitude of actors is producing an increasingly discontinuous and fragmented Concrete City. The Premium City of the elites and the investors, sometimes entirely privatized and gated, is characterized by the active flow of capital of uncertain provenance (Van Noorloos and Kloosterboer 2018, Goodfellow 2020); the Affordable City, propelled by the state and donors, is supposedly built for everyone but in reality destined for the middle and upper classes; and finally, the Low Cost City in the distant outskirts is home both to the poorest who build incrementally and to those hoping to use their small and slowly accumulated capital to become property owners. Premium City with its vertical towers in the city center, Affordable City with its two-story social housing projects and Low Cost City self-build ground level neighborhoods in the periphery: these three urban forms are built with the same cement but represent three capital circuits and three possible and profoundly unequal expressions of the Concrete City. Concrete materializes these inequalities: it is both a source of impoverishment for the most disadvantaged and of immediate enrichment for the most advantaged who pour considerable tons of it. The Concrete City heralds a new phase of capitalism in Africa and has become an emblem of the neoliberal rhetoric of Africa as a winner. It symbolizes its connection to the international financial markets. It is a place where money circulates, but also a place of debt and credit. And where there is concrete, there is power, money, capitalism, corruption, and lobbying.

In this second chapter, I have demonstrated that the Concrete City of West Africa is capitalistic, fragmented, and unequal. But it would be reductive to say that this city is solely the result of global and capitalist processes channeled by profits for some and exclusion for others. As Pinson and Morel Journel (2017) remind us, Marxist theories and neoliberal dogma do not explain everything. The Concrete City is not only an expression of capitalism, nor is it exclusively informal. Instead, I argue that it is something else. The Concrete City also means hope, dream, desire, emancipation. In order to take into consideration the local particularities, it is essential to draw on post-colonial urban studies. The Concrete City is a powerful reality that is also emerging as the outcome of everyday, endogenous, and local processes. These processes are largely driven by the builder-inhabitants, to whom I will turn my attention in the following chapter. As I have explained, the Concrete

City depends greatly on the strong relations between politics and economics, between entrepreneurs and the incumbent authorities, international investors, and domestic companies. But it is also intrinsically linked with how local communities express their attachment to land and to place, with the value they assign to the material and the immaterial, and with the social and cultural symbols that cement, and concrete have become.

Notes

1   Podcast available at: https://www.mckinsey.com/featured-insights/middle-east-and-africa/how-to-win-in-africa.

2   International New Town database available at: http://www.newtowninstitute.org/newtowndata.

3   See *Le Monde*, 10.07.2019, 'Lagos, mégapole tentaculaire du Nigeria, s'enfonce dans les eaux', https://www.lemonde.fr/afrique/article/2019/07/10/lagos-megapole-tentaculaire-du-nigeria-s-enfonce-dans-les-eaux_5487653_3212.html. See also https://www.ekoatlantic.coms.

4   https://www.ekoatlantic.com/milestones/Eko-Atlantic-Milestones-Issue-1.pdf.

5   See Elias Saad's Interview by *The Business Year*, 11.01.2016, https://www.thebusinessyear.com/nigeria-2016/strong-position/interview.

6   As part of this government project, homes will also be built in Porto-Novo (250), Parakou (500), and in 11 other cities around the country. https://simaubenin.com/projet-logement. See the promotional video: https://youtu.be/b2Av0_CV64k.

7   See the drone images and the time-lapse images of the city's evolution: · https://youtu.be/RCuiOwh3dMQ.

8   A survey conducted in 2012 with Beninese households living abroad revealed that the majority of sums transferred are intended first for day-to-day consumption (30%) then for a property project (23%), far ahead of education (6%) or health (4%) (INSAE 2013).

9   There is also Decree no. 2005–482 of 4 August 2005, very rarely applied, in which Article 2 stipulates that: "The design and construction of any socio-community infrastructure, of any social housing, of any service building, must demonstrate that 25% of its cost comes from the use of local materials or materials produced under a Beninese license."

10   See *Nigerian Tribune*, 01.04.2017, 'Planes And Pyramids: The Surreal Mansions Of Lebanon's Nigeria Avenue' https://tribuneonlineng.com/ planes-pyramids-surreal-mansions-lebanons-nigeria-avenue.

And the video of Miziara https://youtu.be/Pgh5iI94i04.

11   See *Le Monde*, 27.07.2016, 'Panama papers: comment la fortune de magnats indiens du Togo finit dans les paradis fiscaux', https://www. lemonde.fr/afrique/article/2016/07/27/panama-papers-comment-la-fortune-de-magnats-indiens-du-togo-finit-dans-les-paradis-fiscaux_4975374_3212.html.

12   The name "*Parcelles Assainies*" [sanitized plots] recalls the 1970s World Bank program in the 1970s to distribute plots with pre-installed sewage and water connections (Osmont 1995).

CHAPTER 3

The Social Life of Concrete

The story of the Three Little Pigs has shaped the imaginations of millions of children. This eighteenth-century fairy tale, revisited and adapted by Walt Disney in 1933, teaches us that houses made of wood and straw are useless – that only houses built of bricks and cement can protect us against the wolf and therefore, metaphorically, against any danger. In French-speaking West Africa, children learn to read and write with *Mamadou and Bineta's Book of reading French for African schools* (Davesne 1996). Lesson 55 is entitled "The beautiful houses in my village": "In my village, there are not only huts: there are also beautiful and solid houses whose walls are built with bricks and cement and whose roofs are covered with tiles or corrugated iron" (*ibid.*: 76). The pupils are then invited to copy and memorize the new words: bricks, cement, tiles, and corrugated iron. Concrete houses are "naturally" beautiful. In both the tale of the Three Little Pigs and the alphabet book, and in the collective imagination they have fed, concrete is valued for the superior durability and protection it is able to provide for the household.

This third chapter proposes to explore concrete houses and blocks of cement as lively materialities of city life (Fontein and Smith 2023). I pay attention to the production of the city from below, a "subaltern urbanism" (Roy 2011) grounded in the agency of individuals to shape their living spaces, notably through the act of building. Following a postcolonial approach and the work of urban anthropologists and sociologists, I analyze the perspective of the people who live in these concrete houses. This analysis allows me to offer a portrait of social life in contemporary urban Africa. This chapter is inspired by the ethnographic turn in global metropolitan studies which sheds light on what urban dwellers do and say (Roy and Ong 2011: xv). It will draw on the personal accounts of individuals to understand their relationship to cement blocks, to their houses, to their neighborhoods, and to the city. It thus aims to explore the day-to-day practices that underpin the Concrete City,

Concrete City: Material Flows and Urbanization in West Africa, First Edition. Armelle Choplin.
© 2023 John Wiley & Sons Ltd. Published 2023 by John Wiley & Sons Ltd.

those that take place in parallel with – and on the margins of – the spectacular urbanism and capitalistic processes of megaprojects. It will be an opportunity to decipher the bottom-up urbanization that relies on practices of autoconstruction (Caldeira 2017; Gastrow 2017), which have been described in numerous ways: incremental urbanism (van Noorloos et al. 2020), popular urbanization (Streule et al. 2020), plotting urbanism (Karaman et al. 2020). Many scholars have analyzed the act of building, especially in African cities, and have revealed the individual fates and collective destinies, social bonds, political relations, subsistence processes, and profit motives which arise from it (Nielsen 2011; Pinard 2016; Melly 2017; Morton 2019). To report on these various dynamics, I listen directly to the owners whose building projects I followed over the course of my three years of fieldwork, as well as to the tenants of several areas of Cotonou, Porto-Novo, Accra, Lagos, and Lomé with whom I spoke during my field research. The objective is to bring out some common features of construction imaginaries without claiming to understand and reduce the complexity of the diverse communities that inhabit the Gulf of Guinea (Fon, Yoruba, Ibo, Mina, Ebrié, Tui etc.). In addition to field surveys, I analyze the literature, music, and films set in Lagos or Accra as valuable sources for understanding the identities and imaginaries that are being redefined by the metropolitan experience and the internationalization of African cities (Mbembe and Nuttall 2004; De Boeck and Baloji 2016; Adeniyi-Ogunyankin 2019).

These life stories demonstrate that concrete is a commodity and a business, as well as a socio-technical object linked to modes of social and political organization (Akrich 2010). In line with Bruno Latour's (2005) actor–network theory, objects can be enlisted and have an agency of their own, allowing and constraining the possibility of action. Concrete is one of these objects: it shapes daily social relations, kinship hierarchies, and gender relationships. I investigate these relations, drawing on science and technology studies, the anthropology of techniques, and gender studies. I examine the role of women, often invisible in the construction sector, because there is too little research on gender and construction in the South and in African cities in particular. This part delves into material intimacies: building, constructing, commissioning a building are certainly about skills but also and above all refer to a culture of building that melds technical and social aspects. The act of construction with concrete itself is completely interwoven with discourses on modernity. As the architectural historian Adrian Forty (2012) reminds us: "Concrete tells us what it means to be modern." In contemporary urban Africa, concrete feeds imaginaries of modernity; it is not only a technical and innovative object, but also a source of success and envy, a mark of appropriation and opposition. It is heavily charged with desire, emancipation, and emotion. Far from being a passive and inert material, I propose to unveil the "social life" of concrete, to use Appadurai's expression (1986), and its considerable influence on human lives.

Caution – Work in Progress!

Reinforcing iron, gravel piles, cement bags, and wood scaffolding: the West African urban corridor is an immense construction site. Alongside the materials piled up in a corner of the plot, bare-chested men and teenagers toil together, mixing sand, cement, and water. A little way off, a guard ambles about. He has the unkempt look of the "bushman cousin" newly arrived from the village, probably summoned by the family in the city to guard the materials. Who are these men (and occasional women) who populate the construction sites? Who do they work for? And for what? Why do some projects get finished, while others grind to a halt? In the last 30 years or so, these construction sites have attracted a great deal of scholarly attention, with researchers focusing on self-built and compound housing in Africa (Antoine et al. 1987; Canel et al. 1990; Bertrand 2011). The plot owner may sometimes do the construction himself or get help from family and friends. Usually, however, he will hire a construction pieceworker. This is the dominant approach on most sites, creating multiple jobs and social relations linked to concrete.

Concrete – Child's Play?

In my childhood, I spent many an afternoon "playing concrete" with my brother, in a sandbox that my father made for us. "Playing concrete" meant mixing sand with soil, and a bit of cement and water. Then, armed with trowels, we would stir the gooey mix over and over, and pretend to dry bricks and build walls. Of course, they never held together. Some 30 years later, I found my father teaching my oldest son, age 9, how to "make concrete." Echoing my father's words, my son later proudly repeated to me his new-found recipe for concrete: "You mix a bit of cement, double the sand, gravel, and water. You see, it's easy."

These memories come back to me as I roam through the building sites in the outskirts of Cotonou, Porto-Novo, and Lomé, speaking to all kinds of people who tell me that using concrete is "child's play". As opposed to other building materials, concrete is widely accessible, cheap, and adaptable to the builder's financial resources. The enthusiasm for this material also emanates from its apparent simplicity. Mixing cement does not require a steady electrical power source nor does it require formal training or literacy. In Cotonou, most people, young and old, women and men, know the proportions for mixing cement into concrete to make bricks – one wheelbarrow of cement, two wheelbarrows of sand, three wheelbarrows of gravel. Pictograms on the bags sold are there to remind people of the proportions: one can make up to 30 blocks per 50 kg bag (Figure 3.1).

In reality, making concrete is a lot more complex. Adrian Forty (2019) reminds us that, "the greater part of the world's cement production is used by people with no professional or technical training: self-builders and small-scale constructors." This is the paradox of cement: it is highly complicated to produce but, once bought and "ready to use," it is easy to handle. Or at least it seems this way. As a site foreman named Bonaventure pointed out, pouring concrete requires certain skills. I met Bonaventure at the dissertation defense for my student Oliver, who had been researching the construction sector in Abomey-Calavi. Bonaventure's background is unusual. He has a Master's degree in chemistry and biology from University of Abomey-Calavi, but runs his own construction business: "When I was seven, I started helping my father, who was a builder. I helped him out during vacations. My father passed on his skills to me" (interview, Abomey-Calavi, 2019). After finishing

FIGURE 3.1   Bag of cement with pictograms, 2020. Source: Courtesy of H. Dato.

school in 2013, he came to earn a degree in Cotonou, where he rented a small room near the university. The landlord soon put him in touch with a site foreman who gave him a job: "Alongside my studies, I helped on building sites to earn money. Then my landlord gradually began to give me construction jobs on his own property, then recommended me to his friends as a site foreman."

There are several levels of knowledge involved in construction. While common sense means that everybody more or less knows how to mix cement, in practice there are not many people capable of building a simple wall. Moreover, the skills needed are not the same in a village compared with a city, where people know how to build multi-story houses. Bonaventure explains that "in town, one in two houses has an upper floor, while in the village its only one in ten. And while in the village you can make up to 40 blocks per packet, in Cotonou the number is closer to 30." In the city, customers have bigger budgets, and the usual practice is to employ a skilled worker. Some owners employ acquaintances or cousins or builders from their home village, who all cost less and are more trustworthy than skilled workers. These village builders are generally given accommodation by the owner until the work is finished. Some of them, once they have learned the trade, end up settling in the city.

For Ernest and Claude, site foremen who I met in Fidjérossé, most customers "broadly know what materials you use to make cement, the different phases in the construction of their house, but that's as far as it goes". It is not enough to know how to make a brick. There is also the correct drying time, the different steps to follow, planning the laying of the concrete – in other words, specialized skills. "As professionals, we don't give the customers too much detail about our techniques, because they will use them to hire their own piecework bricklayers and tell them: Do it like this, this is how it should be done," Claude explained, "when it works, they'll say that they built without using skilled builders, but the structures aren't made properly. They endanger the workers, the neighbors." Claude and Ernest do not mess around when it comes to rules and standards. In the event of a problem, they could be sued and risk their reputations.

Claude is at the site, watching his workers: "There are six apprentice bricklayers, and two apprentices who prepare the rebar. They are in training. My job is to make sure that everyone does their job properly." The apprentices are young. Maybe 10–12 years old, and not yet strong enough to lift buckets of cement and wheelbarrows full of sand. The apprentices provide unskilled labor: they stop school very young (before 13) to follow a site foreman, generally a member of the family or someone they know, who will agree to train them. They are not paid. On the contrary, the family pays the foreman to take them under his wing. The first year of apprenticeship is spent observing then, in the second year, they start building walls under the attentive eye of the foreman and, finally, in the third year they do it on their own (Gra 2019). This apprenticeship could be much shorter, but then the foreman would forfeit three years of payment. Construction sites are very hierarchical, and everyone has a set role: the site foreman, the one with the know-how, is at the top, while the bricklayers and apprentices, right at the bottom, simply carry out orders (Figure 3.2). Laborers get paid 2,000 francs CFA a day. The foreman – who may also be the layout designer, the site manager, and the works inspector – is paid per stage: 350,000 for the foundations, 200,000 for the ground floor, 100,000 for the slab. "That excludes materials," Claude explained, "out of that, I pay the workers, and keep the rest for myself."

Standing next to Claude, Ernest takes out his smartphone and proudly shows us the plans of the future house that he drew himself with Archicad, a free open-source 3D software application: "On the ground floor, we're going to build two apartments to rent. The first floor is for the owner, he explains. He lives in Switzerland. He wants something a bit European, with bay windows to let the light in." In front of the windows are Greek style columns, and the walls are tiled. Ernest is paid 8–10% of the total value of the work. He has recruited skilled workers. "There's the head bricklayer, the plumber, the glazier, the carpenter . . . The head bricklayer can't read these drawings in 3D, so

FIGURE 3.2   Worksite, Fidjerossé, 2018. Source: M. Lozivit.

I explain things in a different way. We understand each other. We've worked together for a long time."

Like in most projects, taxes have not been declared in this one, which is a cause of enormous losses to the state. In Benin, there are few builders who have an IFU (tax identification number). "If I had to pay taxes, I would have to increase my prices, so I would have fewer customers," Bonaventure argues. However, if he had to choose, he would prefer to do things by the book, because it "tells owners that you are trustworthy. They know that if there's a problem, you can't just do a runner, they'll be able to find you." Indeed, bad workmanship and mistakes are common – inadequate foundations, rusty steel, sloping floors – and few architects and engineers in working-class and peripheral areas. It is worth noting that owners invest less when the building is intended for rent rather than personal use.

However, in tracking the progress of several sites, I found that the sector is becoming increasingly organized: skills are starting to spread, and standards are beginning to be respected. In this respect, the metaphor of "child's play" may no longer apply.

Concrete Block: The Ingot of the Poor

The term *brique* is used in Francophone Africa to refer to manufactured concrete blocks, usually simply called "blocks" in Anglophone Africa. Broken or crumbling blocks are a frequent sight, because builder's often use poor quality cement and sand, because there are insufficient quantities of cement, and because of the local environment. The close proximity to the lagoon means that buildings have to be adapted and special care taken with foundations. In reality, few buildings are inspected by people who know much about this fragile environment. Builders often use lagoon sand, even though its high salt content can cause rusting in rebars and reinforcing steel. Surprisingly, people do not attribute much importance to the type of cement: they rarely discriminate among brands and seem to know little about the different qualities and ranges. "What do we sell? We sell strength!" claimed the managing director of the SCB Lafarge factory (interview, Onigbolo, 2017), who also noted that the most widely sold cement is CPJ 35.[1] And CPJ 35 is precisely the cement singled out by his competitor, the director of Nocibé, who does not rate its quality very highly: "This type of cement hasn't been around in Europe for 30 years. Since 1994, there have been clearly defined international standards, which are followed all around the world. We are a long way behind here: these standards are not met" (interview, Massé, 2018). CPJ 35 corresponds to CEM II 32.5, in other words the weakest cement, the one recommended for small jobs. For its part, Dangote sells 42.5R cement, "Dangote 3X"

("*Xtra strong, Xtra life and Xtra yield*"), which is stronger than the CPJ 35 cement sold by its competitors SCB Lafarge, SCB Bouclier and Cimbénin.

The quality of the blocks also depends on how they are manufactured. At the start of a construction project, the owner has three options: either the site foreman makes the blocks himself; or the blocks are bought ready-made from a brickyard; or the owner employs a block maker to come and make them in situ. The last option is chosen by the poorest households when they are beginning a building project but have not yet put together enough money. They are content to buy one or two bags of cement to make a few blocks, and the ingredients are mixed with a shovel, since concrete mixers are very rare. The bricks are then dried in a corner of the plot. They deteriorate quickly and are sometimes of poor quality. As Bonaventure explains: "If the blocks have already been made, I have to test them before using them. And I am often obliged to remake them." He does not want to construct a dangerous building with poor quality blocks and then to be held responsible for the problems. He reports that some owners try to save money by reducing the quantities of cement and reinforcing steel, and other builders are quite happy to change the proportions and weaken the binding agents. Bonaventure has no time for these unscrupulous and risky practices: "Some customers ask us to make more blocks to reduce the costs. The problem is that the blocks don't last as long. They crumble more quickly, and the building can collapse."

Poor block quality and distrust of block makers are the reason why breezeblock manufacturing firms are proliferating. This market is aligned with the emerging property development business. It targets private individuals who want to build their own houses, as François explained:

> There are too many problems on construction sites to get your own blocks made: you never know how much cement your builder is using to make the blocks. It's well known that some of them make the blocks with less cement and keep the rest for themselves. And often the blocks are of bad quality, and break. Personally, I prefer to buy ready-made blocks. It puts my mind at rest. I don't have to spend my time checking on my builder.
> (interview, Abomey-Calavi, 2016)

Mr. Jihad, owner of the firm SOREMAC, is one of Cotonou's leading building materials wholesalers. He has just opened SOCIMAT, a block manufacturing firm in Calavi. His aim is to set up a property development company that he can supply with blocks and building materials. He is currently developing partnerships with the bank, *Société Générale*, that helped him buy the land and open the hardware store and brickworks. He is also backed by the Heidelberg group:

FIGURE 3.3   Block seller in the suburbs of Lagos, 2018. Source: A. Choplin.

> Heidelberg financed the storage units for the brickworks. They also allow us to use the Heidelberg Cement label to sell our bricks. In return, they have the right to monitor our sales, the quality of the product. The label is a guarantee of quality. By buying ready-made bricks, customers can save on cement. A house normally requires 40 to 50 tons of cement, but there is a lot of waste here when opening the bag and mixing the cement. Material gets wasted. Building a house here takes 100 tons!
>
> (interview, Cotonou, 2018)

Buying ready-made blocks reduces construction costs. In Nigeria, block sellers gather in large numbers on both sides of the main roads and in the outskirts of cities, much more than in Benin or in Togo (Figure 3.3). Breeze-block could be considered the "ingot of the poor": like a gold bullion for the wealthy, a concrete block is an object that allows poor people to hoard money. And its quality reveals the wealth of the person who is building.

The Plot and the Block

I Build (with Concrete) Therefore I Am

> "I want my own place" – "If you havent built, you don't exist, even if you have loads of money" –

> "Home is the only place you feel comfortable" – "You need to have a house before doing anything else."

These short phrases, drawn from conversations with residents across West Africa, that punctuate my field notes are a reminder that most people in the region dream of owning a plot of land. And more than just land, a plot with a building on it. In West Africa, having "your own place" (*avoir "son chez"*) relates to the notion of ownership and is a means to purchase belonging in the social category of "owners" and "acquirers." In Cotonou and Lomé, in particular, the "obsession with owning your own home" is very evident (Assogba 2014). Even more than being an owner, building your own home is a mark of social recognition – it brings respect and pride, especially for people able to build houses beyond a single-story (Coralli and Houénoudé 2013). It is therefore common to find a sign in the middle of a plot indicating the name of the owner and arranged around it the clues to a future construction site like bags of cement or concrete blocks. A number of studies have shown the importance of building in Senegal (Pinard 2016; Melly 2017), in Tanzania (Mercer 2014), in Ghana (Cassiman 2011), in Congo (De Boeck and Baloji 2016), and in Mozambique (Nielsen 2011). In Accra, several residential forms coexist – collective structures like the compound, the family house, and the self-contained flat – where unrelated households live as tenants (Bertrand 2011; Ardayfio-Schandorf et al. 2012).

The desire to build and own a private house, with or without a formal land title, is one of the main driving forces behind the production of the West African city. The consequence of this dynamic is to increase the sale of and speculation on land. In peripheral areas, land prices have risen precipitously. In the town of Abomey-Calavi, prices rose 10-fold between 2000 and 2010 (Glélé 2015). Prices vary depending on flood risks, proximity to the road, and also whether or not there is a recognized land title. Owning property remains complicated, since it is difficult to acquire formal land titles in the region (cf. for Lagos, Sawyer 2016; for Benin, Lavigne Delville 2010; Chabi 2013; Simonneau 2017; for Accra, Bertrand 2011). In Benin, only possession of a *Certificat de Propriété Foncière* (land ownership certificate) (Act 2013-01 of 14 January 2013) confers legal ownership of a property. However, most dwellings do not have one. Land insecurity is high and is linked to the continuing existence of a customary law in which the village elders, chief, or council decide on the allocation of land to new "acquirers." The latter are given the right to occupy the land, but not a formal land title, which would require a registration procedure and therefore state recognition. As a result, in African cities, as in most cities in the Global South, informality has become the rule rather than an exception, both in business and property related activities, as a response to insecurity (Roy 2005; Murray and Myers 2007; Watson 2009). Informal landholding is not confined to the inhabitants of shanty towns. The middle and upper classes practice it with equal regularity. For example, in her novel *Americanah*, the writer Chimamanda N. Adichie (2013) offers a subtle account of the dodgy transactions that she observes in Lagos in Nigeria's middle class.

People build to stop being tenants equally as much as to become owners. Renting is often seen as a real constraint, characterized by submission to and dependency on landlords. In the absence of legal provisions governing tenancies, landlords frequently abuse tenants by raising rents and carrying out evictions without notice. The fifth of the month, rent payment day, is a date feared by all tenants. For many, the experience can be painful. As one resident, Edgard, recalls: "When I couldn't pay on time, because I hadn't yet received my wages, the landlord would hassle me, right in front of my kids. Even today, that is still a painful and unforgettable memory" (interview, Cotonou, 2018).

People often talk about a sense of insecurity. As another resident, Lina, explained, "the landlord doesn't understand when you have problems paying, if your daughter has been ill the month before and you had to buy medicine" (interview, Cotonou, 2018). In addition, becoming a tenant is expensive: tenants must pay a deposit for water and electricity, and generally six months' rent in advance to protect landlords from defaulters. In Lagos and Accra, it is common to ask for six months or even a year of rent in advance. For example, in the second episode of the web series entitled *An African City*, the heroine Nana Yaa, a returnee who has just come back after studying in England, is looking for an apartment in Accra. The agent shows her an apartment for rent at $2,000 a month and tells her that she has to pay cash for two years up front. Similarly, in the novel *Americanah* (Adichie 2013), the heroine Ifemelu finds an apartment in an old house that she must renovate completely, and she is nevertheless required to hand over a check for two years of rent. In certain neighborhoods, rents are close to or even higher than those in major western cities. Richard Grant (2009) describes how in Accra real estate bubbles coexist without any connection between them: the market for properties for expatriates working in the mines and the oil industry, as well as for returnees and the leading elites, is completely out of alignment with local realities and demand. This practice of requiring six months' rent in advance in Ghana and in Nigeria has spread to Benin and Togo under the influence of migrants, completely disrupting the local market. As a result, some people decide that, rather than paying such an advance, they will buy a plot in the outskirts of Lomé or Lagos, or else buy cement, as Bienvenue explains: "If your rent is 50,000 francs CFA a month (€75), you have to put down a year upfront, 600,000 francs CFA, then a deposit of 100,000 for water and electricity. That makes 700,000 francs CFA. Well, that's the price of a piece of land or 10 tons of cement."

In order to escape this climate of insecurity and conflict, many people choose to build their own house. As soon as the opportunity of acquiring a plot arises, they don't hesitate to buy: "It may be tough, but at least you have your own house. And it's better to suffer to become a homeowner yourself than to be hassled by a landlord," argues Galbert, who has just moved into his house, as he put it, in a hurry: "I moved in before I had completely finished. I've covered the window openings with metal sheets until I find the money to buy windows. It's still better than being a tenant" (interview, Cotonou, 2018).

The Incremental City: "Building Bit by Bit"

In Benin, in order to describe how their homes are currently – or rather, perpetually – under construction, homeowners in Benin often say that they are building their houses "bit by bit" (*un peu, un peu*). In West Africa, the city is built day-by-day, brick by brick, depending on the often intermittent revenues of poor urban households. West African cities are therefore incremental cities, as described in many studies on the informal neighborhoods and peripheral areas of other Southern cities (McFarlane 2011; Caldeira 2017; Van Noorloos et al. 2020). Schmid, Karaman, Sawyer, and Streule theorized these urban dynamics by drawing on the cases of Lagos, Kolkata, and Istanbul, and they developed expressions like "popular urbanisation" and "plotting urbanism" (Streule et al. 2020; Karaman et al. 2020; Sawyer et al. 2021). "Popular urbanisation" (Streule et al. 2020) is defined as "a people-led process of land appropriation and settlement building based on collective action, self-organisation and the labour of inhabitants" (Streule et al. 2020), whereas "plotting urbanism" (Karaman et al. 2020) is "characterised by more individualised strategies of urban development and intensification of land use, strong processes of commodification and often a marked socioeconomic differentiation between property owners and tenants." These terms describe both the collective dynamics employed by the poorest people who build to survive, as well as more structured dynamics employed by developers and small owners to take advantage of land reserves by converting them into financial assets. These two strategies emerged in my field research. Plotting strategy (converting farmland into housing plots) is a very profitable and very common practice. It is employed by many elected officials because it is often the only way to bring money into local authority coffers. "New urban worlds" (Simone and Pieterse 2017) thus take form as a result of land deals organized sometimes by the authorities, by small landowners, or by customary chiefs turned property developers (Bon 2021; Sawyer et al. 2021). Yet these urban worlds also take form as a result of local people making do and very often doing "without."

All these non-coordinated and sometimes opposing dynamics lead to the mix of improvisation, tinkering, and insecurity that Simone and Pieterse (2017) call "makeshift." Incremental urban production is clearly identifiable in the urban interstices of the corridor, for example in the poor sections of Accra documented by Jonathan Silver (2014), as well as in the outskirts of these cities. Claire Mercer (2020: 79) speaks of "incremental efforts" in reference to middle-class populations who build their houses on the edges of Dar es Salaam. In the Global South where social security is inexistent and access to the banking system is difficult, buying bags of cement, investing in concrete is a way to hoard. As Norbert, a taxi driver with very irregular income, explained: "When I have some money in my pocket, I try to buy bags of cement, which I store on my plot. I know that if I keep the money in my pocket, someone will ask me and I will not be able to save it" (interview, Abomey-Calavi, 2017). Building piece by piece is a way to stockpile money (Agossou 2011), to face economic insecurity, and to anticipate the insecurity of retirement when there is no more money coming in. A bag of cement is seen both as a short- and a long-term investment: if it costs 3,500 francs CFA to buy, it is worth potentially much more once the powder is mixed with water and sand. Once turned into concrete, it transforms from land to real estate and ultimately into an inheritance. "When I am no longer around for my children, the house will still be here," explains François, who has just completed his house project. Igor, another homeowner, similarly asserts: "here, to make money, you buy a plot of land, you build a property and you rent it out" (interview, Abomey-Calavi, 2016).

Building is therefore a way of "preparing the future" and "preserving the future" for one's children (Nielsen 2011). As Norbert summarized to me, building then becomes the main objective in life: "During the day I think about cement. At night, I dream of cement." He explained that "Everybody wants their own place" (*son « chez »*). As soon as you start working, you want your own place, so you tighten your belt. You save bit by bit first to buy the plot, then to build your house. In the end, often, you finish everything when you reach retirement and that's when you die, just when you finally take possession of your property." Norbert's philosophy affirms that building is a lifetime project, one in which only respectable people have concrete graves.

In the dozen home building sites I tracked between 2016 and 2018, the owners explained at length how their homes "weighed too heavily on their minds" because of conflicts with neighbors, heirs, with other possible acquirers, and particularly with builders who were often accused of padding prices, working slowly, or stealing equipment. Getting a house requires the owner to monitor progress, possibly for several years. Giving up is common (around 15% of sites in our field areas). The main reason is building costs, which owners often underestimate at the start. They are well aware of the price of construction materials, but they forget to include the costs of equipment – a block mold, for example, or, less commonly, a cement mixer or labor costs (10% of the cost of construction). Ultimately, while cement is the biggest single cost item, buying it represents only 30% of the total cost. The time-scale of construction is far from linear and difficult to anticipate, as Morten Nielsen (2011) has demonstrated in the case of houses in Maputo built from scratch (*casa de raiz*). I met François, a caretaker, in 2016. He bought his plot, located in Calavi, in the suburbs of Cotonou, in 2004. It took him three years to pay off the price of the land (1.5 million francs CFA) and six years to save enough to start construction in 2010. "I bought a ton of cement and ask a mason to come to make the blocks. Then another ton later on. After the blocks, I waited to find more money" (interview, Abomey-Calavi, 2017). In all, between buying the land in 2004 and moving into the house, almost 14 years went by. He estimates that he spent 2.5 million francs CFA, "and it still isn't entirely finished."

When I met Elinor, she was 26 years old and the owner of a fabric store in one of Cotonou's busiest shopping streets. She dreamed of building her own house. She acquired a plot in Ouédo, in the periphery, where the government has started constructing public housing developments. On our first visit in September 2017, she explained that she does not need an architect because, she says, "I had all the plans in my head" (interview, Ouédo, 2017). Elinor expressed confidence in her ability to manage the project: "I have a good site foreman. At the beginning, I was there a lot and guided him to get what I wanted." But she also manages many aspects of the construction herself – it is Elinor, for example, who purchases building materials from the nearest hardware store (Figures 3.4, 3.5, and 3.6).

A year later, with the work nearing completion, Elinor confesses that she had remained openly skeptical, and highly scrutinous, of the foreman to prevent him from raising the prices or keeping materials for himself. "For example, I avoid bringing money to the site. Otherwise, you're tempted to give them what they ask for," she explained. "As far as possible, I avoid letting them work on their own." To elaborate, she shared an anecdote: "One day they needed gravel, the foreman told me 75,000 francs CFA, so I gave him the money. But on the way back, nearby, I met a seller who told me it was 55,000 a ton. I took back the money and went to buy the gravel myself."

Elinor claims that she is always on her guard: "At the beginning the workers told me that they needed six tons of cement for the compound wall. We counted the number of bricks per square meter needed for the whole length of the plot, and it came out at four tons! And it was the same for

FIGURE 3.4   Elinor's site in 2017. Source: M. Lozivit.

FIGURE 3.5   Elinor's site in 2018. Source: M. Lozivit.

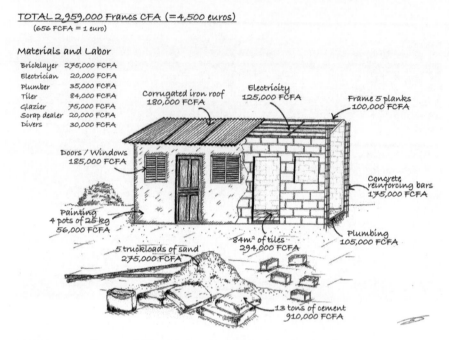

TOTAL 2,959,000 Francs CFA (=4,500 euros)
(656 FCFA = 1 euro)

Materials and Labor

Bricklayer   275,000 FCFA
Electrician   20,000 FCFA
Plumber   35,000 FCFA
Tiler   84,000 FCFA
Glazier   75,000 FCFA
Scrap dealer   20,000 FCFA
Divers   30,000 FCFA

Corrugated iron roof
180,000 FCFA

Electricity
125,000 FCFA

Frame 5 planks
100,000 FCFA

Doors / Windows
185,000 FCFA

Concrete
reinforcing bars
175,000 FCFA

Painting
4 pots of 25 kg
56,000 FCFA

84m² of tiles
294,000 FCFA

Plumbing
105,000 FCFA

5 truckloads of sand
275,000 FCFA

13 tons of cement
910,000 FCFA

FIGURE 3.6   Costs of Elinor's house 2019. Source: D. Bertrais.

the reinforcing steel." These issues are everyday events on the sites: "If you're not careful," she went on, "it'll cost you an arm and a leg! And if you're a woman on your own as well, you have to show that you know what you're doing if you don't want to be cheated." When everything was added up, she spent almost 3 million francs CFA for the building (i.e., €4,500 for a house), whereas she had initially calculated the cost at around 2 million. On top of this was the price of the land, 5.8 million francs CFA in all (i.e., almost €9,000). She adjusted her schedule as she went along: "As soon as I had a bit of money, I would buy sand or cement."

Galbert, another home builder, described a similar approach to incremental construction: "You never finish your house. With a few end-of-year bonuses, you buy cement and go on spending until there are tiles everywhere." In Lagos, the writer Chimamanda Ngozi Adichie (2019) offered a similar portrait of her childhood home: "my house had required some arcane engineering, sand-filling, leveling, to prevent the possibility of sinking. And during the construction, my relatives stopped by often to check on things. If you're building a house you must be present, otherwise the builders will slap-dash your tiling and roughen your finishing. This is a city in a rush and corners must be cut."

These projects and stories show that home building is a lifetime long pursuit. They also reveal the vitality of all these small, informal businesses linked to construction and, at the same time, they reveal the fragility of this incremental city which relies on individuals to be their own builders, their own developers, their own employers, and to depend on monetary and/or hierarchical relationships. The slightest crisis, whether local (political tensions), regional (border closures), or international (economic slowdown or collapse in the price of materials) has an immediate impact on these jobs and these relationships, as well as on the city they produce. In this way, an individual's life can be understood from the perspective of the bags of cement (s)he has accumulated and bricks (s)he has built over the course of a lifetime.

Right to Concrete for a Right to the City

After food, cement is the second product that people in West Africa buy to tackle the hazards of urban life and its emergencies. It is therefore a haven commodity that people store when they can and offer as a gift when possible. For example, migrants send money to their families back home to pay school fees or buy bags of cement. And during wedding ceremonies, cement is regularly part of the gifts offered in the dowry.

Cement has long been a factor of social distinction, especially between the rural environment – the village or the bush – and the urban environment. Colonists and Africans alike have mapped this dual distinction onto a similar binary between "traditional" and "modern." In many regions across the continent, clay, straw, and timber are understood as traditional materials associated with the village (Piot 1999; Cassiman 2011), where the countryfolk live. For example, the word "*gletanu*" in the Fon language translates literally into "the ones who come from the fields," but it is more commonly used to refer to a person thought to be ignorant. Conversely, urban dwellers consider cement, sheet metal, and tiles as "modern" aspects of the city – and by extension to civilization. They also associate such materials with people who can read and write and are "evolved" (*éduqué* in French – educated or *akowé* in Fon). This distinction between the cement city and the earth village persists, even in national statistics (Table 3.1). In the same way, Benin's Ministry of the Environment and Sustainable Development distinguishes between "traditional housing" (earth walls and thatched or corrugated iron roofs) and "modern housing" (walls built with cement-based blocks, cement and sometimes tiled floor, corrugated iron, slab or tiled roof).

In the public imagination and in official definitions, cement is a feature of the city, of modernity, of wealth, and of civilization; just as straw, earth, and bamboo are perceived as attributes of the village, using these materials is similarly perceived as a backward practice associated with poverty.

TABLE 3.1 Distinction rural and urban area in Benin.

	Rural	Urban	Cotonou
Cement walls	24	63	86
Earth walls	61	26	7
Metal roof	80	84	81
Grass roof	16	5	5
Slab roof	–	–	13
Cement floor	46	76	81
Earth/sand floor	49	17	–
Tiled floor	1	6	14

Source: INSAE, General Census of Population and Housing (RGPH) (2013).

As a consequence, the use of so-called "traditional" materials carries connotations in the urban environment: straw and bamboo are perceived as temporary and associated with the poor and marginal populations who live in illegal dwellings in areas of squalor (Figure 3.7). Indeed, the non-durability of construction materials is one of the five criteria applied by UN Habitat in its definition of slums (UN-Habitat 2003). A map of Cotonou which shows the percentages of houses built with cement walls and floors is enlightening. The districts with the lowest percentage of cement houses are precisely located on the edges of the lagoon which regularly flood. They correspond to the most precarious neighborhoods in the city, such as Placodji or Ladji in Cotonou (41% bamboo housing). In Lagos, the poor district of Makoko is similarly known for its wooden houses on stilts. Yet far from being recent developments in these cities, poor and autoconstructed areas on the edges of lagoons are in fact the oldest districts, and they are inhabited by the original populations (*Xula* and *Toffins*) (Ciavolella and Choplin 2018; Choplin and Lozivit 2019). Local materials are often understood as a sign of precariousness, and the authorities similarly see them as a signal that these precarious neighborhoods are merely villages of "backward" populations who have no place in a modern city center.

Acquiring bags of cement and building structures out of concrete has particular significance in neighborhoods marked by high levels of economic insecurity. And this insecurity is accentuated in areas with heavy and recurrent rainfall. During the three months of annual flooding, which can sweep everything away, concrete is often the only thing that remains. When they can, households cover the earth floors with concrete, and then build concrete walls. Many urban residents understand concrete homes as "permanent and

FIGURE 3.7   Concrete house: the end of precariousness, Cotonou 2018. Source: A. Choplin.

durable," and they therefore require little maintenance. As one local proverb puts it, "Brick doesn't rot!" Georges is the chief of Ladji, an informal neighborhood located on the banks of a lagoon. For him, "building with concrete is the only way to stay out of the rain and the rising waters. And you don't have to rebuild the houses, like dirt houses after every rainy season." Corrugated iron is also gradually replacing grass roofs, which decompose quickly and are a fire risk. These uncertainties and vulnerabilities explain why most households, even poor ones, generally have a half bag of cement stored somewhere.

Given the recurrent evictions across West Africa (Gillespie 2016), the use of permanent materials and structures – such as concrete – often forms the basis of claims for greater integration into the city and for urban citizenship. In Maputo, for example, cement was historically restricted to colonial settlements. David Morton (2019) has interpreted the use of cement among urban residents in Maputo as a political act of defiance and protest addressed to the authorities. Claudia Gastrow (2017: 233) offers a similar analysis of concrete construction in Luanda's informal neighborhoods: with the use of concrete, "houses could no longer simply be dismissed as anarchic, but had to be taken seriously as objects of good urbanism, through which demands and rights could be articulated." Permanent structures, strong foundations, multi-story buildings symbolize the legitimacy of presence. In this sense, concrete embodies the right to be and remain in the city – a first step toward a right to the city (Lefebvre 1968). Georges, the chief of Ladji, reminds us that this informal neighborhood is regularly threatened with eviction. He argues: "The government cannot evict us, as if we didn't exist. We have invested a lot of money to build concrete houses. If we didn't have the right to stay, if it wasn't our place, we would never have spent so much money" (interview, Cotonou, 2018). Especially in shanty towns, building in concrete makes it possible to legitimize one's presence, to break away from the precariousness of wood and sheet metal and to no longer be at the mercy of eviction policies and floods. Gabriella Körling (2020) reaches similar conclusions in her study of the peripheral areas of Niamey where permanent structures are a way for citizens to be recognized as "productive" and "respectable."

Other studies on urban materiality have explained how various documents, technologies, infrastructures, and consumer products can underpin claims to civic legitimacy. In this way, concrete is part of "the political materiality of cities" (Pilo' and Jaffe 2020): the various documents, technologies, infrastructures, and consumer products which shape socio-political life in the city. Writing about Brazil's favelas, Francesca Pilo' (2020) showed that paying the electricity bill is a way to integrate, to feel as if one is part of the state and part of the city. Sylvy Jaglin (1995) has identified similar processes of escaping precariousness through access to electricity in South Africa. For Jaglin, "the struggle for electricity, like the struggle for a house made of durable materials, is ultimately a struggle for the right to the city." In Accra, Lomé, and Cotonou, I made the same observation and reach the conclusion that, in informal neighborhoods, a life without concrete means being in the city without having a right to it. Concrete blocks are used to underpin claims to political legitimacy as citizens. They materialize the "right to the city" and one's belonging to it.

Afropolitan Modernity, Imaginaries, and Experience

Desire and Success

Concrete is a highly-coveted object: it is an object of aspiration, emotion, and desire. These desires are fed by the new models of success and power in Africa: footballers, pastors, and singers are developing new pathways to accumulation and to an ostentatious material culture. Their success is embodied in the accumulation of iconic objects, often beginning with the private villa and later joined by the vehicle, the video, and the veranda – what is known as the four "V"s (Banégas and Warnier 2001), urban attributes of success that have replaced those associated with the village: the three "B"s of bicycle, bou-bou, and *boeuf* (oxen in English) (Bredeloup 2007). As Julie Archambault (2018, 2021) has argued, in Mozambique, cement bags are becoming new currencies of exchange and markers of attention. They have even come to be an important gift given in romantic relationships, like the mobile phone in the 2000s. Lovers offer each other bags of cement as a declaration of love, as a "durable" proof of their commitment to each other.

Desires reflect collective processes and are "formatted" by class, age, and gender. For many young men (18–30), their first desire is to own a motor-bike. This is a source of autonomy, of independence from family, and a source of status, notably with girls. The articles by Guive Khan-Mohammad (2016) and Giorgio Blundo (2018) on the symbolism of Chinese motorbikes help to understand the social and political trajectory of this object that is now indissociably linked with African cities. The song "Moto Moto" (motor-bike motorbike) by the famous Ivorian singer DJ Arafat, star of *coupé-décalé* music, who died tragically in a motorbike accident in 2019, is exemplary of the social imaginary associated with this object. In the clip, a parade group of highly sexualized young women are depicted sitting astride high-powered motorbikes. DJ Arafat sings about the need to own and control these pow-erful metal bodies, as well as those of the women straddling them. After the age of 30 – once the motorbike is bought and paid for and the man has a more or less stable job – the next step is to start building. Getting a house built is something of a rite of passage into the world of mature and responsible adults, and it allows young men to gain the title of "head of the family" (Bertrand 2013). Completing this rite brings recognition from fam-ily and from urban society, both of which operate on a capitalist mode of accumulation. In Lagos, Lyndsay Sawyer (2016) describes the social pressure on people in the middle classes to have built or purchased their own home once they reach their middle-to-late thirties. For the Beninese geographer Moïse Chabi (2013: 266), "building constitutes an instrument for measuring social success and the position that the individual merits within the family," especially for the Yoruba community from the 1970s onwards in Nigeria and then in Benin in Porto-Novo and Cotonou. He recalls that many Yoruba musicians in Nigeria celebrate the importance of the big house, with Yoruba expressions such as "He has built a house that is beyond comprehension" or "He has built house upon house" (*ibid.:* 266). To demonstrate success and at the same time to achieve property security and to be autonomous, those are the main reasons why some people want to own a piece of land and a permanent house and to move to the outskirts of the city, much more than the desire to escape urban pollution and crowds, or to have a big compound. Once a man has a motorbike and a house, it will be time to think about a car. Then it is finally time to retire and, for anyone with a bit of money, to build again, generally on or nearby one's own plot in order to rent and generate new income. In an urban society marked by uncertainty and financial insecurity, renting property is one of the few ways to guarantee a regular income for the "twilight years." As a result, people never stop building.

These different objects of desire and markers of success coincide with clearly identified stages in life. Following this path seems self-evident, and any change is perceived as imprudent or ill-considered. This is how Bienvenue, a direct descendant of the Abomey royal family (therefore "well-born") and now a professor at University of Abomey-Calavi, describes his family's heated reactions to his "irrational" choices:

"When I was a tenant on the outskirts of Calavi, I got fed up with traveling to the city center by *zem* (motorbike taxi). I could no longer stand the pollution, the fatigue, the fear of accidents. I decided to buy a car. It was a decision my family couldn't understand. I was considered foolish to buy a car before putting a roof over my family's head. My uncles said Why buy a car before you've got your house? You will be parking your car in front of somebody else's house!"

Yet Bienvenue fondly recalls of his uncles that, "they didn't leave me in peace until I began building my house." His family's reaction shows how desires are socially formatted, conditioned, and structured. Insofar as "building their own place," as one resident put it, is a priority for many urbanites (and villagers) and the main mark of social recognition, anyone who does not follow this model is deemed suspect or irresponsible. As a Fon proverb puts it: "The tenant should not plant flowers in front of the landlord's house."

Women at Work! Virility, Gender, and Emancipation

"My husband is capable" is the name of a well-known wax fabric that West African women wear to display their husband's strength and to repel rivals. Being a capable husband means being a good breadwinner, providing your family with a roof and protecting them within concrete walls. Being capable for a man means building a permanent home. In West Africa's patriarchal societies, activities – like spaces – are highly sharply divided by gender: while the house and the domestic sphere belong to women, construction is seen as belonging to men. A man's strength is measured in the number of plots he acquires and the number of tons of cement he has poured. This is a recurrent theme in everyday life, as in Moïse Chabi's (2013) description of a tenant's issues with his lodgers. After a falling out, the latter insult the tenant and mock him as an "incompetent who can't even get a block made" (Chabi 2013: 297).

Concrete offers a lens through which to explore the material basis of social and gendered relations. Yet the materiality of the construction sector in the Global South has received limited attention. Critical analysis of the relationship among materials, infrastructure, and gender has only recently emerged (e.g., Archambault 2021). Concrete contributes to the assertion of social and sexual power as indicated by the emblems of the cement manufacturers' brands: many of them imply strength, such as a *bouclier* (shield) or a *cuirasse* (breastplate), others to powerful and dominant animals such as *buffle* (buffalo), *bélier* (ram), elephant, and eagle (Figure 3.8). Anyone who builds with concrete is seen as both virile and tough. Advertisements for cement and construction materials feature men with large bellies, a sign of success referencing the manager or civil servant comfortably settled in his air-conditioned office, secure in his important post and with his secure salary that will allow him to buy the necessary building materials to construct his own concrete home. The belly distinguishes him from men obliged to do backbreaking work in the fields, whose hollow bellies scream hunger. This protuberance becomes a symbol of wealth, as it does in Émile Zola's *The Belly of Paris* (2006[1st edition 1873]), a novel that portrays the contrasts between the "fat" and the "thin." In Africa as elsewhere, today as it did in the past, the body expresses a person's position

FIGURE 3.8 Cement bags: the elephant/ram/buffle logos, 2018. Source: Lafarge Nigeria, LafargeHolcim Ivory Coast Group, Cimtogo HeidelbergCement Group.

in society. In Ghana, middle-class transnational migrants are referred to with a hint of mockery as "Burgers," a reference to the bodily corpulence that supposedly connotes their success (Nieswand 2014). During a plane trip from Amsterdam to Accra, I was seated next to a Ghanaian woman named Berenice, who told me that she lived in the Bronx neighborhood of New York and that, in Ghana, "people call us Burgers because some immigrants live in the United States. Ghanaians in the home country think that we are fat because we only eat burgers. They also think that we have fat wallets" (interview, 2016). In Benin, female shopkeepers are called "*bonnes dames*" (buxom ladies), and pictures of "gogo" women with generous curves circulate on WhatsApp groups. Lina, a Togolese woman, complained to me about being too slim which, in her view, prevents her from finding a husband. And she imagines this husband as a big man as well, hard as concrete, solid as the foundations of the house she dreams he will build for her.

These bodies and these people are the infrastructures on which urban society rely (Simone 2004). This is particularly true in "corporeal cities" like Kinshasa (De Boeck and Plissart 2004), "where stone and concrete are in short supply or crumbling, the city turns to another material, the human body." Cities across the Gulf of Guinea display a similar style of social relationship and a similar mode of governmentality which are often expressed through corporeal metaphors. In this region of the world, the "politics of the belly" continue to determine many socio-economico-political relations. The expression, formulated by the political scientist Jean-François Bayart (1993), is a reminder that the state is perceived as providing access to privileges and resources for the members of one's clan. Although developed through an analysis of Cameroon, "the politics of the belly" is valid for countries throughout the Gulf of Guinea, where power and dominance are exercised by whoever consumes, swallows, devours concrete – like men consuming food prepared by women. Indeed, the sexual division of roles is clear: a strong man's job is to cover spaces with concrete while his wife's, in return, is to fill his belly. To do this, women strive to prepare dishes that fill their husbands' stomachs. *Ougali* in Kenya, *to* in Burkina or *pâte* in Benin are terms that refer to substances that are low in nutritional value but heavy to digest, and settle in the stomach to make it hard over time.

In West Africa, as elsewhere across the world, the construction sector and construction sites are masculine places: nearly all builders in this sector are men. Even very young men (Figure 3.9). Historically, the cement and concrete industry has been a male-dominated field whereby women presence is below 15% (source: Global Cement and Concrete Association). In Ghana, 3% of workers employed in the construction sector are women. Nevertheless, the sector is expanding and lucrative. Some NGOs' have launched initiatives to

FIGURE 3.9   The cement bag: between burden and emancipation for young people, Ganvié, 2018. Source: A. Choplin.

go beyond gender stereotypes and make this sector attractive for women with little education and low investment.[2] Women often play a major but invisible role in house construction (Eyifa-Dzidzienyo 2012). In Bamako, women are deeply involved in the real estate market – they buy land, commission construction, hire builders, manage the accounts – though they rarely participate in the physical labor of concrete construction (Bertrand 2001). Most women I encountered in Cotonou, Lomé, Lagos, or Accra generally know the price of a bag of cement, how to mix concrete, and the different stages of construction (Figure 3.10). And of the dozen building projects I followed during my field research, three were supervised by women. It is common for a woman to be both owner and client, and to play an active part in the process of building, monitoring progress, supervising the construction sites, and negotiating the prices of materials. Elinor is one such woman who is familiar with the construction process. She finished the construction of her house in December of 2018. "For the floor," she recounted, "I'm thinking of laying a floating timber plank floor. I'm even wondering whether to do it myself. I've seen the carpenters working, and I reckon I could do it." She confessed: "I wanted to build in order to have my own house, not to be dependent on anybody. I am happy because I have a house, my house. Even if I am not yet married, my family respects me."

FIGURE 3.10 Women and Concrete, Cotonou, 2018. Source: Courtesy of A. Hertzog.

Echoing Elinor's desires for independence, Rita (55 years old) described how she "started building after my husband's death, so that I wouldn't have to be beholden to his family." And Raymonde, another resident of Cotonou, recalls that "it was tough, but now I've had my house built, I'm no longer dependent on anyone else" (interview, 2018). In a patriarchal system dominated by fathers, brothers, and oldest sons (Bertrand 2013), many women build homes on their own as a way to unyoke themselves from such familial hierarchies. Concrete is the key to independence, the mark of the younger son's emancipation from his older brother, the wife's from her husband, the widow's from the family. And the peripheral areas where people are building their homes in turn become places of emancipation for young households. Here, they can live in neutral spaces, away from social and family control, unobserved behind high concrete walls.

Concrete Palace, or Walter Benjamin in Lagos

"For many people, modernity is embodied in the white man. So, we have to imitate the white man, build the same houses as him, out of cement. Even if it is hotter and unsuitable. We imitate, but not as well," sighed Gérard, a historian living in Porto-Novo. In an imaginary inherited from modernist colonial architecture (Herz et al. 2015; De Boeck et Baloji 2016; Hoffman 2017), being modern and "evolved," as people say locally, means living in a concrete house. Antoine et al. (1987) corroborate this idea in their study of Abidjan: "Since independence, the idea of modernization has been embodied in houses made out of cement breezeblocks with corrugated iron roofs."

The analysis of the links between modernity and urbanization has fueled many works on Africa. First, the Manchester School/Rhode Livingston Institute, through the work of Gluckman (1960), addressed this issue of modernity driven the emergence of new urban perceptions and experiences in the Copperbelt in the 1950–1960s. Later, the anthropologist James Ferguson (1999) examined the "expectations of modernity" in the Copperbelt too. He explored the social and cultural responses to the economic decline of the region in the 1980s and narratives of urbanization, modernity, and social change. More recently, Jennifer Robinson (2013) addressed the question of modernity and the urban experience by mobilizing Walter Benjamin's work on modernity at the turn of the twentieth century. To reread Benjamin, as Jennifer Robinson (2013) suggests, and to compare Accra, Lagos, or Lomé with late nineteenth century Paris or Berlin, is an invitation to think about the new, home-grown African "metropolitan condition" which is emerging in urban spaces in new dimensions and forms. A century earlier, in *The Arcades Project*, Walter Benjamin (2012) realized that the introduction of the metropolitan consumer into the global market designated a key moment in the metropolitan experience.

In West Africa, concrete seems to have become an avatar of modernity and of the contemporary metropolitan condition, like glass in the Berlin of Walter Benjamin's childhood. As Philippe Simay (2006: 15) observed from Benjamin's writings, "the supreme and paradoxical quality of glass is to make things darker, but also to clarify the relations between interior and exterior, family structure and individuality, eros and sexual repression, exploited and exploiter." It is easy to transpose these remarks to the concrete wall which, in its variations of thickness, of granularity, of hardness, expresses social relations of domination, poverty, and exclusion. At the end of the nineteenth century, modernity was embodied as glass and steel and epitomized by the Crystal Palace, a palace of cast-iron and glass, erected in London for the first Universal Exhibition of 1851. The historian of anthropology, George Stocking (1987), saw this building as a metaphor for the discovery of the world in the Victorian era. For Riccardo Ciavolella and Eric Wittersheim (2016: 25), "the transparent glass structure shows all the diversity of human production concentrated under a single roof, thus bringing together, and hence rendering comparable, what was originally disconnected and unrelated." Modeled on Crystal Palace, the Grand Palais – inaugurated in Paris in 1900 – and the city's numerous glass-covered arcades became symbols

FIGURE 3.11   A Concrete Palace, Porto-Novo, 2019. Source: Courtesy of A. Guillot.

of openness and discovery of the world, which would later come to inspire Walter Benjamin.

If Benjamin were to stroll through the streets of Paris or London or Lagos or Lomé today, he would see that concrete has today replaced glass as the dominant material of urban modernity – the Crystal Palace has given way to the Concrete Palace and altered the experience of the modern city (Figure 3.11). While the glass façades of the Crystal Palace and other transparent structures of the era were symbols of openness to others and to the world, of ecstasy and of envy – as described in Baudelaire's 1862 poem *The Eyes of the Poor* – the tall opaque walls of today's Concrete Palace instantiate closure, exclusion, self-protection, withdrawal. Although glass today remains an iconic material – in the towers of Dubai or Eko Atlantic City alike – it is generally tinted and blocks the unencumbered gaze. Behind concrete walls, Africa's city dwellers protect themselves from natural hazards, such as floods, but also from the power and the unknown otherness of the city itself, which is not fully under control, be it in its forms, its functions, or in its extensions. To borrow Simmel's words, concrete could be said to offer a certain form of "protection of subjective life against the violence of the Big City" (Simmel 2005). Because, as Benjamin recalled, the metropolis is experienced as a disruption of the human *sensorium*: as a protection against this assault, concrete reassures.

Six-Bedroom-Villas

These *"extrêmement chambrées"* [excessively roomed] villas, as they are called in Bénin and Togo, are a source of constant surprise. Every kind of shape and variety of layouts, like the people who have them built (Figure 3.12). A symbol of wealth and a promise of social distinction, the ideal villa has come to populate "afropolitan imaginations" (Adeniyi-Ogunyankin 2019), from those used as settings in the Nigerian film industry (Haynes 2016; Jedlowski 2019) to those in the decorative Chinese posters sold in the streets (De Boeck and Baloji 2016: 212). Neoclassical in style and inspired by British mansions, West African villas are adorned in cold marble and plaster ceiling moldings, fake Greek columns and balustrades, tiled floors and walls, and decked out with multiple satellite dishes connecting them to the world. The materials are generally imported, a reminder of "the transnational and privileged experience" (Melly 2017). The villa is permeated with decoration, with so-called "Western-style" furniture that is in fact generally bought from stores owned by Levantine merchants, in a style ultimately closer to that of Eastern rather than Western elites. These villas are ideally occupied by a couple with two children. The model is a radical departure from the traditional layout of the West African house and family compound: it no longer offers a communal courtyard but small rooms furnished with cold and uncomfortable fake leather sofas, but is instead modeled after so-called "self-contained" homes where most social activities take place indoors (Gra 2019).

FIGURE 3.12   A six-bedroom-villa, Accra, Ghana, 2018. Source: A. Choplin.

This is the model of the ideal villa propagated by the media (Cassiman 2011). Films, advertisements, video clips, soaps, and novels all spread references to this concrete imaginary, part of the "ostentatious material culture" that "builds the [social] hierarchy" (Warnier 1999). Diaspora and returnees alike play a fundamental role in the dissemination of these architectural models and Afropolitan lifestyles. In 2005, the West African novelist Taiye Selasi coined the term "Afropolitan." Selasi wrote about multilingual Africans with different ethnic mixes living around the globe – as she put it "not citizens but Africans of the world." A CNN article titled "Who Are Afropolitans"[3] reminds us that the term refers to – but also criticizes – this new global class of successful, urban, intelligent, culturally aware, and savvy 30-somethings, who often come from the diaspora rather than the continent's metropolises. This diverse community plays a crucial role in defining the continent's new urban imaginaries. These imaginaries are nourished by another vision of African cities characterized by buildings mushrooming everywhere, processions of powerful cars caught in the traffic jams of new business districts, international banks and brands flowering at every street corner, and huge villas aligned behind high concrete walls topped with barbed wire. For example, in the web series *An African City*, each episode begins with shots of Accra. We see the wide avenues, the interchanges, and the cranes that suggest buildings under construction, the arrival of foreign capital, and the emergence of a capitalist and consumerist society. The female directors and producers – themselves of Ghanaian origin and diasporic returnees – have chosen to focus on the forward-looking African city, the city where money flows and the women are beautiful and intelligent, modern, and classy. They frequent restaurants and big hotels in the trendy Osu and Oxford Street districts (Quayson 2014), a stone's throw from "Sodom and Gomorrah" (the name given to Accra's biggest slum) and from the famous Agbogbloshie e-dump (an open-air graveyard of electronic waste from Europe). But these themes are not limited to Ghana: the Senegalese web series *Maîtresse d'un homme marié* (mistress of a married man) similarly follows the lives of women in Dakar's emerging middle class. And in the novel *Americanah*, the heroine is hard put to recognize the booming city of Lagos. She finds that her first lover has become a rich entrepreneur, a broker of real estate deals. They meet in private clubs – trendy restaurants where people "brunch," taste French or Italian cuisine, or consume hamburgers, panini, and frozen French fries. . . everything except local fried rice and plantains.

In all these cases, the heroines are "returnees," middle-class and upper-class young women who have returned to Accra and Lagos after a decade in the US or the UK, to take advantage of the economic boom in their countries, eager to profit from all the opportunities for success that lie before them. These places recall those that provide the backdrop for the successful Nigerian movie, *A Wedding Party*. Fifteen million spectators across the world watched this comedy about two rich Ibo and Yoruba families aiming to marry their children and who, as a result, spend their time in all the chicest places in Lagos: the malls, hotels, and restaurants where international standards hold sway. In this film, as in the novel and the series, the emphasis is on the symbols of success: the car (SUV, preferably Japanese or German), air conditioning, the generator whose size provides clues to the family's wealth (Rateau and Choplin 2021), the business class flights to Europe or the USA and, of course, the villa. As the journalist Jean-Philippe Rémy says about Lagos: "A man's success is judged by a social algorithm that combines the size of his car with that of his generator (and sometimes too the tallness of his wife's hats)."[4]

These novels and television series reflect many of the same cultural experiences as the research on the middle and upper classes in Africa (Adeniyi-Ogunyankin 2019). In both the research and in new cultural production in West Africa, the concrete villa has become an architectural signal used to display a new way of life and a certain vision of the continent – one of Afropolitanism, whose values are interwoven with those of Africapitalism: entrepreneurship; philanthropic business; a property boom fueled by borrowing; and a consumerist and hedonistic urban society a long way from the frugal modesty of village life. The Afropolitan elites and the diaspora say that they want to help make the city more beautiful. However, in the quest to break with certain stereotypes – particularly the Africa of armed conflicts, terrorist threats, famine, slums, and poverty – other clichés have emerged to create a picture of a binary Africa: stereotypical images of young women and men who seem to be imitating Western standards. These superficial characters appear as only interested in money, sex, and freeloading in a city that has become a film set, one increasingly attractive to foreign investment but less and less livable for the large majority of the population who manage with little money.

Concrete Fetishes and Voodoo

Genius Loci – the spirit of the place. In West Africa, the links between homes, rituals, and religious practice are strong (Griaule 1954; Cassiman 2011; Gra 2019). This is especially true along the Gulf of Guinea, where the voodoo religion has a strong influence on the Fon and Yoruba communities. For many in the region, regardless of religion, places are inhabited by genies, spirits, and the souls of former slaves who have returned to wander their former land. Respect must be given and offerings made to all these spirits (Brivio 2012). Houses are places that are full of these forces: they are believed to shelter the spirits of the ancestors and ghosts charged with protecting the family.

In the Fon language, the word for house is *xwé*. It refers to the physical building but also, more symbolically, to the place of protection, confidence, and safety that shelters the family. When building a house, it is customary for followers of a blend Christian, voodoo, and pagan rituals to bury the spirit of the house – the *xwéli* – on the threshold in the belief that it will protect the household and give it the power to grow in numbers and in space. When the house is consecrated, regular prayers are said to nourish its spirit and to "push back the palisade" – in other words, to make the house grow. The enlargement of the *xwécé* – often translated into French as "*mon chez*" and roughly equivalent in English to "my place" – is a sign of a healthy family and finances, of fulfillment, and of good company.

The spirit of the house (*xwéli*) is not just a piece of light-hearted superstition. Building a house entails different rites of consecration: burying the spirits, raising altars, and sprinkling with blood – generally the blood of a chicken or a cock (Bertin 2021). Building your own house is a deeply personal act, as is the spirit of the house that inhabits and is believed to protect it. It is in this same house that its owner will be buried. His tomb will be placed in the middle of the house, close to the spirit that watches over the household (Noret 2010).[5] And once there is enough money, the tomb is covered in concrete and, if possible, with tiles (Brivio 2012). This means that the house ceases to be a simple object or common place. While as a piece of property it has a market value, it also has a sacred, symbolic value. In this respect, all houses are unique, differing from each other through the presence of the spirits of the house and of the ancestors who inhabit it. How then can a house be transferred or sold on the property market, when the spirit of the family and the bodies of one's forebears are buried there in perpetuity? Spirits can be exhumed, by means of certain complex rituals, but house owners prefer to avoid this in case the awakening of the spirits goes wrong.

Bertrand, who has just finished his house, explains: "Your spirit is there, you can't just rent it to anyone." Even the term used to refer to the owner, *xwéto* – literally the owner of the house – says a great deal about the powerful ties that bind a man or, less commonly, a woman to the house that (s)he has built. The situation is different for houses built to rent, which are not believed to become home to anyone's voodoo or to the spirits of the ancestors. In contrast with the village, where there are many rituals and altars (Gra 2019), the presence of fetishes and ancestors in the home is less common in cities.

Moreover, concrete offers a form of spiritual protection that renders this practice less necessary. To be surrounded by concrete walls is already, in a way, to be sheltered. In this respect, concrete is compatible with spiritual belief. In the house of the voodoo chief of the lake village of Ganvié, I saw a drawing of a concrete house on the wall. "That is the house of my dreams," the chief explained, spilling a few drops of *sodabi* (palm liquor) on the cement floor, "to honor the ancestors" buried beneath. In this drawing, the concrete house is surrounded by grass and a grazing horse – a marked contrast to the house on stilts in which he lives.

A growing number of voodoo fetishes are covered with concrete (Tassi 2019). Cementing a voodoo is first a way to protect it, especially against heavy rains (Figure 3.13). It is also a way to honor it with the importance it deserves. Using imported – and therefore expensive – materials like cement or tiles is a mark of respect. Conversely, keeping a fetish in a temple made of local materials signals a loss of power and reputation (Sinou and Agbo 1995, p. 131). However, some local people are said to condemn the practice of cementing fetishes because it prevents them growing. It is believed that a fetish is nourished by means of ceremonies and offerings, and therefore needs to fatten in order to stay alive. "People no longer come to consult this *legba*

FIGURE 3.13 Cemented voodoo, Porto-Novo, 2018. Source: A. Choplin.

(protective fetish) because there is too much cement. The legba no longer absorbs. There is no more flow and no more spirit" (interview with Gérard, Porto-Novo, 2017). According to this view, a concrete fetish is a dead fetish.

Conclusion

In this third chapter, I have offered an exploration of West African construction sites and the cultural aspirations and modes of dwelling in concrete homes. I approached these complex practices by reporting conversations with landlords and tenants on their day-to-day lives in a West African city, and by giving a voice to city dwellers to express their dreams, uncertainties, desires, and fears around their concrete urban futures. The stories I collected during my field research revolve around the building plot, the house, the concrete block. The house, the way it is built, its foundations, as well as its finishing touches together tell the story of the person who built it. The concrete block itself is therefore an object that bears witness to someone's life. It stores intimate memories and relations.

Drawing on critical socio-anthropological, postcolonial, and Science and Technology studies, I have revealed how the generalization of concrete has transformed urban lives in West Africa. Concrete is an excellent prism for reading the construction of cities and the social relations being redefined in them. It is a central social object through which to analyze gender relations (as a symbol of virility), patriarchy (by reinforcing the place of men in society), relations between generations (as an object of negotiation), and religions (as a link between material and immaterial forces). I examined these social relations and their links to urban materiality and the role of women in the construction sector. Through this analysis, I have shown that women are mostly invisible but not entirely excluded from it. My initial findings call for further research on the links between urban materiality and gender. It also calls for in-depth research on construction sites as a place to read the relationships of domination, the hidden dynamics of human exploitation and domination.

This section therefore complements the previous two chapters which, in contrast, focused on the top-down forces driving the concrete business (cement capitalists, development projects). On the one hand, city dwellers reproduce economic processes of capitalism from the bottom up – individuals claim the Concrete City, where the symbolic apparel of success and domination is expressed through material construction and land ownership. The Afropolitan diaspora and elite define capitalist urban imaginaries in which concrete cities are places of material ostentation and consumption. On the other hand, my analyses further an understanding of the importance of local cultural values, forces from below which are also driving the increasing demand for this material. Marxian analyses of the Concrete City reveal important aspects of the contemporary urban experience, but they cannot explain everything. The Concrete City cannot be reduced to an avatar of capitalism. Scholarship in critical urban studies has shown that housing is an eminently social and political act. Many homeowners understand building with concrete as a way of claiming rights, asserting a social position, or achieving upward social mobility. Concrete is reassuring – it legitimizes land occupation for individuals who do not have property titles, and it allows them to hoard money when they cannot afford to open bank accounts. As a means of incremental construction, it is adaptable to the builder's financial resources. For the poor and vulnerable, in an informal land market where the risk of eviction is high, building in concrete promises to put an end to precarity; it offers protection and security in a word of uncertainty. From this perspective, popular demand for cement and concrete blocks are political actions and claims to citizenship in the postcolonial city.

This chapter has demonstrated that, although inert, concrete plays a major role as a binding agent between the urban and the rural world, between men and women, between young and old, between the visible and invisible spheres. This nonhuman, non-living object is central to the lives of millions of African city dwellers. The objects derived from cement and transformed into concrete – powder, bags, bricks, walls – are at the heart of a "world of relationships" (Söderström 2014), for both the most intimate, local relations and the most global connections. It shows that the built environment is essential to social life, values, and hierarchies specific to the coastal communities of the Gulf of Guinea. Concrete is now part of West African cultural identity and is appearing as a singular horizon of African cities and societies. Yet this consensus also seems to be crumbling. Many have turned against concrete, and new critiques of this ubiquitous material have emerged. In the following section, I will consider how the Concrete City – the icon of modernity and economic development – has also become the symbol of an ecologically uninhabitable world.

Notes

1   There are three categories of cement: CPJ 35, which corresponds to CEM II 32.5, which is not very strong, 42.5R (3X) (CEM II-AL) which is for everyday use, while 52.5R (CEM I) is restricted to big structures (slabs, bridges).

2   See Ethel Seiwaa Boateng, 2020, Women at work: engaging young women in construction in Ghana. *Align.* https://www.alignplatform.org/resources/women-work-engaging-young-women-construction-ghana.

3   See Mark Tutton, 2012, Young, urban and culturally savvy, meet the Afropolitans, *CNN* https://edition.cnn.com/2012/02/17/world/africa/who-are-afropolitans/index.html.

4   See Jean-Philippe Rémy, 2019, Lagos, le laboratoire de l'impossible, *Le Monde.* https://www.lemonde.fr/afrique/article/2015/03/27/lagos-le-laboratoire-de-l-impossible-conquerante_4602863_3212.html.

5   The idea of being buried in a municipal cemetery is relatively recent and associated with urbanization. Normally every Beninese is expected to have their own "home" within the country, and to be buried there. Abomey is thus a city full of funeral rites where the great families come to be buried (Noret 2010).

CHAPTER 4

Uninhabitable Concrete

The Uninhabitable

The uninhabitable: the architecture of contempt or display, the vainglorious mediocrity of tower blocks, thousands of rabbit hutches piled one above the other, the cutprice ostentation of company headquarters

The uninhabitable: shanty towns, townships

The hostile, the gray, the anonymous, the ugly, the corridors of the Metro, public baths, hangars, car parks, marshalling yards, ticket windows, hotel bedrooms

Georges Perec, Species of Space (1997: 89–90)

Among the list of spaces that Georges Perec labels as "Uninhabitable," we could add the Concrete City. Concrete cities epitomize many of the contradictions of our ultra-capitalist world and self-destructive society: on the one hand, they are created to shelter and protect human beings; but on the other hand, they are created from an extractive, polluting, energy-intensive industry which is destroying the planet. The existence of the Concrete City raises the question of its habitability, particularly in humid tropical areas like parts of Africa. As Danny Hoffman (2017) illustrates of Monrovia, the concrete architecture inherited from the modernist movement is "uninhabitable." More broadly, the proliferation of these concrete cities puts into question the notion of the habitability of the planet, which is at the heart of many ongoing debates on the Anthropocene (Latour 2021; Mbembe 2020).

Since the 1950s, development institutions, construction companies, and ordinary urbanites have all expressed enthusiasm for concrete. The Concrete City itself has come to symbolize promises of progress, modernity, and capitalist prosperity. But recently, it has also sparked many criticisms. In this final chapter, I shed light on these criticisms concerning the social

Concrete City: Material Flows and Urbanization in West Africa, First Edition. Armelle Choplin.
© 2023 John Wiley & Sons Ltd. Published 2023 by John Wiley & Sons Ltd.

and environmental effects of increasingly concrete landscapes. At a time of global climate change and rising ecological awareness, concrete contributes to urban heat islands, soil impermeability, and an ever-greater demand for air conditioning. It also requires limestone extraction, immense amounts of the diminishing resources of gravel and sand (UNEP 2019, 2022), the release of harmful particle pollution into the air, and the proliferation of rubble and ruins.

In a popular video online, one resident of the village of Ewekoro in Nigeria named Mrs. Babalola complained that, in her area, "We eat cement, we drink cement."[1] The video was part of the "Responsible Business Initiative" campaign on which the Swiss people voted in autumn 2020. It accused the Franco-Swiss multinational LafargeHolcim of endangering the health of the village where its cement plant is located with the harmful particles emitted (Figure 4.1). The aim of this ultimately unsuccessful grassroots initiative was to force big Swiss firms and their subsidiaries to respect human rights and the environment. In October 2020, Greenpeace published a report that held LafargeHolcim responsible for more than 120 cases of environmental pollution and human rights violations in 34 different countries.[2] At the same time,

FIGURE 4.1   LafargeHolcim, Ewekoro, Nigeria, 2017. Source: A. Choplin.

during the autumn of 2020, in Vaud Canton in Switzerland, environmental activists set up on Mormont Hill exploited by Holcim. The first Swiss ZAD (*Zone à Défendre*, a French expression referring to an area occupied by activists who intend to blockade a project) was created to denounce the extension of the quarry. In March of 2021, police evicted the ZAD. And in June of 2021, 400 Extinction Rebellion activists invaded concrete stations in the Greater Paris area to block the construction of several new transport infrastructure across the region. These recurrent actions and criticisms mark a turning point in the enthusiasm surrounding concrete. It has now become clear that concrete is under attack because the energy-intensive cement industry is one of the most polluting of the world, responsible for 8% of global annual gas emissions (IPCC 2022).

In this last chapter, I explore the tremendous environmental impact of concrete. I bring together literatures often separated in the analysis of contemporary urbanism. I mobilize works of engineering sciences that raise technical questions about this material (Habert et al. 2020): Can cement be replaced and with what material? Can and should we instead build with earth, wood, or straw? Is it possible to produce green cement? And how might the construction sector be transformed? I address these questions from a West African perspective, which I combine with the critical perspective of the social sciences by drawing on recent work in the field of urban political ecology (UPE). UPE helps elucidate how social, political, economic, and ecological processes are reshaping urban landscapes in a context of capitalism (Swyngedouw and Heynen 2003; Keil 2005). Cities are thus considered as "urban metabolisms" (Barles 2010; Gandy 2014) in constant interaction with their environment, animated by flows of materials shaped by social and political trade-offs (Heynen et al. 2006). Different processes underly the production of the Concrete City and its life cycle, namely extraction, excavation, construction, destruction, recycling, and landfilling. It is now well known that concrete is ecologically unsustainable and does not age well: the lifespan of steel-reinforced concrete is only 50–70 years (Forty 2012; Fry 2013).

But, beyond these gray horizons, the ecological transition is a source for new green expectations. This last chapter is also an invitation to discover the collectives and individual initiatives launched by architects, engineers, NGOs, academics, and ecological activists as they open up new paths by building differently with diverse materials, and as they envisage other ways for humans and nonhumans to coexist. In doing so, they are devising more ecological alternatives to this increasingly concrete world, and they are imagining the possibility of a post-Concrete City and the re-creation of a habitable planet.

(De)Construction and Destruction

Collapse, Rubble, and Ruins

On March 22, 2021, the façade of a building at Riviera Bonoumin in Abidjan collapsed, killing 13 people, including 7 children. It was the second building collapse in 10 days. The following day, the Ivorian government published a press release condemning "acts of civil irresponsibility in the domain of real estate construction."[3] A year later, Abidjan is still mourning its dead due to repeated building collapses: seven dead in February 2022, six in March 2022. A few months earlier, a Ghanaian academic criticized the spate of building collapses in Accra (Boateng 2021). In Lagos, 112 cases were recorded between 1978 and 2008 (Windapo and Rotimi 2012). In 2021, the destruction of the Ikoyi tower in Lagos killed 40. In Ibadan, building collapses are – along with electrocutions, explosions, and fires – among the 10 leading causes of accidental death (Adelekan 2020). Building collapses are recurrent across the continent, where it causes several hundred deaths each year (Smith 2020; Smith and Woodcraft 2020; Boateng 2021). Structures are built quickly, by underqualified builders, often with poor quality materials, without respecting proportions and international norms, and without building permits. For Constance Smith (2020: 18), who conducted a study on building collapses in Kenya, these collapses are dramatic symbols of the interweaving of "fake architecture" and opaque economies in the context of Nairobi's booming but "murky construction industry" and "semi-licit property speculation." They also remind us that behind the apparent simplicity of concrete, technique and technology remain paramount. Concrete is the result of a clever combination of water, sand, rubble, and cement, and the quality of the structure depends on this dosage – something that many in West Africa often overlook.

These tragic events in African cities – like those that have recently occurred in Europe – are indicators of the potential obsolescence of concrete. The collapse of Genoa's Morandi Bridge in 2018, which killed 43 people, revealed to the world that although concrete had long been promoted as solid and eternal, it is actually quite fragile. After this use-by date, buildings and infrastructures require large-scale maintenance operations. Every time a tower, bridge, or balcony collapse in Europe (e.g., in Angers [France] in 2016 killing 4 young people and injuring 14 others), the cause is always the same: a lack of maintenance which accelerated cracks in concrete foundations and consequently infiltration and waterproofing problems. As a result, water then begins to degrade the reinforcing steel and pieces of concrete come loose. In France, buildings are only insured for 10 years after their construction and are not technically checked after this period. This dramatic situation in

Europe, as in the United States of America, is provoking a new set of questions about concrete. In Europe, the central concerns are about repairing, restoring, and conserving concrete. But is this possible in Africa where concrete is the material of the poor? In a context where financial resources are limited, who will pay for the repairs to the buildings when, in a few decades, the region's concrete has reached the end of its life? And further, existing evidence suggests that the life of cement will be shorter across the continent due to the poor cement dosages and low-quality materials widely used in the mixing of concrete. These financial constraints therefore suggest that the Concrete City in West Africa is likely to live and to die.

The question of the physical deterioration and the possible collapse of the Concrete City raises the question of rubble and ruins. In his inspiring work on modernist concrete buildings in Monrovia, Danny Hoffman explains that our "goal is to learn to inhabit ruins" (Hoffman 2017: 4), especially the modern city ruins. Writing about the end of the world and the possibilities of living in the ruins of capitalism, Anna Tsing explains that "in order to know the world that progress has left us, we need to track the shifting patches that are now part of landscapes in ruin" (Tsing 2015: 303). The relics of concrete could be among these patches that can be found more or less everywhere in the world. For example, there are hundreds of concrete latrines across Accra, Cotonou and Lagos which now go unused because they are unsuited to local needs. It is pointless to look for the person who holds the key to the toilets and who now maintains sole control of access to them. Some barely legible writing tells you that these toilets were donated by small French towns under former decentralized cooperation agreements, or by long vanished NGOs. I wonder what may grow on these patches, in the midst of this concrete where heat and smells persist.

What happens to this concrete once its social life is over? The end-of-life of objects is an essential question because, as Jean Baudrillard (1970) asserts, "consumer society needs its objects in order to exist, and more specifically it needs to destroy them." This looming obsolescence of concrete lends urgency to the question of the future of its rubble. In turn, rubble is directly linked with the question of urban metabolism, the measurement of inward and outward flows, and the insistence on the importance of recycling (Barles 2010). Indeed, there is a need for further reflection on the "circulation of flows of materials, energy and waste," and in particular on the end-of-life of materials such as concrete and its rubble (Garcier et al. 2017). More generally, these ideas derive from research in UPE that looks at the social relations of power to extract and distribute resources and materials such as water (Swyngedouw 2004; Kaika 2005), waste (Njeru 2006; Pellow 2007) or energy (Verdeil 2014). Surprisingly, the raw materials of the city, such as limestone, clay or gravel, have attracted little scholarly attention but this is emerging as a topic of in-depth research (Mongeard 2017; Augiseau and Kim 2021). In the Global South, there is a growing scholarly research in the field of UPE (Lawhon et al. 2014) that includes interesting work on construction materials in Zanzibar (Myers 1999) and on sand in Accra (Dawson 2021). However, the question of construction materials flows and their waste is rarely addressed. Laëtitia Mongeard (2017) notes that, given the growing quantities of waste in circulation, demolition has become a specific construction sector activity because it demands an extensive process of sorting, crushing, and disposal. However, concrete rubble recycling varies greatly from one country to another: in Brazil, less than 1% of rubble is processed, as compared with 10% in China and 90% in Japan and Europe (Jappe 2020). In Europe, rubble is reused as ballast material for roadbeds. In Switzerland, the construction firms make their money not only by extracting limestone, gravel, and sand, but also by filling in the resulting holes with materials from excavation and demolition sites[4]. The recycling and storage of construction waste appear to be a new and lucrative market. Across West Africa, construction waste is not processed locally and is therefore difficult to recycle. Numerous obstacles still remain to the establishment of a rubble recycling sector. But at the same time, the reuse chain is already very active and well organized, especially for steel and plastic: the investigations I carried out in Benin showed that these materials are collected in Cotonou by Indian and Chinese companies and sent to Asia by boat. Reuse channels are a full part of the material flows and the functioning of the city.

Research on urban metabolism and the circular economy analyses the entire construction cycle and raises the possibility of employing a commodity chain approach (Mongeard 2017). As a result, researchers but also private companies now approach the construction and deconstruction of a building as a single process. They use tools such as Life Cycle Analysis (LCA) to measure a building's carbon footprint by quantifying the greenhouse gas emissions during all the phases of its "life": production of the raw materials, construction, operating life, and disassembly (Tirado et al. 2022). In France, reports by building firms like Vinci record that construction accounts for 60% of greenhouse gas emissions, of which 56% comes from the production of the materials, and operational life accounts for 40%. In Switzerland, in the canton of Geneva, a new law voted in 2022 requires companies to calculate the carbon footprint of a building before its construction. The initial choice of materials is therefore fundamental and has become a recurrent debate, particularly following a series of heatwaves in Europe. Dark colored materials – coatings like tar, asphalt, and gray concrete – absorb solar rays and therefore exacerbate atmospheric heating. They maintain and accentuate the action of cities as heat islands and are a contributory factor in exposing city dwellers to dangerously extreme temperatures, which are increasingly frequent across Africa, especially in West Africa (Rohat et al. 2019; Gough et al. 2019). Moreover, in that same tropical environment, the use of concrete accentuates the risks of flooding. Too often attributed to climate change, such floods are in fact a consequence of urbanization and the laying of impermeable concrete surfaces, which prevent natural water flows and drainage. In Dakar, the problem has been clearly demonstrated in the district of Pikine, where individuals have built on former wetlands (*Niayes*) (Leclercq 2022), but where concrete remains resistant to water.

The spread of concrete is also linked with air-conditioning, and vice versa. Indeed, it is difficult to live in buildings that have been designed not for natural air flows and ventilation, but for artificial cooling. A symbol of wealth and success, a factor of social distinction in the same way as concrete and generators, air conditioning has become widespread in the tropics (Sahakian 2014). In Nigeria, it is common to stay in hotels where you can adjust the temperature of the air conditioning but cannot open the windows. It is a vicious circle, and the ecological cost is considerable: the warmer it gets, the more we use air conditioning to stay cool, and the more this contributes to global warming.[5] The Concrete City raises the fundamental issues of thermal comfort. We have seen that the Concrete City is multifaceted and that only certain parts of it – such as the Premium and the Affordable City – are air-conditioned and can offer this thermal comfort. The Concrete City requires the use of air-conditioning, which is energy-intensive and increases the carbon footprint. "Cooling" makes our concrete cities habitable while at the same time making the planet uninhabitable. The circle is vicious. The Concrete City is thus the source of new thermal inequalities, and, in a context of climate emergency, it is at the heart of the debate on climate justice.

Sustainability and Greenwashing

In response to the growing objections, cement manufacturers have begun to publicize their own efforts to protect the environment. Referring to the UN Sustainable Development Goals (SDG), they all claim compliance with international standards and commitment to environmental protection. Their websites – showcases of greenwashing that all tout their green credentials in their color codes – highlight the firms contributions to sustainable development. While the companies flaunt their green programs, it remains difficult to find figures about the environmental impacts and damage caused by the cement industry, or even to find maps showing the location of the big limestone and sand extraction sites.

In India, in June of 2019, several big cement firms partnered with the World Business Council for Sustainable Development (WBCSD) and launched the Indian Cement Sector Sustainable Development Goals. UNIDO (United Nations Industrial Development Organization) supported this program which aimed to outline how the Indian cement industry could contribute to sustainability. For its part, Dangote claims to be trying to minimize the environmental impact of its activities (Dangote Cement Plc *Annual Report Document* 2021: 34). Other concrete companies have published "sustainability reports" and publicize their different "sustainable projects" through foundations. The LafargeHolcim foundation is particularly active in this respect, running a big conference on sustainable materials every three years. At the last meeting in Cairo in 2019, almost 350 experts, academics, engineers, and architects – among them the British architect Norman Foster and the Burkinabe Francis Kéré (Pritzker Prize 2022) – met to talk about concrete and how to limit its impact on natural resources.[6] The foundation also awards $2 million prizes, the LafargeHolcim Awards, for the most innovative architectural structures in terms of sustainability. It also funds the chair in sustainable construction at Swiss Federal Institute of Technology in Zürich (ETH), which pursues fundamental research on sustainable materials and new environment-friendly concretes. Other companies are researching alternatives to the use of fossil fuels which, in cement production, are responsible for significant greenhouse gas emissions. Bringing coal from Russia or South Africa by boat to fuel West African power plants is equally unsustainable. In Europe, some plants are working on the use of oils, chemical solvents, animal flours, or industrial by-products like blast furnace slag to fuel the kilns. In Senegal, Sococim Industries is experimenting with jatropha plant as a biofuel to replace coal. Others are looking at using waste as fuel, but in the absence of waste sorting, this option is for the moment little used, in particular in Africa, where fuel diversification is a major issue for the future.

In parallel, the cement manufacturers claim to be making major efforts on particle emissions in the attempt to meet international standards. The CEOs of these companies I interviewed during my field research said that they had installed air filters in order to meet air pollution standards and protect local people, as is required for environmental compliance certificates and by Health Safety Environment (HSE) services. In one interview, the director of the Lafarge Onigbolo plant reported no problems with nearby residents and, in contrast, argued that his plant contributes to the development of the region and to the financing of infrastructures (schools, hospital, water tower, electrification). The press, however, tells a very different story.[7] The populations living around Onigbolo report daily problems with air pollution, in particular when the electric filters fail, and a thin white coating is said to cover the entire area. Existing environmental research and regulations elsewhere in the world have long recognized that the production of cement releases other pollutants into the air (e.g., nitrogen oxides, sulfur dioxide, hydrogen chloride, hydrogen fluoride, and dust). In addition, local populations complain about the pollution caused by the diesel generators used to offset load shedding on the power grid. They find it hard to breathe properly with the dust and vapor they are forced to inhale. Beninese government has recorded similar complaints in Cotonou city center, in Placodji, next to the SCB Bouclier plant (Figure 4.2). Until recently, the Ministry of Labour was located in an old colonial building very close to the cement works. The employees went on strike in protest against the dust emanating from the plant. Today, the ministry staff have left, abandoning this neighborhood to the poor who have now contracted respiratory disorders. SCB Bouclier claims to have responded to these criticisms by installing 18 fabric filters and a misting system to contain the dust, reduce particle emissions, and purify the air. However, one only has to walk in the neighborhood to see that it is entirely covered in a fine layer of cement powder. The same is true in Nigeria, as is revealed in the "Responsible Business Initiative" video which accuses LafargeHolcim of smothering the village of Ewekero in dust and causing health problems for many local people (lesions on the liver, lungs, and spleen). But the side effects of cement

FIGURE 4.2   SCB Bouclier Factory, Placodji: a cement plant in the downtown of Cotonou, 2018. Source: M. Lozivit.

are not always well known. A REACH guide study produced in the 1980s by the World Bank demonstrated the carcinogenic effects of cement. However, the study received little publicity. Some scholars in West Africa say that the cement lobbies tried to stop its dissemination.

Sand: Rarer than you Think

This title is borrowed from Pascal Peduzzi (2014), director of the Global Resource Information Database (GRID), which is part of the United Nations Environment Programme (UNEP). In a co-authored report, Peduzzi describes sand and gravel as the "unrecognised foundational material of our economies" and the second most-exploited natural resources in the world after water (UNEP 2019). In the last report published in 2022, Peduzzi's team starts by warning: "You cannot withdraw 50 billion tons of sand out of the environment without generating an impact on the environment and society (…). Today, we use a bit more than 17 kilograms of sand per day for everybody on planet Earth. We are totally dependent on this material, yet it is really a non-recognized hero for development" (UNEP 2022). The report brings 10 strategic recommendations to the attention of governments and many other stakeholders from industry, civil society, and users of sand in or-der to avoid the sand crisis. Similarly, the industry's demand for water poses problems for water access in cities with arid, desert climates and in cities with limited hydraulic infrastructures. The use of sand has tripled over the last two decades, reaching between 40 and 50 billion metric tons a year. The report contains a warning: this resource is becoming so scarce that it is expected to run out in the next 30 years. This situation has led to a sharp rise in the interest in and the development of "sand mafias." In India, these sand mafias control access to the quarries and to the resale market (Mahadevan 2019). This strong demand for sand is linked to urbanization. Peduzzi explains that "because of the frenzied development of new dams, roads, buildings, and factories, China has used more sand in the last four years than the US has in the last century" (UNEP 2022). He also notes that wind-formed desert sand is too smooth for construction. So, despite being in the heart of the desert, Dubai's artificial islands were built with sand imported from Australia. Similarly, Singapore imported sand from Malaysia, Indonesia, Vietnam, and Cambodia.[8]

In Africa, the sand business is crucial because large quantities of sand are required to make concrete blocks. The mass use of sand raises questions about the future of the fragile coastal and lagoon zone of the Gulf of Guinea. As the names imply: Lagos, city of the lake, of the lagoon; Togo (from *To* – water – and *Go* – edge), water's edge; Cotonou, backwater of death. In response to coastal erosion, the different countries have legislated to ban the uncontrolled extraction of marine sand, which is also highly corrosive because of its high salt content. However, while the direct extraction of sand on the coast has stopped, people now dig a few hundred meters back, in the lagoon area. This has caused major disruption to the lagoon ecosystem and the destruction of fish life, a problem highlighted in a number of papers, videos, and blogs. For example, the project "Shifting Sand–Lagos communities count the cost of dredging" has highlighted the consequences of sand exploitation on the Lagos coastline – some quarries are abandoned once their resources are exhausted, leaving a pitted and damaged landscape, and sand extraction now competes with less profitable agricultural activities (Mendelsohn 2018).[9] In the case of Greater Accra, Katherine Dawson (2021: 11) has shown that agricultural activities are challenged by sand: "sand destined to become the city is extracted from land which is increasingly commodified." Around Lomé, fields of maize and manioc and oil palm plantations have gradually given way to sand extraction (Konlani 2015). And even though it is officially forbidden to extract sand within 20 meters of any building, underground extraction below these buildings continues. As a result, some houses collapse from erosion during the rainy season. While extraction is often small-scale, it is also done by large companies with state licenses. So far, no study has been done on the short- and long-term impacts of these extraction processes.

The populations living near sand extraction zones often file formal complaints against extraction companies. In Togbin, in the suburbs of Cotonou, flooding has become worse during the rainy season. The sole main road is often submerged for several weeks, and the flow of trucks disrupts traffic circulation, making certain tracks unusable. Residents in this area are demanding compensation for these issues and blame the sand extractors who, for their part, deny any link between the extractive industry and the problems raised. Indeed, the CEO of Minex-Bénin claims to be a social benefactor: "We have built box culverts, laid cobbles, built schools, funding 30 or even 40% of the costs."[10] And the firm DG/ABE similarly argues that "sand dredging not only benefits developers but also local populations and the state, which is able to pursue construction projects." The firm goes on to say that dredging is even "responsible for drying out the environment in certain areas." The inhabitants have the impression that the sand lobby can do whatever they want, while denouncing the sand mafia, which is often only an informal activity allowing the poorest to subsist. Complaints have also been filed in Lagos, near the Eko Atlantic City project. Whereas the developers are happy that the floods have diminished in this part of the city, the inhabitants of the adjacent neighborhoods argue that the sea wall is deflecting powerful waves toward them (Mendelsohn 2018).

In West Africa as well as in Europe, more and more complaints are addressed to the concrete industry. The world is discovering and beginning to be concerned about concrete's environmental impact. In Africa, it is particularly visible: rubble is already part of the everyday urban landscape. Whereas the Concrete City grows continuously outwards and upwards, it is at the same time falling into ruin under the combined effects of lack of maintenance, collapses, land speculation, and evictions. Yet there are also emerging initiatives that seek to show that it is possible – and necessary – to build and live otherwise.

Green Expectations: Alternatives to Concrete?

In 2017, Madiana Hazoume, a Beninese civil engineer and advocate of raw earth construction, advanced a new proposal for the continent's future: "Let's say goodbye to the all-concrete culture in Africa."[11] Aware of the environmental impact of the construction sector, citizens across Europe and Africa like Madiana Hazoume are developing a new critique of concrete and, in response, are articulating new claims for more inclusive and less polluted cities. These movements are reminiscent of the work of the Egyptian Hassan Faty (1973), who demonstrated that it is possible to build for the poor by reintroducing traditional Nubian architecture into the city of New Gourna. Yet across much of the continent these kinds of ancient practices and materials have been replaced by concrete. Several residents in West Africa with whom I spoke recognized that it would be better to build a home like they do in the villages: houses made of earth, straw, or banco (fermented mud) which stay cool when the sun is at its hottest. Many in the region recognize that building with timber and mud rather than with concrete, which requires ventilation and/or air conditioning in hot environments, would be more sensible. There is, however, a renewed interest in these alternative materials: in March 2022, the Burkinabe architect Francis Kéré, one of the promoters of vernacular architecture and wood and earth materials, was awarded the Pritzker Architecture Prize (the highest distinction in architecture). The idea of a transition to more sustainable building materials with a lower carbon footprint is therefore becoming a central part of the profession. Many are now putting into question well-established building practices. Initiatives have been launched here and there, by policy makers, by individuals, and collectives in both professional and academic worlds, but also in the private sector. Cement manufacturers are looking for new ways to transform one of the most polluting industries into a sustainable and green one. Both interesting and original, these initiatives provide a glimpse into a possible world. While technical innovations are often thought to primarily emanate from industrialized countries, architects and builders across Africa are themselves innovating modernized forms of traditional architectural practices.

Heritage and Vernacular Architecture

François is all smiles as he waits for me at the entrance to his plot. I have come to visit him and see his new house on the outskirts of Cotonou. He told me how happy he was to see his sacrifices bear fruit in the form of a home. But he also confessed to one of his homes central flaw's: "the problem is that it is too hot inside. At night, I get up to sleep outside because its too much for me. But outside, there are the mosquitoes" (interview, Abomey-Calavi, 2016). François has built an uninhabitable house. His story is common. Many people across West Africa report that they often sleep badly because of the intolerable heat accentuated by concrete. This is definately not a material adapted to the tropical climate. A villa I rented in a wealthy neighborhood in the economic capital of Benin offered a similar climatic experience: it was a furnace. The architect (if there was one) seemed to forget to allow for airflow between the rooms. A villa for which the architect had the clever idea to isolate the roof with a slab of black tar, a material which readily absorbs the sun's rays – zero thermal inertia.

So, looking at François dwelling-as-furnace, I think back to the coolness of the bamboo houses in the floating village of Ganvié and to the houses of Tata Somba, earthen boxes in North Benin now listed as a UNESCO World Heritage site. I recall the stone houses of Chinguetti and Wadan, caravanserai nestling in the heart of the Mauritian Sahara, where I once stopped to enjoy a little coolness; the pyramids of Meroe in Sudan where I had been fortunate enough to spend a night, and where I had even felt a little cold; the Dogon villages clinging to the Bandiagara escarpment in Mali; the mud and grass "dome-houses" of the Musgum people of North Cameroon, sketched so magnificently by the geographer and anthropologist Christian Seignobos (2018). It must be comfortable there, as in the Afro-Brazilian houses of Porto-Novo, Ibadan, Aného, Lagos, and Lomé (Figure 4.3). And as in the colonial forts of Ouidah and El Mina, where European slave traders used to live, protected from the heat.

The centers of the port cities of the Gulf of Guinea are bursting with these remarkable and airy buildings, a reminder of the constant exchanges between Latin America, Africa, and Europe. One such place is the Afro-Brazilian neighborhood in Ouidah nicknamed "Brazil," described by Alain Sinou (Sinou and Agbo 1995: 110):

> "The walls of the main habitations are made of bricks fired using a kiln built for this purpose to bake the clay. In order to bind the bricks, they make a cement using a very old technique little used on this coast, which consists in crushing and then baking shells collected by the sea.

FIGURE 4.3   Afro-Brazilian houses, Ibadan 2018. Source: A. Choplin.

(…) Some roofs are covered with tiles imported from Brazil. The Afro-Brazilians are inspired by the fazendas, the dwellings of their former masters (…). In order to build their businesses, they are quite happy to send their employees to train in Brazil, to make up for the shortage of labour (…). This community maintains numerous connections with America."

The legacy to be preserved is immense. For the city of Porto-Novo alone, the School of African Heritage has identified 597 buildings in need of preservation (Mengin and Godonou 2013). However, as in many other neighboring localities, and despite the establishment of a plan for historic preservation, the municipality, and the local populations have little interest and few resources to devote to the protection of these sites (Coralli and Houénoudé 2013). Alain Sinou and Bachir Oloudé note that "Brazilian inspired houses have no more value for a Porto-Novian than a building made of earth or of concrete" (Sinou and Oloudé 1988: 159). The anthropologist Saskia Cousin (2013: 447) concurs, explaining that these colonial buildings are perceived as "old stuff" or, as one could also put it, "old colonial stuff." Only new buildings made of cement carry social prestige. This explains why many buildings are in an advanced state of dilapidation, often following family disputes but also in the absence of builders possessing the expertise in Afro-Brazilian architecture needed to restore them. The loss of skills is a major issue. In Porto-Novo, Gérard Bassalé, a historian at the head of a cultural association that seeks to publicize local heritage, explains: "You can't find workers locally, we had to bring architects and builders from Brazil to renovate certain Afro-Brazilian houses."

In Porto-Novo or in Ibadan, this question of heritage, of vanishing skills, and of the use of local techniques and materials raises broader questions about "vernacular" architecture. The term has come back into common use through certain manuals, texts and, manifestoes – in particular through the *Atlas of Vernacular Architecture of the World* (Vellinga et al. 2007), which features the African continent on the flyleaf. In the preface to *Learning from Vernacular*, the architect and stage designer Patrick Bouchain (2010) recalls that "the term 'vernacular' comes from the Latin *vernaculus,* which means "indigenous, domestic," from *verna*, referring to "a slave born in the house"." For Bouchain (*ibid.*: 4), "the first thing that recognizing vernacular cultures would do is therefore to restore peoples reduced to slavery to their place in the shared house of the history of human beings." This is a definition that speaks particularly powerfully to West Africa, which was bled of millions of individuals who were first enslaved and then transported to the Americas. These vernacular architectures are a reminder of thousands of years of good sense which remain marginalized.

Back to Earth, Back to the Local

Throughout West Africa, a growing number of initiatives seek to find alternatives to all-concrete buildings and to offer solutions both to the demand for affordable housing and to the need for thermal comfort. These initiatives spread knowledge about the benefits of building with local and renewable materials which are easy to use, widely affordable, and generally require less cement – like mud (Figure 4.4). In 2015, for example, UNESCO launched the "Terra Award," a global prize awarded for contemporary architectures using raw earth. Every year, the "Terra Award Sahel +" prize – the African version of the "Terra Award" – goes to the best projects and initiatives built using raw earth (Vandermeeren 2020). In Europe and America, but also in Africa, various networks and initiatives launched by architects, NGOs, and supported by donors and academic institutions are promoting alternative methods of construction. The research center CRAterre (International Centre for Earthen Architecture) based in Grenoble (France), is developing projects across the world with the Compressed Earth Block (CEB) technology, which is emerging as a potentially viable option in terms of price and sustainable

FIGURE 4.4 Mud houses, Comé, Benin 2017. Source: A. Choplin.

objectives. This CEB technology was developed in the 1950s in Colombia thanks to the engineer Raul Ramirez who designed a press that could produce blocks from moist earth made up of a mix of clay, silt, sand, and small gravel (Sémond et al. 2016). Cement or lime are commonly added to increase water resistance. The blocks are then dried for several days or weeks, depending on the climate. CRAterre proposes the use of local resources and short supply circuits, not only as an answer to the challenge of sustainable development but also as a source of local employment. In this way, ecological construction is a matter of international solidarity.

In West Africa, CRAterre has trained many masons and entrepreneurs who are now promoting earth construction through the use of CEB.[12] In Dakar the civil engineer Doudou Deme has created *ElemenTerre*, a company specialized in the production blocks made with earth. In the Sahel area, since the 1980s, the association *La Voûte Nubienne* (The Nubian Vault) promotes the use of adobe – a technique that originated in Nubia in Egypt – which can be formed into arches and domes. This material can be incorporated into walls allowing buildings to be roofed without the use of timber or corrugated iron. The website has records of 4,200 completed projects; training provided for 950 apprentices, builders, and craftsmen; and 44,700 beneficiaries. Boubacar Ouilly, coordinator of the organization in Burkina Faso, notes that the average indoor temperature of a mudbrick house built by *La Voûte Nubienne* would be 25 °C, compared with 35 °C for a cement house.[13] It would cost 30–60% less to build than a house made with concrete blocks.

The FACT Sahel + is another extremely active network on social media: it aims to bring together African and European builders, architects, artists, students exploring more sustainable ways of building, especially earth construction. On Facebook and WhatsApp, several hundreds of members – overwhelmingly from Africa – send pictures of their constructions sites, exchange about technical solutions to develop a low-carbon sector, participate in online debates about alternatives to concrete. At present, initiatives appear to be dispersed and limited to only a few individuals. But the emergence of these networks and exchange platforms could quickly change the situation and give visibility to these ecological alternatives (Figure 4.5). The

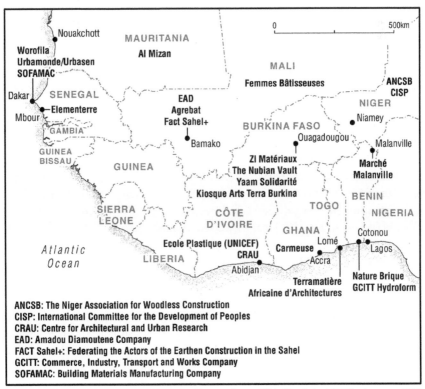

ANCSB: The Niger Association for Woodless Construction
CISP: International Committee for the Development of Peoples
CRAU: Centre for Architectural and Urban Research
EAD: Amadou Diamoutene Company
FACT Sahel+: Federating the Actors of the Earthen Construction in the Sahel
GCITT: Commerce, Industry, Transport and Works Company
SOFAMAC: Building Materials Manufacturing Company

Sources: Personal Data Choplin Lozivit & Vandermeeren 2020

FIGURE 4.5 Map of alternative construction initiatives, 2020.
Source: Adapted from A. Choplin, M. Lozivit, M. Irving, personal fieldwork data.

mud houses in Djenné (Mali) is a reminder these structures can last a long time (Marchand 2016). In Burkina Faso, the Yaam Solidarité Association, with the Help of UrbaMonde and CRAterre, is active in a working-class area of Ouagadou on the development of housing with local materials. In Dakar, the NGO UrbaSEN/UrbaMonde is developing the *Fédération Sénégalaise des Habitants* to promote the fabrication of blocks made with typha. Researchers in the AE&CC (*Architecture, Environment and Construction Cultures*) unit at the University of Grenoble have partnered with CRAterre and the International Abbé Pierre Foundation to compile a study of recent experiments of this kind (Cankat et al. 2019). This study demonstrates that it is possible to produce houses with eco-materials, with the participation of the inhabitants and in precarious urban contexts. This exploration of local construction is taking place in several other places: CRAU (centre for architectural and urban research) in Ivory Coast; the African Fabber School, which produces low-cost and off-grid houses in Cameroon; *L'Africaine d'architecture* developed in Lomé by Sename Koffi Agbodjinou who revisits the concept of neo-vernacular architecture. In Ivory Coast, schools are being built with recycled plastic bricks (funded by UNICEF). The Swiss Agency for Development and Cooperation (SDC) has also supported a number of projects, including the urban market in Malanville in northern Benin, built of local materials (CEB) by the Swiss NGO Contact. The French Development Agency also supports a project of eco-construction (e.g., PECOBAT – *Project Eco-construction Bâtiment*) in Mauritania.

This movement toward a return to mud and stone (i.e., to construction with locally available materials) is also spreading in Europe, as evidenced by the initiative undertaken by Terrabloc, a Geneva company that supplies CEBs in Switzerland. In France, the "*Les Bâtisseuses*" collective promotes the reuse of materials; building with local earth, wood, and straw, as well as the role of women in construction. Some architects are also arguing for a return to the local. For example, Gilles Perraudin is laying the foundations for a locally-based "situated architecture" by using stone, *pisé* (rammed earth), and wood in his buildings. But "localness" is ambiguous since cement manufacturers, starting with Dangote, boast of producing locally when in fact they import gypsum, petcoke, and other adjuvants. For Olivier Moles, who has been a member of CRAterre for 25 years as a teacher and researcher at the Grenoble Advanced National School of Architecture, cement produced in Africa cannot be considered a local material: while it is true that the limestone is extracted locally, the energy and fuels that drive the kilns are not. Moreover, profits do not benefit the local population. According to Olivier Moles, it is important "to understand what resources are available, in particular geo- and bio-sourced materials, the environmental constraints (notably subsoil, climate, and density), local demand, relations between the inhabitants, where the energy comes from and what are the environmental and social impacts on the area, where the profits go. Using local materials entails trying as far as possible to reconcile all these constraints. That is why there is no recipe and no type of material that is right everywhere and in everyplace" (interview, 2020).

"Tropicalizing" Construction

"I would have liked to build a thatched roof, but it's too expensive," Édith confided when I visited her charming guesthouse in Abomey, the former royal capital of Benin. Édith is a strong woman of sturdy character. She built the guesthouse on her own, using local red ferruginous clay mixed with cement. The rooms are cool, the natural ventilation well-designed. Édith did not use an architect but instead drew on her common sense and memories, recalling the cool houses of her childhood. The house and its wide and comfortable front patio appear nearly perfect, save for the big rusty eyesore that looms over the rooms. Édith had to resign herself to a corrugated iron roof because, as she put it, "straw is too expensive." It is expensive to maintain, both in cost and time: because of the heavy rains, the roof must be repaired regularly and replaced roughly every five years. In addition, Édith explains that there are not many people left with the skills to repair a grass roof. She had done her calculations: corrugated iron imported from Nigeria would be much cheaper in the long term than local straw.

Elinor, another woman who had built her own house, was similarly obliged to revise her plans. At our first meeting on the site of her future house in 2017, she explained that she would build the roof with natural materials. A year later, at my second visit, I noticed that the roof was now made of corrugated iron. To lay a thatched roof, she would have had to fetch large quantities of the raw materials from the Porto-Novo and Ouidah regions, transport it, and then employ several people to do the work. The thatcher estimated the cost at 2 million francs CFA (including 200,000 for transport). "At that price, I could build another house or buy a plot, it's much too expensive, so I chose corrugated iron," she explained. These accounts show that local natural materials are now beyond the reach of ordinary people. The same is true of stone, which has become a scarce material in the region, especially on the coast: you have to travel almost 300 km north to find stone (Dassa area in Benin or Abeokuta in Nigeria). And people in the region who know how to carve stone are few and far between, which makes it an expensive, even luxury, product.

Only a small West African elite who have traveled and spent time outside the continent are beginning to recognize the effectiveness of local materials and to use them. Many across Africa still associate straw, stone, and mud with the poverty of rural villages. Romarick, an architect who trained in France and has since returned to Benin, explained that, "when I suggest straw and bamboo to my clients, they refuse. They say: 'Oh no, those are village materials. Wood is for the bush, not for the city.'" It is only recently that these materials have become markers of social distinction. Their prices are increasing, inflated by demand from this well-heeled elite. Using these materials also requires significant expenditure to pay for their regular repair. So-called modern construction techniques using concrete, though initially more expensive, are perceived as a better investment because they last longer. And as we have seen, the choice of cement is not just a question of money. Nonetheless, some think otherwise, that the solution will only come through the rediscovery of the surrounding natural resources. Victor Kidjo is one of these. This Beninese engineer, trained in Belgium, heads the firm *Nature Brique*, located near Abomey, which employs 40 people. His objective is to "democratize construction" and reduce its fixation on cement: "you can't build with concrete in a hot and humid country, especially a country that is brimming with clay" (interview, Cotonou, 2018). Kidjo explains that to make bricks, he needs clay, water, electricity, and fuel for the kiln. He has chosen charcoal locally produced with palm kernel shells. As he notes: "it is 100% organic and burns at 950 °C. CO_2 emission rates are 0.02%, well below cement plants." His mud blocks are cheaper than cement blocks (7,000 CFAF per square meter for one mud block, compared with 18,000 for cement). His biggest challenge: upscaling production and finding energy sources to fuel the kiln and the artificial dryer. He is thinking about mounting a large, off-grid solar power plant on the roof to supply his energy needs: "If I can't get help, I'll go to China on my own to buy one there."

Maureil Smith – director of the firm which built Cité Bethel, GCITT – has worked for decades in South Africa (Figure 4.6). During this time, he became the representative of Hydraform, a South African firm that produced houses made of local materials in the aftermath of apartheid. He wants to promote the use of CEBs in West Africa, as well as Moladi technology, in which large plastic formwork panels are filled with mortar or earth. He is the Chairman of the Community of Manufacturers and Layers of Local Building Materials, an association largely dedicated to organizing the different actors in the field and to training, but which also promotes local materials with political decision-makers. However, the structure created "on the initiative of the Ministry of the Living Environment and Housing" in October 2017 has

FIGURE 4.6   Self-blocking compressed earth block house, Ouédo CGITT Bethel, 2020. Source: Courtesy of H. Dato.

attracted only a few entrepreneurs (among them Victor Kidjo of *Nature Brique*) and self-employed builders. Bonaventure, the site foreman we met on the building sites of Cotonou, would like to develop his skills in earthen construction because, as he put it, "red brick houses are cooler than cement houses." And although he would like to enter this market, "the brickmaking machines are too expensive."

There are numerous challenges and constraints in the return to local earthen construction: uncompetitive prices, a market controlled by powerful lobbies, limited interest on the part of local populations dubious about construction techniques that are reminiscent of the rural world, lack of skills and technical capacity, very high maintenance costs, volume difficulties. Very often, the use of local materials does not go beyond the experimental stage. On the production side, it is difficult to rationalize supplies of raw materials and power. Under these circumstances, all the initiatives – whether emanating from NGOs, donors, researchers, or even contractors – can bring change by raising awareness of more sustainable ways of building. According to

Olivier Moles from CRAterre, "producing locally with affordable materials and positive local impacts is technically possible. But it is important for local people to have the tools to judge, for knowledge to be disseminated. This requires training and the transfer of skills. And the most affordable materials need to become respectable again." Change will perhaps come through support from the big companies – the same companies that are responsible for polluting practices but have the technical and financial muscle to test and introduce new materials, rules, and standards. The influence of the elites is also essential in order to change habits. As Mr. Smith points out: "If people with money start building big villas using earth, they show that it is a desirable material. Then, the rest of the population will want to follow. If the rich use it, why not everyone else?"

Other initiatives encourage experiments with plant fiber, a "living" material derived from renewable natural resources (reeds, flax, hemp, typha) which was for a long time the main material used in West Africa to construct homes. While it is not very strong and is permeable to water, air, and mosquitoes, it is an effective temperature regulator in buildings. In addition, it has little environmental impact: the supply chains are short since the materials are processed and used near where they are collected. At a time when architects in Europe are bringing straw back into fashion by combining timber frames and straw insulation, and when international organizations are supporting the production of sustainable bamboo and rattan, the recent rediscovery of typha reeds (bulrushes) in West Africa as a construction material raises interesting prospects.

Typha is a kind of fast-growing reed that flourishes in wetlands and is considered an invasive plant. It became particularly prolific in the 1980s in the Senegal River basin, Nouakchott, and Dakar in the wake of repeated floods. In Mauritania, as in Senegal, NGOs like Gret have conducted experiments to convert this invasive plant into fuel (typha charcoal) and into a building material (Anger and Joffroy 2014). Since 2015, the Senegalese government has been supporting these initiatives at the prompting of the UNDP-GEF unit, with the aim of reducing energy consumption in buildings by means of typha-based thermal insulation materials.[14] The Senegalese firm *Elementerre* and the Worofila Association for earthen architecture partnered with the NGO UrbaSEN (Senegalese branch of the Swiss NGO urbaMonde) to develop typha and clay-based construction. UrbaSEN/urbaMonde has been working since 2006 in the peripheral areas of Dakar affected by flooding: the NGO has set up a participatory project to help the inhabitants to rebuild – and improve – the homes destroyed by the floods (Chabot et al. 2018; Leclercq 2022). Since 2010, thanks to the *Fédération Sénégalaise des Habitants* (FSH – Senegalese Federation of Inhabitants), a savings group created by UrbaSEN, more than 800 houses have been rebuilt.

Supplying a stock of good quality construction materials, at guaranteed and subsidized prices is another possible solution for providing housing in precarious neighborhoods. This project, set up in Senegal by UrbaMonde/UrbaSEN, suggests that subsidizing the production and purchase of bricks would be a solution. Victor Kidjo at *Nature Brique* in Benin holds a similar view. According to Mr. Kidjo, agreements need to be made with banks: once an individual has saved up 100,000 or 200,000 francs CFA at the bank, the bricks could be manufactured at the factory then delivered directly. This would reduce construction costs and the waste of money caused by interminable construction processes during which materials deteriorate. This social system would have the advantage of bypassing prohibitive bank interest rates.

Intervening upstream at the point of manufacture; supporting and subsidizing the manufacture of earthen blocks and the use of plant fibers; creating banks of local materials that would stabilize prices and encourage good quality building: these are potential ways to help the most vulnerable households and to provide affordable and decent housing. Raw earthen bricks, typha, Nubian vaults all form integral parts of these West African initiatives which are contributing to the production of local knowledge and to the rediscovery of compressed earth brick, to the use of rubble and sludge, and to the manufacture of mud cement and stabilized earth blocks. They show other ways of building, and the vitality of individuals who have formed new networks to limit the impact of the construction sector on climate change. They are raising the prospect of a different kind of city. But the challenge is immense. Everything must start from first principles: converting people away from the fixation on concrete, converting experiments into products for all, increasing production to reduce costs, and innovating in the concrete industry.

Toward Innovation in the Concrete Industry

Taking into consideration the United Nations Sustainable Development Goals (SDG) – e.g., sustainable cities and communities (SDG11), responsible consumption and production (SDG12), and climate action (SDG13) – in the production of concrete would require a radical transformation of the construction sector. But the sector remains constrained from embracing novel trends toward decarbonization. Nevertheless, several possibilities are being explored by scientists and cement manufacturers to transform the cement industry, turning it into a more sustainable model to reach the Zero Carbon objective for 2050. The challenge is enormous: producing one ton of Portland cement is equivalent to producing one ton of CO_2. Manufacturing cement clinker involves heating limestone and clay to very high temperatures (1,450° for 48 hours), and 90% of greenhouse gases for concrete production are emitted during this stage (Habert et al. 2020). Considering the extreme pollution produced by this combustion, some scholars are exploring alternatives to lower the carbon footprint of cement: they are producing less energy intensive binders with a similar effect to Portland cement, producing cold cement by other chemical reactions, and capturing CO_2 during the construction stage. Others propose to reduce cement in construction and use building materials such as raw earth.

For instance, Van Damme and Houben (2018) explain that the use of earth remains limited in modern buildings, because of the absence of codes and standards. Moreover, there is still little information about the performance of earthen buildings and few engineers and builders are trained in their design. All these obstacles result in high costs and challenges that are incompatible with the scale of the demand. Van Damme and Houben also point out that cement is often added to raw earth as a stabilizer to increase its strength and water resistance. In their view, the outcome of this systematic use of cement as a stabilizer is often to turn raw earth into poor quality cement, which undermines the ecological benefits of earth as a building material. They recommend that architectural practices should change and that work should be done to develop new methods of stabilization and other binding materials which would have the same stabilizing characteristics as Portland cement but would be more environmentally friendly (Marsh et al. 2020). This is what Professor Guillaume Habert who holds the chair in sustainable construction at Zürich ETH in Switzerland – is working to achieve (Habert et al. 2020). With his Togolese colleague Gnanli Landrou, he is investigating ways to reuse the earth extracted when digging foundations, which is generally treated as rubble. They have developed a process that converts the extracted clay into cement-free concrete, which can be poured while still fresh and dries rapidly. This technology is reportedly 2.5 times cheaper and 20 times less energy-intensive than cement production.[15] At *École Polytechnique Fédérale de Lausanne* (EPFL), Professor Karen Scrivener has developed the Limestone Clay Calcined Cement (LC3) which emits less carbon dioxide than traditional cement. The purpose of this project, supported by The Swiss Agency for Development and Cooperation (SDC), is to investigate a different type of clinker that would emit less CO_2. Aircrete could also be a solution to explore as it is a lightweight building material with interesting qualities (high compression strength, buoyancy, and thermal insulation), and some experiments have been tried in Dar es Salaam (Degani 2020).

The cement industry is interested in these technical and technological advances and recognizes that it is urgent to reduce the environmental impacts – in particular greenhouse gas emissions – associated with the production and use of cement (Marsh et al. 2020). But the cement and concrete industry is reluctant to change well-established practices whose transformation would require high investments. At the same time, as social demand grows for more sustainable housing, cement companies are planning to begin the sale of ecological, green, decarbonized cement. It would not only reduce controversies and provide a response to climate change imperatives but would also open up new markets. However, we must be aware that these possible innovations and intense technical debates are developed in the Global North, by researchers and companies sometimes without any link to the building contexts in the Global South. And although solutions are being developed, they will take a long time to be implemented in Africa.

Putting African Architecture on the Map

In June of 2017 at a round table on sustainable architecture in Abuja, Nmadili Okwumabua, a young Nigerian architect, found it hard to hide her irritation. She described how, when she arrived in the United States to train as an architect, she wanted to conduct a research project on African architecture. Her teachers, she said, countered that, "it is not really architecture." In response to this lack of recognition, Okwumabua has since created "The Community Planning & Design Initiative Africa" (CDPI Africa), which aims to bring together communities and regional architects, has launched an annual architecture competition focusing on African architecture, both modern and inspired by local examples. A similar initiative has been launched in French-speaking Africa by the AfrikArchi collective and its chair and founder Romarick Atoké with the goal of supporting the creativity of young African architects. The Terra Award Sahel + competition is part of this movement, as is the ArchiAfrika project launched in Accra by the architect Jo Addo. The latter wishes to regenerate the decaying district of Jamestown, the historic heart of Accra, and to this end has set up an office in an old Afro-Brazilian house, where he regularly invites African architects and thinkers to speak. Still in Accra, the Ghanaian-Scottish architect and novelist Lesley Lokko has recently founded the African Futures Institute, a school of architecture and public events platform to rethink architecture from Africa, considered as the "laboratory of the future".

Yet, the situation is about to change: in 2021, the publication of the rich seven-volume *Architectural Guide Sub-Saharan Africa* (Meuser and Dalbai 2021) invited professional architects to rediscover and recognize the importance of African techniques and materials for building.[16] Moreover, in March 2022, the Burkinabe architect Francis Kéré was awarded the Pritzker Prize (the equivalent of the Nobel Prize for Architecture). He is the first African to receive it, which marks a significant change in the international

FIGURE 4.7   Primary school Gando, Burkina Fasso. Source: Kéré Architecture.

perception and recognition of African architecture. Against the current architectural trends that glorify concrete, Francis Kéré promotes vernacular know-how and calls for the (re)use of local materials such as earth and wood (Figure 4.7). According to Kéré, even the most deprived people have a right to comfort and beauty.[17] In his speech at the LafargeHolcim conference in 2019 (he won the LafargeHocim Award for sustainable construction in 2012), Kéré reminded the audience that, "for Burkinabes, a school is something that comes from France. As a result, it must be made of glass, concrete, and steel. That raises a problem: all we do is reproduce poor quality copies. Instead, I would like to use the material that is most available: clay. That is how we will progress."[18] In addition to Francis Kéré, other architects are making their voices heard, such as the Ivorian Issa Diabate, the Nigerian Mariam Kamara, the British-Ghanaian David Adjaye, the Togolese Sename Koffi Agbodjinou, or the Ghanaian-Scottish Lesley Lokko (who was appointed the curator of the 18th Venice Biennale of architecture in 2023). They seem to share certain values and this same attraction to the rediscovery of local identities, know-how and materials. Mariam Kamara deplores the obstinate insistence on copying of Western architecture and instead argues for the pursuit of a renewed artistic and architectural identity on the continent. In an interview given to *Jeune Afrique* magazine in 2018, she calls on Africans to "imagine our own future, invent our own modernity… That is the minimum of respect we owe ourselves."[19] Issa Diabaté follows the same line. He reminds us that "everything that comes from the West is considered better, we copy Western models to the point of forgetting what we did well before. As if building with concrete implies that we are more advanced. This has to change."[20] Architecture, he argues, must take into account the local context: "cement is not bad in itself, but it has to be adapted to other materials and to the local context, so to the bioclimatic system."

Most of the famous African architects call for a shift away from Western models and to a revival of local knowledge. Yet most have been trained in Europe or North America. It is therefore necessary to create training courses in Africa linked to the local urban contexts. Few schools of architecture exist in West Africa. The Kumasi School of Architecture in Ghana, the first of its kind, opened in the region in 1957. In Francophone Africa, EAMAU (African School for the Architectural and Urbanistic Professions), present in Lomé since 1976, has found it hard to produce enough practitioners for the subregion. Because of the scarcity of courses, the fees are often prohibitive for an ordinary student (around €5,000 for three years at EAMAU). Families that have the resources therefore prefer to send their children to study architecture in Europe or America. There are few courses in these schools on local materials and techniques or which seek to democratize and spread knowledge about vernacular architecture. The CRAterre Association, through its UNESCO chair, is developing multiple initiatives and open access on-line courses in the region. Building with earth is still considered to be "non-modern," for poor people and therefore not very lucrative. Young graduates prefer to respond to the needs of clients who want sealed and air-conditioned concrete houses. Jean-Paul Houndeffo, of the Beninese Order of Architects, is looking at ways to encourage these types of knowledge and the use of sustainable materials. "For the moment," he noted, "we are content with the Eco-Trente label, where the aim is to incorporate 30% of sustainable solutions, either on the site during construction, or afterwards when the structure is in use (waste recycling, solar panels, water management)."

Architecture is a matter of training and transmission, but also of responsibility. In his work on Addis Ababa, Marco Di Nunzio (2019) explains that architects have a responsibility in the production and growth of inequalities. But he also argues that some are already trying to break with the trend in which architects act as handmaidens to capitalism. The emerging critique against concrete is also supported by some African architects who insist that designing more sustainable ways of living and inhabiting is a global emergency. These architects play a key role in reviving lost skills and recognizing the importance of vernacular architecture and by raising awareness of more sustainable ways of building. The redemption of the Concrete City may therefore come through these subversive architects and their experimentation with different techniques for construction (Vandermeeren 2020).

Conclusion

Over the last twenty years, concrete has emerged as the main material of West Africa's new urban horizon. In this last chapter, I have shown that, beyond being a symbol of wealth and modernity, concrete can also be a source of anxiety, and "solastalgia," to use this term that evokes the eco-anxiety associated with the climate change (Albrecht et al. 2007). This last section has focused on concrete's socio-ecological concerns. In a context of global warming, the future of the Concrete City is worrying, and the confidence in concrete is crumbling. This critique of concrete raises the question of how this obsolescent material – which is not adapted to the West African bioclimatic system – is amplifying climate injustice. One of the main challenges of the twenty-first century will be coping with concrete's deterioration and looming collapse of the Concrete City.

This reflection is nourished by research on urban metabolism: it sheds light on these material flows reshaping the interactions between societies, territories, and environments. Building ecologically by limiting the depletion of natural resources like sand and limiting greenhouse gas emissions has become an urgent imperative for policy-makers, firms, scientists, and civil society – ordinary people are making claims for a more sustainable city. Architects and engineers are increasingly turning away from all-concrete construction and are proposing more rational and ecological alternatives. Some advocate the reuse of materials and the recycling of stone and building site waste to promote the circular economy in the construction industry. In Africa, a new critique of concrete is emerging which calls for the recognition of African architecture and point out the existing extractivist practices by Africapitalists like Dangote. A first mark of recognition is the Pritzker Prize awarded to the innovative Burkinabe architect Francis Kéré. This prize marks a real turning point in which Africa has finally appeared on the world map of architecture. It is also a recognition of other building cultures and ways of living and inhabiting more sustainable and in line with the local context.

But African architects alone cannot make a difference. Public policies should support alternative construction through financial incentives, the imposition of standards and norms, and the provision of training, particularly for masons and craftsmen working on building sites. The change could happen through learning, sharing, and transmission of knowledge in schools that are affordable to everyone (schools of architecture, but also of urban planning and landscape). In parallel, earth, wood, straw, and rubble should no longer be perceived only as materials of the poor, but instead as the materials of the future. This section has also highlighted the role of private companies in an environmental transition toward a green construction industry. They are essential players because the decarbonization of the construction industry has massive social and environmental costs.

Finally, in exploring these possible alternatives of environmental transition, I have underlined the crucial role of social demand for a fairer city and a less polluted living environment and building materials. Within and between Africa as in Europe, connections must be made to rethink the entire construction sector and cement industry and to reinvent the global culture of construction. This culture needs to reconnect the artistic and artisanal aspects of construction, practical and theoretical knowledges, as well as reconnect contractors, craftsmen, architects, and the academic world, which at present operate in silos. The social image of concrete is changing. This sociotechnical product, perceived as a symbol of modernity and progress, has also transformed into an icon of unsustainability, obsolescence, and uninhabitability. The point is not to ban concrete but to use it more rationally – for example, it remains an essential element of certain parts of the construction process, especially in pouring foundations. In Europe, many building sites could economize on cement. And in Africa, standards could be reviewed to encourage more sustainable construction. Given the fact that the Concrete City is destined to crumble into ruins within 50 to 70 years, Africa and the Global South will be a crucial place from which to imagine new habitable spaces and urban futures.

Notes

1   See the video: https://responsabilite-multinationales.ch/etudes-de-cas/holcim-met-en-danger-la-sante-de-tout-un-village.

2   See Holcim-Report: Eine Skandal-Recherche von Greenpeace Schweiz Erscheinungsdatum: Oktober 2020. https://www.greenpeace.ch/de/publikation/60009/der-holcim-report/.

3   See the Ivorian government website: http://www.gouv.ci/_actualite-article.php?recordID=12070.

4   See *MatéRhône Project* : Extraction, circulation and recycling of building materials in the Rhone Valley and the documentary film *Des Tours et des Trous. Construire Genève de demain*, directed by H. Blaszkiewicz & A. Choplin, 2022 : https://www.unige.ch/gedt/recherches/projets/materhone/.

5   See *The Guardian*, 29.08.2019, The air conditioning trap: how cold air is heating the world https://www.theguardian.com/environment/2019/aug/29/the-air-conditioning-trap-how-cold-air-is-heating-the-world.

6   See the report of the 6th International LafargeHolcim Forum – Cairo 2019, https://src.lafargeholcim-foundation.org/dnl/e949f24c-4983-440b-a99f-3dbc8e70c3a3/Foundations-23.pdf.

7   See 'Pollution de l'environnement: SCB-Lafarge menace la santé des populations de Pobè et environs', *Cotonou.com*, 19.08.2017, http://news.acotonou.com/h/101471.html

8   See Vince Beiser, *The Guardian*, 27.02.2017, Sand mining: the global environmental crisis you've probably never heard of, https://www.theguardian.com/cities/2017/feb/27/sand-mining-global-environmental-crisis-never-heard and *BBC*, 02.05.2016, Even desert city Dubai imports its sand. This is why. https://www.bbc.com/worklife/article/20160502-even-desert-city-dubai-imports-its-sand-this-is-why.

9   https://pulitzercenter.org/node/15995

10 Newspaper *La Nouvelle-Expression*, 09.09.2016.

11 See Madiana Hazoumé, *The Conversation*, 02.03.2017, En finir avec le tout-béton en Afrique, https://theconversation.com/en-finir-avec-le-tout-beton-en-afrique-72556.

12 See also ¨the "Atelier Matières à Construire Amacò" [Amacò Building Materials Workshop], created by CRAerre graduates around INSA [national institute of applied sciences] in Lyon, which provides training courses in building with earth both in France and abroad.

13 Podcast *7 milliards de voisins*, 09.05.2019 available at: http://www.rfi.fr/emission/20190509-maison-individuelle-reve-cauchemar-villes.

14 PNEEB Typha Project (National Programme for Energy Efficiency in Buildings).

15 The Sustainable Construction Chair at ETH also works with IG Lehm, an organization that promotes earthen construction in Switzerland, and hosted the THINK Earth! exhibition, staged with CRAterre and Amacó.

16   See also "Africa's iconic architecture in 12 buildings," By Ijeoma Ndukwe, BBC, 13.10.2021.

17   See *The Guardian*, 15.03.2022, https://www.theguardian.com/ artanddesign/2022/mar/15/it-is-unbelievable-francis-kere-becomes-first-black-architect-to-win-the-pritzker-prize.

18   https://src.lafargeholcim-foundation.org/dnl/e949f24c-4983-440b-a99f-3dbc8e70c3a3/Foundations-23.pdf.

19   See *Jeune Afrique*, 27.09.2018, Urbanisme: Mariam Kamara, l'architecte « made in Africa », http://www.jeuneafrique.com/mag/632797/culture/ urbanisme-mariam-kamara-larchitecte-made-in-africa.

20   Interview in The Wave Unesco radio program with Amélie Esséssé, Romarick Atoké (Dicember 2021). https://open.spotify.com/episode/5 sHjm994CRpmqJESfi7F87.

Conclusion
Concrete Utopia

Gray Gold

Concrete, plague or plenty?
Good for evil?
Sure, with you I can build a shelter.
Sure, with you I look rich

But did you know that you pollute?
That you enrich men who exploit the greed of others?
That you change our landscapes into gray wastelands?
But unfortunately concrete
You are one more example
Of our so-called development

All this to resemble the West

This poem was written by Mansour Diallo, a 14-year-old student, after hearing me talk about my research in a lesson at the Lycée Montaigne in Cotonou in 2018. It perfectly encapsulates the multiple contradictions of concrete. Where there is concrete, there is power, money, capitalism, corruption, lobbying, degradation. But there is also hope, dreams, desire, and emancipation.

By bringing together critical urban studies, postcolonial approaches, and science and technology studies, this book has taken measure of this crucial material in Africa and, by extension, elsewhere in the world. It was not intended as a manifesto against concrete, but as an invitation to think about the urban world emerging out of the gray matter that surrounds us. Adopting the "follow the thing" approach, this journey through West Africa's cities provided a glimpse of concrete and its major role in politics, in economics, and in societies in the Global South. Concrete appears as one of the most visible forms of West Africa's contemporary urban development. It gives shape to a new urban form that I have termed the Concrete City and that is unfolding along the West African corridor, and beyond.

Concrete City: Material Flows and Urbanization in West Africa, First Edition. Armelle Choplin.
© 2023 John Wiley & Sons Ltd. Published 2023 by John Wiley & Sons Ltd.

The West African Corridor: An Urban Laboratory

At the end of 2018, when I was preparing to leave Cotonou after almost three years, I took a final trip along the corridor to take one last note of the region's urban change. In Accra, the immense Nkrumah Circle interchange was now open to traffic. In Lomé, the first villas in the Mokpokpo "social" housing estate had just been constructed. In Cotonou, at the entrance to the channel, the informal neighborhood of Akpakpa Dodomé had been demolished and its residents evicted to make way for a forthcoming residential and tourist complex. In Porto-Novo, the construction of the massive future National Assembly of Benin was on standby. Over in Nigeria, the Eko Atlantic City Marina was beginning to take shape. Apart from these big projects, I realized that the region's cities had profoundly transformed: all along the coast a denser fabric of buildings had emerged. The construction sites I photographed on my arrival three years earlier had become houses, shops, and warehouses. Other projects have since been launched.

As I was completing this book at the end of 2022, the pandemic prevented me from returning to West Africa. So, I had to content myself with discussing with my colleagues and students, and I observed the region's cities through the aerial images available on Google Earth. The Accra and Cotonou seafronts had been cleared of slum dwellers but the spaces released were still empty. Eko Atlantic City was the same: the island remained empty save for the two Pearl Towers visible on the map. In Porto-Novo, works on the National Assembly had been abandoned: the capital has its white elephant – or rather gray elephant, given the tons of concrete that disfigure the entry to the city. A new Assembly will be erected in another site: the building, mostly in wood and inspired from the palaver tree, has been designed by the Burkinabe architect Francis Kéré. But more generally, numerous large projects seem to be on standby, like portents of a post-COVID economic crisis. On the other hand, urbanization continues along the corridor and the density is still rising. No space seems to be left empty.

Seen from the sky at a macro scale, the corridor resembles an immense stream of concrete, with its 40 million inhabitants, soon to be 55 million, concentrated in a vulnerable environment. It is the manifestation of an unprecedented and planetary, uncontrolled and uncontrollable urbanization. Here as elsewhere, states and the private sector (including cement manufacturers and investors) support the pursuit of this continuous urbanization which, from Abidjan to Lagos, reveals the imprint of capitalism and neoliberalism. Concrete is the product of this capitalist machine that works in the remote corners of the planet, including in the little-known urban areas of Africa. The classic neo-Marxist analyzes on the neoliberal city, on planetary urbanization, and on the urban hypertrophy that characterizes the Global South help to explain these ongoing transformations in the corridor. Material and capital flows are redeployed through and in space in a way that is both massive (it is all we see) and discrete (it is so obvious and pervasive that we no longer see it).

Thus, concrete is a fantastic entry point for understanding the evolution of late capitalism in West Africa. Concrete has been a privileged material of development since colonial times and has become an essential medium for liberalization, extraverted accumulation, and connection to international financial flows. When linked to the construction industry and the real estate market, it becomes a means of capital storage and investment, particularly resilient in economically unstable countries. Concrete fully accompanies the marketing discourses on "Africa Rising" and Africa as "the last frontier of capitalism." Yet these discourses must be relativized and even deconstructed. For Alexander Beresford (2016), who also questions and nuances this optimistic "Africa Rising" discourse, one central question remains: "If Africa is indeed 'rising,' who benefits from it?" After having followed the concrete chain, it is possible to assert that elites in the construction sector benefit from this neoliberal discourse. Achille Mbembe (2015) also invites us to question this form of contemporary capitalism in Africa. For him, these discourses have above all allowed Africa to become "a region where some of the most advanced formal and informal experiments in neoliberal deregulation have taken place." These neoliberal trends are translated into new spatial forms. For Mbembe (*ibid.*), this "frontier-type of capitalism is organized around enclaves (especially mining enclaves), islands and bubbles … It is a capitalism of multiple nodal points, of scattered patterns, of spatial growth combined with neglect and decline. This form of capitalism is mostly extractive." Concrete is this extracted material underlying the construction of these disconnected enclaves. This is very visible when circulating along the Gulf of Guinea. Audacious megaprojects are being built in city centers and innovative new cities and gated communities are springing up on peripheries. In all respects, the Concrete City appears as the backbone of the neoliberal policies that are unfolding in West Africa.

But I propose to go further and say that the Concrete City is also much more than an avatar of capitalism. It is necessary to go beyond the single reading of the transformations of African cities through large real estate projects, new cities, and foreign investments to take into account the more ordinary and popular dynamics of the city's making (Choplin 2020a,b; Karaman et al. 2020; Sawyer et al. 2021). Useful as they are, the theoretical frameworks on the neoliberal city are hard put to capture the multiplicity of the factors that underpin the production of the urban: they are sometimes broadly overarching or too general and/or abstract (Storper and Scott 2016). Southern cities, and African cities in particular, are under-represented in these studies. As Beresford (2016) suggests for Africa, divergent nature of capitalist development coexist, with old patterns of dependency that remain and new patterns of accumulation. This exploration of the Concrete City has demonstrated the existence of these parallel trends and has highlighted how global forces (including the cement business) interact with local structures to create distinctive configurations of urbanization. The Concrete City is as much the city of the rich and of speculative urbanism as it is the city of the poor who have found refuge there. And between the capitalistic enclaves, in the interstitial spaces, concrete makes the link: it is the material of ordinary urbanism, mirroring the daily aspirations of the inhabitants who are simply looking for a decent place to live. Behind this unique material, across the urban corridor, I observed strong contrasts between the cities and urban spaces, which are not impacted to the same degree by the neoliberal and entrepreneurial turn.

Although drone and satellite images reveal a 1,000 km of continuous concrete, West Africa's urban corridor is not a single entity. This close-grained enquiry reveals that it is comprised of a diversity of urban contexts, local political and economic regimes, and a complex network of spatial configurations. The urbanization process does not solely reflect the dominance of big cities. While the boundaries between the "rural" and "urban" are today increasingly blurred in the context of planetary urbanization, the urban itself is not uniform – it remains diverse and heterogeneous. Lagoon-side villages exist alongside built-up suburbs and dense urban centers (Figures C.1 and C.2). While the growth of Lagos in the last 20 years has certainly been spectacular and emblematic of the path followed by many megacities of the South, some small and mid-sized towns have continued to grow in area and influence, whereas others show signs of decline. The urban system is one of contrasts – while some places gain and profit from urbanization, others decay. For example, the historic precolonial and colonial hearts of Porto-Novo, Grand Popo, and Aného are experiencing zero growth and, in some instances, even losing population. Houses in these cities are falling into ruin. Old urban areas are in decline and the boom in land and real estate prices varies in intensity from one place to another. And the rural world has not totally disappeared. On the contrary, it is has become increasingly interwoven with the urban world.

Traveling along this corridor shows also that political geographies remain consequential. Attempting to cross from Nigeria to Benin or from Togo to Ghana is a lesson in the importance of borders – it is the entry to another state, another city, another world (Chalfin 2010; Nugent 2021). The

FIGURE C.1 The corridor at Cotonou, 2018. Source: A. Choplin.

FIGURE C.2 The corridor at Djègbadji, Ouidah, 2018. Source: A. Choplin.

heterogeneity of this corridor owes much to the different political cultures of states. Nigeria is a federal state in which Lagos State exercises dominance through its physical size and economic power. In Benin, on the other hand, the rivalry between Porto-Novo (the official political capital) and Cotonou (which is the economic capital, but it is where the president of the republic resides) prevents politicians from governing at the metropolitan level. In Togo, the country's small size means that the Lomé agglomeration tends to dominate the whole southern coastal area. As for Ghana, the Accra Metropolitan Assembly, the body that governs the capital, takes little account of developments in Tema, the port city, making dialogue between these spaces complicated. The corridor is composed of cities and rural areas; fast-growing places and others that are entirely marginalized; borders that slow circulation.

This corridor can be considered as a laboratory to observe and analyze contemporary urban change. It is a product of capital and politics, but also and above all of millions of individuals wanting a roof over their heads, seeking to build homes, and to simply exist. It is also the result of informal survival strategies and urban politics. In Lagos, Porto-Novo, Cotonou, Lomé, and Accra, inhabitants are engaged in an everyday experiment – and a redefinition of the very concept of the city in its forms, timescales, and materiality – through their relationship to cement and concrete, substances that bind, link, build, and destroy individuals and spaces. In this book, I have explored several key facets of this urban corridor, which has only recently emerged as an object of scientific inquiry (Choplin and Hertzog 2020). Yet the highly complex nature of this space calls for additional research and collective investigations at different scales – macro and micro, regional and intra-urban – in order to gain a better understanding of the urban future being written in this part of the world. Like the journalist Howard W. French (2022) who wrote an article in *The Guardian* about the corridor he calls the "megalopolis," I am convinced that "coastal West Africa will shape the coming century."

Utopia/Dystopia and Afro/Africanfuturism

In 2018, the release of the blockbuster American movie *Black Panther* gave a glimpse of what could be the future of African urban materiality. In this film, superheroes were African. The film was a global success and contributed to a new popular image of Africa and its cities. It depicted the city of Birnin Zana, capital of the kingdom of Wakanda, as an ancient, hidden, yet technologically advanced, utopia in contemporary Africa. The city's design, form, and aesthetic resemble Eko Atlantic City in Lagos (Figure C.3). Yet unlike Lagos,

FIGURE C.3   Birnin Zana, Wakanda, 2018. Source: *Black Panther* Movie / MARVEL.

Birnin Zana is clean and ordered, highly technological, and it is free of street vendors, poor people, and floating slums (Guitard 2018). Birnin Zana is similar to the elite neighborhoods of contemporary Lagos, such as Banana Island, which are under surveillance and closed to the general public. Crucially, Birnin Zana is a Concrete City: the film portrays an urban metropolis blanketed in the dull gray of dried cement in the middle of the jungle. Yet, the anthropologist Émilie Guitard (2018) reports that the ideal city in *Black Panther* did not entirely meet with approval among Nigerian audiences, who considered it "a bit too 'bushy,' with too much vegetation, and not 'modern' enough." She notes that this imaginary city is a "concrete jungle," in the words of Bob Marley's song, "where life is hardest." But Émilie Guitard reminds us that "many people prefer cement to the jungle" (*ibid.*).

Black Panther, and *Wakanda Forever*, the second *Black Panther* movie released in 2022, must be put in perspective with the Afrofuturist and Africanfuturist movements. Afrofuturism is a cultural current that "combines science-fiction, techno-culture, magic realism, and non-European cosmologies, with the aim of exploring the past of so-called people of color and their condition in the present" (Mbembe 2014: 8). In philosophy, music, arts, and literature, Afrofuturism is shaped by the trajectories of human experiences in Africa and among its diasporas. Africanfuturism focuses more on African cultures, mythologies, and evolutions based in the continent and less on the diaspora influences. Several authors considered as Afrofuturists and Africanfuturists imagine in their works cities in which concrete is omnipresent. This is the case in the emblematic works of Nigerian novelist Nnedi Okorafor (2014). In her science-fiction novel, *Lagoon*, myth and monsters mix, as do ancient histories and new futures. Lagos is invaded by aliens. In the city's urban chaos, a road monster awakens: the Bone Collector, the nickname for the Lagos-Benin expressway, a dangerous stretch of highway where hundreds of fatal accidents have taken place. Okorafor magically brings the road to life as it "rises as a huge snake-like slab of concrete" and turns "into a concrete wave (…) Concrete that smelled of fresh, hot tar… and blood" (Okorafor 2014: 227). This road, which is a section of the West African urban corridor itself, made of bitumen and concrete is here characterized as a monster who swallows up urban inhabitants.

Concrete flues urban utopias/dystopias across Africa. For example, in the heart of Kinshasa, Filip De Boeck and Sammy Baloji follow and film a Congolese doctor who has erected a wildly extravagant fourteen-story health center and wellness complex, which towers over the area's existing low-lying concrete structures (De Boeck and Baloji 2015). This concrete utopia came straight from the doctor's imagination, a realization of his dream to build a modern skyscraper. In front of the camera, he explains this concrete tower "will become a model for everyone…a useful tower, inhabited and habitable." Yet his dream remains largely unrealized: the tower's construction was stalled due to lack of funds, transforming his utopian vision into a living – albeit dystopian – ruin (see Hoffman 2017 for Morovia).

Since the 2000s, Lagos in particular has also become a source of many utopian and dystopian narratives and the new icon of post-modernity. In his documentary film *Lagos Wide & Close,* the starchitect Rem Koolhaas (2007) envisaged Lagos "at the forefront of globalizing modernity." He described it as a city of informality, chaos, and at the same time a city of creativity and resourcefulness which enables residents to conjure the city out of almost nothing. He tends to depict Lagos as a work of art in the making and as a depoliticized and dehistoricized space (Gandy 2005; Fourchard 2011). This approach can lead to a romanticized, even culturalist vision of African cities. It is the opposite of African cities which are the culmination of a long process of maturation and assemblage rooted in the coexistence of the formal and the informal, self-development and state intervention, colonial and postcolonial relations, individual and collective projects, human and divine forces. The Nigerian writer Chimamanda Ngozi Adichie (2019) excels in capturing the thickness of Lagos, describing it as a city "still becoming … in a state of shifting impermanence … forward-looking…head down, hurried, unsatisfied in its own frenzy." For better or for worse, Lagos is asserting itself as the capital of twenty-first century modernity (cf. Benjamin 2012).

Toward A Post-concrete World

In her essay, *Nos Cabanes* ("Our wood cabins"), Marielle Macé (2019) suggests a lighter form of inhabiting the world, far away from the model of the Concrete City. Building a cabin could be a first step toward a larger project that seeks to reinvent collective forms of living. Her essay reminds us that Le Corbusier did not finish his life in the concrete buildings he built in Switzerland and across Europe but in a wooden hut, *"Le Cabanon,"* by the sea on the French Riviera.

At a time of eco-anxiety, collapsology, and solastalgia (Albrecht et al. 2007), the existence of this concreted world, its ruins, and its looming collapse are indicative of destructive human action and of a consumed and exploited nature. Concrete alone condenses all the ambiguity of the human presence on Earth. The very act of producing cement reveals the violence of this relationship with nature: (real) stone is calcined and crushed to produce an artificial one. At the same time, after each publication of The Intergovernmental Panel on Climate Change reports (IPCC 2022), more and more human beings are wondering about the future of the world and imagining its end. They want to understand what they live in, where the materials come from, in the same way that they wonder where their food comes and how it affects the planet around them. This demand for more material knowledge and environmental awareness is driving and forcing a global transformation of the construction economy. This book modestly contributes to the debate by analyzing urban growth and the construction boom which accompanies it in the part of the world in which they are strongest: the Global South. I have tried to take into consideration three dimensions of the city by shedding light on the links between extraction (the holes in the ground dug by excavators), construction (the reinforced concrete towers built by cranes), and the material flows on the ground (the trucks loaded with materials traveling along the corridor). In parallel with a movement to abandon fossil fuels and put an end to "carbon democracy" (Mitchell 2011), the movement to move toward a post-concrete era is becoming stronger. Limestone and sand could soon be added to the list of strategic critical materials and consequently, like rare earths, become friction materials. This awareness echoes the desire and hope to live in a less capitalistic and consumerist world, where we don't need to pour 150 tons of cement every second. It advocates a more virtuous way of building, dwelling and inhabiting in the city. Initiatives for alternative modes of occupation are sprouting around neo-rural communities, urban coopera-tives, and new forms of co-housing that call for a frugal, temporary, and Do It Yourself (DIY) urbanism. It echoes the claim expressed by some architects, like the French architect Patrick Bouchain (2006) who implores us to "build differently" (*construire autrement*), to imagine an architecture of "high human quality," as well as a "democratic urbanism" that would enable individuals and groups to act directly on living spaces.

The construction, consolidation, and multiplication of the Concrete City responds to different demands: social (for housing), political (to govern and consolidate power), and economic (to feed capitalism). At the same time, it reproduces and generates new forms of inequalities between those who can build and those who are forced to live in slums, those who can live in air-conditioned spaces, and those who are forced to live in stifling heat. The proliferation of the Concrete City raises global questions of social, spatial, and environmental justice and entails a reconceptualization of the unequal relations between the Global North and the Global South. In this research, using a postcolonial approach, I showed how concrete epitomized unequal colonial power relations which have persisted into the present – notably, the continued extractivism which dominates the sector. Africa's earliest concrete cities were colonial ones: concrete allowed the expansion of capitalism in the colonies by facilitating the cheap, efficient, and secure development of colo-nial urban enclaves. It is also the result of the imaginary success linked to the West, which concrete embodies. Colonial authorities glorified concrete cities, associated to western modernity, while denigrating African architecture and vernacular ways of living; they denied the very historicity of African cities built with materials perceived as unmodern and temporary. Nowadays, the large western groups and lobbies, and in particular those of construction, logistics, and networked services, still largely dominate.

But the Concrete City that is taking shape today is not just a neo-colonial city dominated by the interests of the countries of the North alone. It is also a postcolonial city that has been re-appropriated and transformed by its inhab-itants who assign concrete new social values. The Concrete City is the result of local particularities, a city that is celebrated and claimed for its comfort and (over)consumption, sometimes with extravagance and excess, with pride and fear. In West Africa, the elites, the middle classes and also the poor who live there want to profit from the "society of affluence and freedom" (Charbonnier 2021) that the West enjoyed before them. It would be unacceptable and unfair to ask people in the Global South to renounce affluence and comfort, to be accountable for their carbon footprint and to pay the environmental debts of the northern world. On the contrary, as Olúfẹmi O. Táíwò (2022) explains, the West should pay reparations to the Global South for slavery, colonization, and climate change crises. This stance is in line with Malcolm Ferdinand (2022) who proposes a "decolonial ecology" drawing on research conducted in the Caribbean. He denounces the different forms of imperialism that have destroyed the landscape and invites us to rethink living together by considering other relationships to Earth and relying on other ontologies. This call echoes decolonial movements more broadly. Arturo Escobar (2020) proposes the expression "pluriversal politics" to show how the struggles and cosmologies of indigenous communities open alternative visions to inhabit the planet, a collective inhabitation in which human beings live alongside nonhumans, both living and nonliving. This issue of a better cohabitation between the living/nonliving, human/nonhuman is at the heart of many contemporary reflections on climate and environment. In *Staying with the trouble*, Donna Haraway (2016: 47) explains that if we want to survive, we will need to behave like the little Californian spider, Pimoa cthulhu, which, "as it weaves its threads, continuously repairs its web, remakes the links or finds it new attachment points." This spider is akin to the matsutake mushroom described by Anna Tsing (2015), which can grow in the ruins of capitalism. And in the human world, the spider and the mushroom resonate with the analogy of the mender employed by Bruno Latour (2021), who contrasts the extractors [*extracteurs*], who perforate and wreck the planet, with the menders [*ravaudeurs*], who are responsible for darning and repairing the world so that the human species can survive and the planet can remain habitable. Achille Mbembe (2020: 25) also addresses this issue of cohabitation and habitability, explaining that "the decisive struggles of this century will be fought around the long-term survival of the human species across the entire surface of the earth." For him, the future of the human species began and will continue to be linked to Africa: "it is on the African continent, the birthplace of humanity, that the question of the earth will now be posed in the most unexpected, the most complex and the most paradoxical way. It is here, indeed, that the possibilities of decay are most glaring. But it is also here that the opportunities for creative metastasis are the most mature" (*ibid.*: 25). Felwine Sarr (2020) proposes the concept of "Afrotopia" to think of Africa and African cities as places of alternatives, of possibilities, and of new imaginaries and ways of being in the world. Mbembe and Sarr (2017) suggest writing the *"Afrique-Monde"* to rethink the world from the African continent, because it already appears to be one of the main theaters where the future of the planet will be played out. According to the United Nations projections, Africa is anticipated to host 40% of the world's population by the end of the century. It is indeed where original ways of being in the world and producing the city are being and will be authored. For the moment, African cities highlight the contradictions of our material and materialist societies: they prefigure both the finitude of our world but also its future. As such, they should be seen as places that contain possibilities – the "creative metastasis" announced by Mbembe – for living and inhabiting together, for living with the human and nonhuman world, with the voodoo spirits or other divinities, with ancient myth and new futures; places in which to listen to what the nature and elements have to say; to feel earth, air, fire, and water rather than the hot surface of concrete; to devise real utopias from this gray matter in order once again to see the world in vivid color.

References

Aalbers, M.B. (2016). *The Financialization of Housing: A political economy approach*. Routledge. https://doi.org/10.4324/9781315668666.

Acey, C. (2018). Rise of the synthetic city: Eko Atlantic and practices of dispossession and repossession in Nigeria. In: *Disassembled Cities: Social and Spatial Strategies to Reassemble Communities* (ed. E.L. Sweet). Abingdon/New York: Routledge.

Adama, O. (2018). Urban imaginaries: funding mega infrastructure projects in Lagos, Nigeria. *GeoJournal* 83 (2): 257–274. https://doi.org/10.1007/s10708-016-9761-8.

Adelekan, I.O. (2020). Urban dynamics, everyday hazards and disaster risks in Ibadan, Nigeria. *Environment and Urbanization* 32 (1): 213–232.

Adeniyi-Ogunyankin, G.A. (2019). "The city of our dream": Owambe urbanism and low-income women's resistance in Ibadan, Nigeria. *International Journal of Urban and Regional Research* 43 (3): 423–441.

Adichie, C.N. (2013). *Americanah*. Alfred A. Knopf.

Adichie, C. N. (2019). Still Becoming: At Home In Lagos. *Esquire*. https://www.esquire.com/uk/culture/a27283913/still-becoming-at-home-in-lagos-with-chimamanda-ngozi-adichie.

Agossou, N. (2011). Paradoxes de l'étalement urbain à Porto-Novo: dynamique démographique et économique vs dynamique foncière. *Les Cahiers d'Outre-Mer* https://doi.org/10.4000/com.6370.

Akindès, F. and Kouamé, S.Y. (2019). L'immixtion « par le bas » des technologies digitales dans la vie urbaine africaine. *Afrique contemporaine* 269-270 (1): 87.

Akinola, A.O. (2019). Rent seeking and industrial growth in Africa: the case of Dangote's cement industry. *The Rest* 9 (1): 6–17.

Akinyoade, A., and Uche, C. (2016). Dangote Cement: An African success story? African Studies Centre Leiden, ASC Working Paper 131/2016, 1–40.

Akinyoade, A. and Uche, C. (2018). Development built on crony capitalism? The case of Dangote cement. *Business History* 60 (6): 833–858. https://doi.org/10.1080/00076791.2017.1341492.

Akinyoade, A., Dietz, T., and Uche, C. (2017). *Entrepreneurship in Africa*. Leiden: BRILL.

Akrich, M. (2010). Comment décrire les objets techniques? *Techniques & culture* 54-55: 205–219. https://doi.org/10.4000/tc.4999.

Albrecht, G., Sartore, G.-M., Connor, L. et al. (2007). Solastalgia: the distress caused by environmental change. *Australasian Psychiatry* 15 (1_suppl): S95–S98.

Anger, R. and Joffroy, T. (2014). *Etat de l'art: Utilisation traditionnelles et contemporaines de fibres végétales dans la construction*. Craterre.

Antoine, P., Dubresson, A., & Manou-Savina, A. (1987). *Abidjan « côté cours »: Pour comprendre la qeuestion de l'habitat*. Paris: Karthala.

Appadurai, A. (1986). *The Social Life of Things: Commodities in Cultural Perspective*. Cambridge: Cambridge University Press.

Appel, H. (2019). *The Licit Life of Capitalism: U.S. Oil in Equatorial Guinea*. Durham: Duke University Press.

Appel, H., Mason, A., and Watts, M. (2015). *Subterranean Estates: Life Worlds of Oil and Gas*. Cornell University Press.

Archambault, J. (2018). 'One beer, one block': concrete aspiration and the stuff of transformation in a Mozambican suburb. *Journal of the Royal Anthropological Institute* 24 (4): 692–708. https://doi.org/10.1111/1467-9655.12912.

Archambault, J.S. (2021). Concrete violence, indifference and future-making in Mozambique. *Critique of Anthropology* 41 (1): 43–64.

Ardayfio-Schandorf, E., Yankson, P.W.K., and Bertrand, M. (2012). *The Mobile City of Accra*. African Books Collective.

Arsan, A. (2014). *Interlopers of Empire: The Lebanese Diaspora in Colonial French West Africa*. Oxford University Press.

Assogba, G. (2014). L'obsession d'habiter sa propre maison à Lomé: quel impact sur la dynamique spatiale? *Les Cahiers d'Outre-Mer* https://doi.org/10.4000/com.6443.

Augiseau, V. and Kim, E. (2021). Inflows and outflows from material stocks of buildings and networks and their space-differentiated drivers: the case study of the Paris region. *Sustainability* 13 (3): 1376.

Aveline-Dubach, N. (2016). Land and real Estate in Northeast Asia, new approaches in an era of financialization. *Issues & Studies* 52: 4. doi: 10.1142/S101325111602001.

Balandier, G. (1985). *Sociologie des Brazzavilles noires*. Paris: Presses de Sciences Po.

Banégas, R. and Warnier, J.-P. (2001). Nouvelles figures de la réussite et du pouvoir. *Politique africaine* 82 (2): 5–23.

Banerjee, A.V. and Duflo, E. (2011). *Poor Economics: A Radical Rethinking of the Way to Fight Global Poverty*. India: Random House.

Banque Africaine de Développement (BAD) (2016). *Rapport Annuel 2016, Département Infrastructures*. BAD: Villes et Développement Urbain.

Barles, S. (2010). Society, energy and materials: the contribution of urban metabolism studies to sustainable urban development issues. *Journal of Environmental Planning and Management* 53 (4): 439–455. https://doi.org/10.1080/09640561003703772

Baudrillard, J. (1970). *La société de consommation, ses mythes, ses structures*. Paris: Denoël.

Bayart, J. F. (1993). *The State in Africa: The Politics of the Belly*. Lodon and New York: Longman.

Bayart, J. F. and Warnier, J. (2004). *Matière à politique. Le pouvoir, les corps et les choses*. Paris: Editions Karthala.

Beiser, V. (2018). *The World in a Grain: The Story of Sand and how it Transformed Civilization*. Riverhead Books.

Benjamin, W. (2012). *Paris, capitale du XIXe siècle: Le livre des passages*, 3e. du Cerf).

Bennett, J. (2010). *Vibrant Matter – A Political Ecology of Things.* Duke University Press.

Bennett, T. and Joyce, P. (2013). *Material Powers: Cultural Studies, History and the Material Turn.* London: Routledge.

Beresford, A. (2016). Africa rising? *Review of African Political Economy* 43 (147): 1–7. https://doi.org/10.1080/03056244.2016.1149369.

Bertin, C. (2021). Building churches for the City-to-come: Pentecostal urbanization and aspirational place-making in the 'rurban' areas of southwestern Benin. In: *Religious Urbanization and Moral Economies of Development in Africa* (ed. D. Garbin, S. Coleman and G. Millington). Bloomsbury.

Bertrand, M. (2001). Femmes et marchés fonciers urbains: mesures et déterminants d'une percée à Bamako, Mali. *Autrepart* 19: 29–48.

Bertrand, M. (2011). *De Bamako à Accra.* Paris, Karthala: Mobilités urbaines et ancrages locaux en Afrique de l'Ouest.

Bertrand, M. (2013). Fils, frères, pères: Masculinités sous contrats, du nord à la capitale du Mali. *Cahiers d'études africaines* 53 (209-210): 323–344. https://doi.org/10.4000/etudesafricaines.17348.

Biehler, A., Choplin A., Morelle M. (2015). "Social housing in Africa: a model to be (re)invented?", *Metropolitics*, URL: https://metropolitics.org/Social-housing-in-Africa-a-model.html

Bigon, L. (2016). *French Colonial Dakar: The Morphogenesis of an African Regional Capital.* Manchester: Manchester University Press.

Blaszkiewicz, H. (2021). Using the flow regimes framework to de-hierarchise the analysis of commercial movements: case studies from the central African Copperbelt. In: *Transactions of the Institute of British Geographers*, 2021. doi: 10.1111/tran.12439

Blundo, G. (2018). Le dragon et le fétiche. Les vies globales des motos chinoises en Afrique de l'Ouest. Conference at the Institut Français du Togo.

Blundo, G., and Olivier de Sardan, J.-P. (2007). Etat et corruption en Afrique. Editions Karthala. https://doi.org/10.3917/kart.blund.2007.01

Boateng, F. G. (2021). Ghana's unstable building problem is about more than lax regulation. *The Conversation.* https://theconversation.com/ghanas-unstable-building-problem-is-about-more-than-lax-regulation-153201.

Bock, S. (2018). *Translations of Urban Regulation in Relations between Kigali (Rwanda) and Singapore.* LIT Verlag Münster.

Bon, B. (2021). Invisible sprawl: land, money and politics at the rural-urban Interface in Kenya. *disP - The Planning Review* 57 (3): 33–49.

Bouchain, P. (2006). *Construire autrement: comment faire ?* Arles: Actes Sud.

Bouchain, P. (2010). Introduction. In: *Learning from Vernacular: Pour Une Nouvelle Architecture Vernaculaire* (ed. P. Frey). Arles: Actes Sud.

Bredeloup, S. (2007). *La Diams'pora du fleuve Sénégal: Sociologie des migrations africaines.* Presses universitaires du Midi.

Brenner, N. (2004). *New State Spaces: Urban Governance and the Rescaling of Statehood.* Oxford: Oxford University Press.

Brenner, N. and Schmid, C. (2015). Towards a new epistemology of the urban? *City* 19 (2-3): 151–182. https://doi.org/10.1080/13604813.2015.1014712.

Brenner, N. and Theodore, N. (2002). Cities and the geographies of "actually existing neoliberalism". *Antipode* 34 (3): 349–379. https://doi.org/10.1111/1467-8330.00246.

Brenner, N., Peck, J., and Theodore, N. (2010). Variegated neoliberalization: geographies, modalities, pathways. *Global Networks* 10 (2): 182–222. https://doi.org/10.1111/j.1471-0374.2009.00277.x.

Bridge, G. (2015). The hole world: scales and spaces of extraction. *Scenario Journal.* 5, https://scenariojournal.com/article/the-hole-world.

Brivio, A. (2012). *Il vodu in Africa. Metamorfosi di un culto.* Roma: Viella.

Buire, C. (2014). Suburbanisms in Africa? Spatial growth and social transformation in new urban peripheries: introduction to the cluster. *African Studies* 73 (2): 241–244.

Byiers, B., Karaki K., and Vanheukelom J. (2017). Regional Markets, Politics and value chains: The case of West African cement. *European Centre For Development Policy Management 216.* Available at: http://www.ecdpm.org/dp216.

Caldeira, T.P. (2017). Peripheral urbanization: autoconstruction, transversal logics, and politics in cities of the global south. *Environment and Planning D: Society and Space* 35 (1): 3–20. https://doi.org/10.1177/0263775816658479.

Calder, B. (2016). *Raw Concrete: The Beauty of Brutalism.* William Heinemann.

Canel, P., Delis, P., and Girard, C. (1990). *Construire la ville africaine: histoires comparées de chantiers d'habitation autoproduits.* Paris: L'Harmattan.

Cankat, A., Awal, H.M., Moles, O. et al. (2019). Co-construire de l'expertise inclusive des connaissances locales. *Afrique contemporaine* 269–270 (1): 283–306.

Cassiman, A. (2011). *Architectures of Belonging/Inhabiting Worlds in Rural West Africa.* Antwerp: BAI publishers.

Chabi, M. (2013). *Métropolisation et dynamiques périurbaines: cas de l'espace urbain de Cotonou.* Thèse de doctorat en géographie: Université de Nanterre.

Chabot, L., Keita, P.A., and Varnai, B. (2018). *Le programme d'appui à la reconstruction de la Fédération Sénégalaise des Habitants – vers un urbanisme participatif et solidaire.* Urbanités.

Chalfin, B. (2004). *Shea Butter Republic: State Power, Global Markets, and the Making of an Indigenous Commodity.* New York: Routledge.

Chalfin, B. (2010). *Neoliberal Frontiers: An Ethnography of Sovereignty in West Africa.* Chicago; London: The University of Chicago Press.

Chamoiseau, P. (1992). *Texaco.* Paris: Editions Gallimard.

Charbonnier, P. (2021). *Affluence and Freedom: An Environmental History of Political Ideas.* Cambridge, UK; Medford, MA: Polity Press.

Choplin, A. (2020a). Cementing Africa: cement flows and city making in the west African corridor (Accra-Lomé-Cotonou-Lagos). *Urban Studies* 57 (9): https://doi.org/10.1177/0042098019851949.

Choplin, A. (2020b). *Matière Grise de l'Urbain, La vie du ciment en Afrique.* Genève: MétisPresses.

Choplin, A. and Franck, A. (2010). A glimpse of Dubai in Khartoum and Nouakchott, prestige urban projects on the margins of the Arab world. *Built Environment* 36 (2): 192–205.

Choplin, A. and Hertzog, A. (2020). The west-African corridor, from Abidjan to Lagos: a mega-city region under construction. In: *Handbook of Megacities and Megacity-Region* (ed. D. Labbé and A. Sorensen), Northampton: Edward Elgar Publishing, 206–222.

Choplin, A. and Lozivit, M. (2019). Mapping a slum: learning from participatory mapping and digital innovation in Cotonou (Benin). *Cybergeo: European Journal of Geography* https://doi.org/10.4000/cybergeo.32949.

Choplin, A. and Pliez, O. (2018). *La mondialisation des pauvres, loin de Wall Street de Davos*. Paris: Seuil.

Ciavolella R., and Choplin A. (2018). *Cotonou(s). Histoire d'une ville sans Histoire*. Cahiers de la Fondation Zinsou, IRD.

Ciavolella, R. and Wittersheim, E. (2016). *Introduction à l'anthropologie du politique*. De Boeck supérieur.

Cirolia, L.R. and Berrisford, S. (2017). 'Negotiated planning': diverse trajectories of implementation in Nairobi, Addis Ababa, and Harare. *Habitat International* 59: 71–79.

Cook, I. (2004). Follow the thing: papaya. *Antipode* 36 (4): 642–664. https://doi.org/10.1111/j.1467-8330.2004.00441.x.

Cooper, F. (1995). *Africa in the World: Capitalism, Empire, Nation-State*. Cambridge, MA: Harvard University Press.

Coralli, M. and Houénoudé, D. (2013). La patrimonialisation à l'occidentale et ses conséquences sur un territoire africain: Porto-Novo au Bénin. *Espaces et sociétés* 152–153 (1): 85–101. https://doi.org/10.3917/esp.152.0085.

Coralli, M. and Palumbo, M.A. (2011). Entre singularité et similitude: Cotonou, une ville en changement. *Lieux communs* 14 (2011): 59–93.

Côté-Roy, L. and Moser, S. (2019). 'Does Africa not deserve shiny new cities?' The power of seductive rhetoric around new cities in Africa. *Urban Studies* 56 (12): 2391–2407. https://doi.org/10.1177/0042098018793032.

Courland, R. (2011). *Concrete Planet: The Strange and Fascinating Story of the world's most Common Man-Made Material*. Prometheus Books.

Cousin, S. (2013). Extensions du domaine de la restauration. Porto-Novo capitale. In: *Porto-Novo: Patrimoine et développement* (ed. C. Mengin and A. Godonou), 441–460. Paris/Porto-Novo: Publications de la Sorbonne/École du patrimoine africain.

Croese, S. (2018). Global urban policymaking in Africa: a view from Angola through the redevelopment of the bay of Luanda. *International Journal of Urban and Regional Research* 42 (2): 198–209.

Damasio, A. (2019). *Les Furtifs*. La Volte.

Dangote Cement Plc (2021). *Annual Report and Accounts 2021: resilience and growth*. Lagos: Dangote Cement Plc. Available at https://dangotecement.com/wp-content/uploads/2022/06/new-Dangote-cement-AR2021.pdf

Datta, A. (2021). Fast Urbanism: Between Speed, Time and Urban Futures. *Transcient space and Societies*. https://doi.org/10.34834/2019.0017.

Datta, A. and Shaban, A. (ed.) (2017). *Mega-Urbanization in the Global South: Fast Cities: And New Urban Utopias of the Postcolonial State*. London: Routledge.

Davesne, A. (1996). *Les premières lectures de Mamadou et Bineta: Livre de lecture et de français à l'usage des écoles africaines: cours préparatoire 2e année*. Edicef.

Dawson, K. (2021). Geologising urban political ecology (UPE): the urbanisation of sand in Accra, Ghana. *Antipode* anti.12718.

De Boeck, F. and Baloji, S. (2015). The Tower. A Concrete Utopia. Notes on a video-installation in (ed. M.J. Holm and M.M. Kallenhauge), 84–88. *Africa: Architecture, culture, identity*. Humlebaek: Louisiana museum of art.

De Boeck, F. and Baloji, S. (2016). *Suturing the City. Living Together in Congo's Urban Worlds*. London: Autograph ABP.

De Boeck, F. and Plissart, M.-F. (2004). *Kinshasa: Tales of the Invisible City*. Ludion: Royal Museum for Central Africa; Vlaams Architectuurinstituut VAi.

De Certeau, M. (1990). *L'invention du quotidien*. Paris: Gallimard.

Degani, M. (2020). Air in unexpected places. *The Cambridge Journal of Anthropology* 38 (2): 125–145.

Deleuze, G. and Guattari, F. (1980). *Mille plateaux*. Paris: Éditions de minuit.

Despret, V. (2016). *What Would Animals Say if we Asked the Right Questions?* Minneapolis (MN): University of Minnesota Press.

Di Nunzio, M. (2019). Not my job: architecture, responsibility and inequalities in an African metropolis. *Anthropological Quarterly* 92 (2): 375–402.

Dobler, G. and Kesselring, R. (2019). Swiss extractivism: Switzerland's role in Zambia's copper sector. *The Journal of Modern African Studies* 57 (2): 223–245, 228.

Dorier, E., Tafuri, C., and Agossou, N. (2013). Porto-Novo dans l'aire métropolitaine littorale du Sud-Bénin: quelles dynamiques citadines? In: *Porto-Novo: patrimoine et développement* (ed. C. Mengin and A. Godonou). Paris: Publications de la Sorbonne.

Dorier-Apprill, E. and Domingo, E. (2004). Les nouvelles échelles de l'urbain en Afrique. Métropolisation et nouvelles dynamiques territoriales sur le littoral béninois. *Vingtième Siècle* Revue d'histoire 81 (1): 41–54.

Drozdz M, Guironnet A., Halbert L. (2021). "Cities in the Age of Financialization", *Metropolitics*. URL: https://metropolitics.org/Cities-in-the-Age-of-Financialization.html.

Dubresson, A. (1989). *Ville et industries en Côte d'Ivoire: pour une géographie de l'accumulation urbaine*. Paris: Karthala.

Ellis, S. and Fauré, Y.-A. (1995). *Entreprises et entrepreneurs africains*. Paris: Karthala.

Escobar, A. (2020). *Pluriversal Politics: The Real and the Possible*. Durham: Duke University Press.

Eyifa-Dzidzienyo, G.A.M. (2012). Social construction and the invisible gender roles in Talensi house construction. *International Journal of Ethnography and Archaeology of the University of München Berlin* 53 (1/2): 86–101. Waxmann.

Ezeoha, A., Uche, C., and Ujunwa, A. (2020). Crossing the borderline in strategic corporate philanthropy: Dangote and the construction of cement roads in Nigeria. *Business Ethics: A European Review* 29 (1): 70–81. https://doi.org/10.1111/beer.12249.

Fält, L. (2016). From shacks to skyscrapers: post-Political City visioning in Accra. *Urban Forum* 27 (4): 465–486.

Fält, L. (2019). New cities and the emergence of 'Privatized Urbanism' in Ghana. *Built Environment* 44 (4): 438–460. (23), https://doi.org/info:doi/10.2148/benv.44.4.438.

Faty, H. (1973). *Architecture for the Poor. An Experiment in Rural Egypt.* The University of Chicago Press.

Fauveaud, G. (2020). The new Frontiers of housing financialization in Phnom Penh, Cambodia: the condominium boom and the foreignization of housing Markets in the Global South. *Housing Policy Debate* 1–19. https://doi.org/10.1080/1051 1482.2020.1714692.

Fayemiwo, M.A. and Neal, M.M. (2013). *Aliko Mohammad Dangote: The Biography of the Richest Black Person in the World.* Houston, TX: Strategic Book Publishing and Rights Co.

Ferdinand, M. (2022). *A Decolonial Ecology: Thinking from the Caribbean World.* Cambridge: Polity Press.

Ferguson, J. (1999). *Expectations of Modernity: Myths and Meanings of Urban Life on the Zambian Copperbelt.* Berkeley: University of California Press.

Ferguson, J. (2006). *Global Shadows.* Duke University Press.

Fontein, J. and Smith, C. (2023). Introduction: the Stuff of African cities. *Africa* 93(1).

Forty, A. (2012). *Concrete and Culture: A Material History.* Reaktion Books.

Forty, A. (2019). 'Concrete? It's communist': the rise and fall of the utopian socialist material. *The Guardian.* https://www.theguardian.com/cities/2019/feb/27/concrete-its-communist-the-rise-and-fall-of-the-utopian-socialist-material

Foucault, M. (1978). La gouvernementalité. Cours du 1/2/1978. In: *Dits et écrits. T. III*, 635–657. Paris: Gallimard.

Fourchard, L. (2011). Lagos, Koolhaas and partisan politics in Nigeria. *International Journal of Urban and Regional Research* 35 (1): 40–56.

Fourchard, L. (2012). Between world history and state formation: new perspectives on Africa's cities. *The Journal of African History* 52 (2): 223–248.

Fourchard, L. (2021). *Classify, Exclude, Police: Urban Lives in South Africa and Nigeria.* Oxford: Wiley.

French, H. W. (2022). Megalopolis: how coastal west Africa will shape the coming century. *The Guardian.* https://www.theguardian.com/world/2022/oct/27/megalopolis-how-coastal-west-africa-will-shape-the-coming-century.

Fry, M. (2013). Cement, carbon dioxide, and the 'necessity' narrative: a case study of Mexico. *Geoforum* 49: 127–138.

Furlong, K. (2020). Geographies of infrastructure 1: economies. *Progress in Human Geography* 44 (3): 572–582. https://doi.org/10.1177/0309132519850913.

Gandy, M. (2002). *Concrete and Clay: Reworking Nature in New York City.* The MIT Press.

Gandy, M. (2005). Learning from Lagos. *New Left Review* 33: 37–53.

Gandy, M. (2014). *The Fabric of Space: Water, Modernity, and the Urban Imagination.* Cambridge, Massachusetts: The MIT Press.

Garcier, R., Rocher, L., and Verdeil, É. (2017). Introduction: circulation des matières, économies de la circularité. *Flux* 2 (2): 1–7. https://doi.org/10.3917/flux1.108.0001.

Gastrow, C. (2017). Cement citizens: housing, demolition and political belonging in Luanda, Angola. *Citizenship Studies* 21 (2): 224–239. https://doi.org/10.1080/13621025.2017.1279795.

Gereffi, G. and Korzeniewicz, M. (ed.) (1994). *Commodity Chains and Global Capitalism.* Westport: Greenwood Press.

Gervais-Lambony, P. (1994). *De Lomé à Harare. Le fait citadin: images et pratiques des villes africaines*. Paris: Karthala, IFRA.

Gervais-Lambony, P. and Nyassogbo, G. (ed.) (2007). *Lomé: Dynamiques d'une Ville Africaine*. Paris: Karthala.

Gillespie, T. (2016). Accumulation by urban dispossession: struggles over urban space in Accra, Ghana. *Transactions of the Institute of British Geographers* 41 (1): 66–77.

Gillespie, T. (2020). The real estate frontier. *International Journal of Urban and Regional Research* 44 (4): 599–616. https://doi.org/10.1111/1468-2427.12900.

Glélé, G. (2015). *La périurbanisation et les dynamiques foncières sur le plateau d'Allada (Sud-Bénin: L'espace témoin de la commune d'Abomey-Calavi)*, Thèse de doctorat, Université d'Abomey-Calavi, Bénin.

Gluckman, M. (1960). Tribalism in modem British Central Africa. *Cahiers d'Études africaines*: 55–70.

Goldman, M. (2011). Speculative urbanism and the making of the next World City: speculative urbanism in Bangalore. *International Journal of Urban and Regional Research* 35 (3): 555–581. https://doi.org/10.1111/j.1468-2427.2010.01001.x.

Goodfellow, T. (2017). Urban fortunes and skeleton Cityscapes: real estate and late urbanization in Kigali and Addis Ababa. *International Journal of Urban and Regional Research* 41 (5): 786–803. https://doi.org/10.1111/1468-2427.12550.

Goodfellow, T. (2018). Seeing political settlements through the City: a framework for comparative analysis of urban transformation: seeing political settlements through the City. *Development and Change* 49 (1): 199–222. https://doi.org/10.1111/dech.12361.

Goodfellow, T. (2020). Finance, infrastructure and urban capital: the political economy of African 'gap-filling'. *Review of African Political Economy* 47 (164): 256–274. https://doi.org/10.1080/03056244.2020.1722088.

Gough, K.V. and Yankson, P. W. K. (2000). Land Markets in African Cities: the case of peri-urban Accra, Ghana. *Urban Studies* 37 (13): 2485–2500. https://doi.org/10.1080/00420980020080651.

Gough, K., V., Yankson, P. W. K., Wilby, R. L. et al. (2019). 'Vulnerability to extreme weather events in cities: implications for infrastructure and livelihoods', *Journal of the British Academy* 7 (S2): 155–81.

Gra, R. (2019). *De la maison de terre à la villa de béton. Transformation des modes d'édifier de terre en pays Lamba rural*, Mémoire de master en anthropologie, EHESS-Goethe Universität.

Graham, S. and Marvin, S. (2001). *Splintering Urbanism: Networked Infrastructures*. Technological Mobilities and the Urban Condition: Psychology Press.

Grant, R. (2009). *Globalizing City: The Urban and Economic Transformation of Accra*. Ghana: Syracuse University Press.

Grant, R., Oteng-Ababio, M., and Sivilien, J. (2019). Greater Accra's new urban extension at Ningo-Prampram : urban promise or urban peril? *International*

Planning Studies 24 (3–4): 325–340. https://doi.org/10.1080/13563475.2019.1664896.

Gregson, N., Crang, M., Ahamed, F. et al. (2010). Following things of rubbish value: end-of-life ships, 'chock-chocky' furniture and the Bangladeshi middle class consumer. *Geoforum* 41 (6): 846–854. https://doi.org/10.1016/j.geoforum.2010.05.007.

Griaule, M. (1954). The Dogon of the French Sudan (Mali). In: *African Worlds. Studies in the Cosmological Ideas and Social Values of African Peoples* (ed. D. Forde). London: Oxford University Press.

Guitard, E. (2018). Le Wakanda de « Black Panther: une Afrique du futur en miniature?, *Carnets de Terrain, Blog de la revue Terrain*, https://blogterrain.hypotheses.org/9982.

Guyer, J.I. (2004). *Marginal Gains: Monetary Transactions in Atlantic Africa*, 1e. University of Chicago Press.

Habert, G., Miller, S.A., John, V.M. et al. (2020). Environmental impacts and decarbonization strategies in the cement and concrete industries. *Nature Reviews Earth & Environment* 1: 559–573. https://doi.org/10.1038/s43017-020-0093-3.

Halbert, L. and Attuyer, K. (2016). Introduction: the financialisation of urban production: conditions, mediations and transformations. *Urban Studies* 53 (7): 1347–1361. https://doi.org/10.1177/0042098016635420.

Haraway, D. (2016). *Staying with the Trouble. Making Kin in the Chthulucene*. Durham: Duke University Press.

Harvey, D. (1989). From managerialism to entrepreneurialism: the transformation in urban governance in late capitalism. *Geografiska Annaler. Series B, Human Geography* 71 (1): 3–17. https://doi.org/10.2307/490503.

Harvey, D. (2001). *Spaces of Capital: Towards a Critical Geography*. New York: Routledge.

Harvey, D. (2016). *Abstract from the Concrete*. Sternberg Press.

Harvey, P. (2010). Cementing relations: the materiality of roads and public spaces in provincial Peru. *Social Analysis* 54 (2): https://doi.org/10.3167/sa.2010.540203.

Harvey, P. and Knox, H. (2015). *Roads: An Anthropology of Infrastructure and Expertise*, 1e. Cornell University Press.

Haynes, J. (2016). *Nollywood: The Creation of Nigerian Film Genres*. The University of Chicago Press.

Heidegger, M. (1951). Building, dwelling, thinking. In: *Poetry, Language, Thought*, translated by Albert Hofstadter. New York: Harper & Row, English version 1971.

Herbert, C.W. and Murray, M.J. (2015). Building from scratch: new cities, privatized urbanism and the spatial restructuring of Johannesburg after apartheid. *International Journal of Urban and Regional Research* 39 (3): 471–494. https://doi.org/10.1111/1468-2427.12180.

Hertzog, A. (2020). *The Lagos Abidjan Corridor – Migration Driven Urbanisation in West Africa*. ETH Zürich PhD.

Herz, M., Schröder, I., Focketyn, H. et al. (ed.) (2015). *African Modernism: The Architecture of Independence*. Zurich, Suisse: Park Books.

Heynen, N., Kaika, M., and Swyngedouw, E. (ed.) (2006). *In the Nature of Cities: Urban Political Ecology and the Politics of Urban Metabolism*. Routledge.

Hibou, B. (1999). *Priviatizing the State*. Columbia University Press.

Hilgers, M. (2012). Contribution à une anthropologie des villes secondaires. *Cahiers d'études africaines* 205: 29–55. https://doi.org/10.4000/etudesafricaines.16957.

Hoffman, D. (2017). *Monrovia Modern: Urban Form and Political Imagination in Liberia*. Durham: Duke University Press.

Huet, J.-M., Chakroun F. (2020). Le Digital Banking en Afrique, BearingPoint, https://www.bearingpoint.com/fr-fr/notre-succes/publications/le-digital-banking-en-afrique.

Idemudia, U. and Amaeshi, K. (ed.) (2019). *Africapitalism: Sustainable Business and Development in Africa*. London: Routledge https://doi.org/10.4324/9781315559346.

Igué, O.J. and Soule, B.G. (1992). *L'Etat entrepôt au Bénin: Commerce informel ou solution à la crise?* Paris: Karthala.

Ingold, T. (2002). *The Perception of the Environment: Essays on Livelihood, Dwelling and Skill*. Routledge https://doi.org/10.4324/9780203466025.

Ingold, T. (2012). Toward an ecology of materials. *Annual Review of Anthropology* 41 (1): 427–442. https://doi.org/10.1146/annurev-anthro-081309-145920.

Ingold, T. (2017). Surface Visions. *Theory, Culture and Society* 34 (7–8): 99–108.

INSAE (2013). *Recensement général de la population et de l'Habitat*. Cotonou.

INSAE (2020). *Grands traits du commerce extérieur du Bénin: Note de publication*. Cotonou.

Jaglin, S. (1995). *Gestion urbaine partagée à Ouagadougou: Pouvoirs et périphéries (1983–1991)*. Paris: Karthala.

Jappe, A. (2020). *Béton: Arme de construction massive du capitalisme*. Paris: Echappée.

Jedlowski, A. (2019). Afriques audiovisuelles: appréhender les transformations contemporaines au prisme du capitalisme global. *Politique Africaine* Karthala 153 (1).

Kaika, M. (2005). *City of Flows: Modernity, Nature, and the City*. Psychology Press.

Kanai, J.M. and Schindler, S. (2019). Peri-urban promises of connectivity: linking project-led polycentrism to the infrastructure scramble. *Environment and Planning A: Economy and Space* 51 (2): 302–322. https://doi.org/10.1177/0308518X18763370.

Karaman, O., Sawyer, L., Schmid, C., and Wong, K.P. (2020). Plot by plot: Plotting urbanism as an ordinary process of urbanisation. *Antipode* 52 (4): 1122–1151. https://doi.org/10.1111/anti.12626.

Keil, R. (2005). Progress report—urban political ecology. *Urban Geography* 26 (7): 640–651. https://doi.org/10.2747/0272-3638.26.7.640.

Kernen, A. and Khan-Mohammad, G. (2014). La révolution des produits chinois en Afrique Consommation de masse et nouvelle culture matérielle. *Politique africaine* 134 (2): 111. https://doi.org/10.3917/polaf.134.0111.

Khan-Mohammad, G. (2016). Ce Made in China qui fait bouger l'Afrique: Motos Chinoises et Entrepreneuriat au Burkina Faso. In: *Entrepreneurs africains et chinois: les impacts sociaux d'une rencontre particulière* (ed. K. Giese and L. Marfaing), 271–303. Paris: Karthala.

Knowles, C. (2014). *Flip-Flop: A Journey through Globalisation's Backroads*. London: PlutoPress.

Knight Frank, K. (2022). *Africa Report 2022/2023 – Real Estate Investment opportunities and insight*. Dubai: Knight Franck. https://content.knightfrank.com/resources/knightfrank.com/reports/africareport/the-africa-report-2022.pdf.

Konlani, N. (2015) Ouverture et exploitation des carrières de sable, une menace du foncier agricole autour de l'agglomération de Lomé (Togo), *Revue de géographie du laboratoire Leïdi* – ISSN 0851 –N°13.

Koolhaas, R. (2007). *Lagos: How it Works*. Lars Muller Publishers.

Körling, G. (2020). Bricks, documents and pipes: material politics and urban development in Niamey, Niger. *City & Society* 32 (1): 23–46. https://doi.org/10.1111/ciso.12240.

Labbé, D. and Sorensen, A. (ed.) (2020). *Handbook of Megacities and Megacity-Region*. Edward Elgar.

Larkin, B. (2013). The politics and poetics of infrastructure. *Annual Review of Anthropology* 42 (1): 327–343. https://doi.org/10.1146/annurev-anthro-092412-155522.

Larmer, M. and Laterza, V. (2017). Contested wealth: social and political mobilisation in extractive communities in Africa. *The Extractive Industries and Society* 4 (4): 701–706.

Latour, B. (2005). *Reassembling the Social: An Introduction to Actor-Network-Theory*. Oxford University Press.

Latour, B. (2021). *Où suis-je ? Leçons du confinement à l'usage des terrestres*. Seuil: Empêcheurs de penser rond.

Lavigne Delville, P. (2010). La réforme foncière rurale au Bénin: émergence et mise en question d'une politique instituante dans un pays sous régime d'aide. *Revue Française de Science Politique* 60 (3): 467–491.

Lawanson, T. and Agunbiade, M. (2018). Land governance and megacity projects in Lagos, Nigeria: the case of Lekki free trade zone. *Area Development and Policy* 3 (1): 114–131.

Lawhon, M., Ernstson, H., and Silver, J. (2014). Provincializing urban political ecology: towards a situated UPE through African urbanism: Provincialising urban political ecology. *Antipode* 46 (2): 497–516. https://doi.org/10.1111/anti.12051.

Le Bris, E. (1987). Usages d'espaces et dynamique du front d'urbanisation dans les quartiers périphériques de Lomé. In: *Famille et résidence dans les villes africaines* (ed. E. Le Bris, A. Marie, A. Osmont and A. Sinou), 13–70. Paris: L'Harmattan.

Leclercq, R. (2022). How does water behave? Unstable milieu and stable Agencements in Dakar's flooded suburbs. *Urban Planning* 7 (1): 21–31.

Lefebvre, H. (1968). *Le droit à la ville*. Paris: Anthropos.

Lefebvre, H. (1970). *La révolution urbaine*. Paris: Gallimard.

Lefebvre, H. (1974). *La production de l'espace*. Paris: Anthropos.

Lihoussou, M. (2017). Dysfonctionnements et entraves à la circulation en Afrique de l'ouest: l'exemple du corridor Abidjan-Cotonou. *Les Cahiers Scientifiques du Transport* 72: 43–66.

Lombard, J. (1953). Cotonou Ville Africaine. *Études dahoméennes* 10: 5–214.

Macé, M. (2019). *Nos cabanes*. Verdier.

Mahadevan, P. (2019). *Sand Mafias in India, Disorganized Crime in a Growing Economy*. The Global Initiative Against Transnational Organized Crime.

Mains, D. (2019). *Under Construction: Technologies of Development in Urban Ethiopia*. Duke University Press.

Marchand, T. H. (2016). The Art of Mud Building in Djenné, Mali. Room One Thousand, 4. Retrieved from https://escholarship.org/uc/item/9zc3j356.

Marcus, G. (1995). Ethnography in/of the world system: the emergence of multi-sited ethnography. *Annual Review of Anthropology* 24: 95–117.

Marsh, A.T.M., Heath, A., Walker, P. et al. (2020). Discussion of "earth concrete. Stabilization revisited". *Cement and Concrete Research* 130: 105991. https://doi.org/10.1016/j.cemconres.2020.105991.

Mbembe, A. (2014). Afrofuturisme et devenir-nègre du monde. *Politique Africaine* 136 (4): 121–133.

Mbembe, A. (2015). Africa in the new century, *CityScapes*, https://cityscapesmagazine.com/articles/africa-in-the-new-century.

Mbembe, A. (2020). *Brutalisme*. Paris: La Découverte.

Mbembe, A. and Nuttall, S. (2004). Writing the world from an African Metropolis. *Public Culture* 16 (3): 347–372. https://doi.org/10.1215/08992363-16-3-347.

Mbembe, A., Sarr, F. (Eds.). (2017). *Écrire l'Afrique-monde: les Ateliers de la pensée, Dakar et Saint-Louis du Sénégal, 2016*. [Paris]: Dakar, Sénégal: Philippe Rey; Jimsaan.

McCann, E. and Ward, K. (2011). *Mobile Urbanism: Cities and Policymaking in the Global Age*. Minnesota: University of Minnesota Press.

McFarlane, C. (2011). *Learning the City: Knowledge and Translocal Assemblage*. Wiley-Blackwell https://doi.org/10.1002/9781444343434.

McKinsey Global Institute (2010). *Lions on the move: The progress and potential of African economies*, McKinsey Global Institute Report, June. McKinsey & Company. Available at: https://www.mckinsey.com/featured-insights/middle-east-and-africa/lions-on-the-move.

Médard, J.F. (1991). L'État néo-patrimonial en Afrique noire. In: *États d'Afrique noire: Formation, mécanisme et crise* (ed. J.-F. Médard), 323–353. Paris: Karthala.

Melly, C. (2013). Ethnography on the road: infrastructural vision and the unruly present in contemporary Dakar. *Africa* 83 (3): 385–402.

Melly, C. (2017). *Bottleneck: Moving, Building, and Belonging in an African City*. University of Chicago Press.

Mendelsohn, B. (2018). Making the urban coast: a geosocial Reading of land, sand, and water in Lagos, Nigeria. *Comparative Studies of South Asia, Africa and the Middle East* 38 (3): 455–472.

Mengin, C. and Godonou, A. (2013). *Porto-Novo: Patrimoine et développement*. Paris/Porto-Novo: Publications de la Sorbonne/École du patrimoine africain.

Mercer, C. (2014). Middle class construction: domestic architecture, aesthetics and anxieties in Tanzania. *The Journal of Modern African Studies* 52 (2): 227–250.

Mercer, C. (2020). Boundary work: becoming middle class in suburban Dar Es Salaam. *International Journal of Urban and Regional Research* 44 (3): 521–536. https://doi.org/10.1111/1468-2427.12733.

Meth, P., Goodfellow, T., Todes, A., and Charlton, S. (2021). Conceptualizing African urban peripheries. *International Journal of Urban and Regional Research* 45 (6): 985–1007.

Meuser, P. and Dalbai, A. (ed.) (2021). *Architectural Guide Sub-Saharan Africa.* Berlin: DOM publishers.

Migozzi, J. (2020). Selecting Spaces, Classifying People: The Financialization of Housing in the South African City. *Housing Policy Debate* 30 (4): 640–660.

Miller, D. (2005). *Materiality.* Duke University Press.

Mintz, S.W. (1986). *Sweetness and Power: The Place of Sugar in Modern History.* New York: Penguin Books.

Mitchell, T. (2011). *Carbon Democracy.* Verso, London, New-York.: Political Power in the Age of Oil.

Mizes, J.C. (2016). Who owns Africa's infrastructure? *Limn* 7: 2016. https://limn.it/articles/who-owns-africas-infrastructure-2.

Mizes, J. C. and Donovan, K. P. (2022). Capitalizing Africa: high finance from below. *Africa* 92 (4): 540–560.

Moghalu, K.C. (2013). *Emerging Africa. How the Global Economy's « Last Frontier » Can Prosper and Matter.* Londres: Penguin Books.

Mongeard, L. (2017). De la démolition à la production de graves recyclées : Analyse des logiques de proximité d'une filière dans l'agglomération lyonnaise. *Flux* 108 (2): 64–79.

Morton, D. (2019). *Age of Concrete. Housing and the Shape of Aspiration in the Capital of Mozambique*, New African histories. Athens: Ohio University Press.

Moser, S., Côté-Roy, L., and Korah, P.I. (2021). The uncharted foreign actors, investments, and urban models in African new city building. *Urban Geography* 43 (8): 1252–1259. https://doi.org/10.1080/02723638.2021.1916698.

Mukhopadhyay, P., Zérah, M.H., and Denis, E. (2020). Subaltern urbanization : Indian insights for urban theory. *International Journal of Urban and Regional Research* 44 (4): 582–598. https://doi.org/10.1111/1468-2427.12917.

Murray, M.J. and Myers, G.A. (2007). *Cities in Contemporary Africa*, 1e. Palgrave Macmillan.

Myers, G. (1999). Political ecology and urbanisation: Zanzibar's construction materials industry. *The Journal of Modern African Studies* 37 (1): 83–108.

Myers, G. (2011). *African Cities.* Alternative Visions of Urban Theory and Practice, Londres: Zed Books.

Myers, G. (2015). A world-Class City-region? Envisioning the Nairobi of 2030. *American Behavioral Scientist* 59 (3): 328–346.

Myers, G. (2020). *Rethinking Urbanism: Lessons from Postcolonialism and the Global South.* Bristol University Press.

Naipaul, V.S. (1979). *A Bend in the River.* Pan Macmillan.

N'Bessa, B. (1997). *Porto-Novo et Cotonou (Bénin): Origine et évolution d'un double urbain.* Thèse d'État: Université Michel de Montaigne-Bordeaux III.

N'goran, A., Fofana, M., and Akindès, F. (2020). Redéployer l'État par le marché : La politique des logements sociaux en Côte d'Ivoire. *Critique internationale* 89 (4): 75–93.

Nielsen, M. (2011). Futures within: reversible time and house-building in Maputo, Mozambique. *Anthropological Theory* 11 (4): 397–423. https://doi.org/10.1177/1463499611423871.

Nieswand, B. (2014). The burgers' paradox: migration and the transnationalization of social inequality in southern Ghana. *Ethnography* 15 (4): 403–425. https://doi.org/10.1177/1466138113480575.

Njeru, J. (2006). The urban political ecology of plastic bag waste problem in Nairobi, Kenya. *Geoforum* 37 (6): 1046–1058. https://doi.org/10.1016/j.geoforum.2006.03.003.

Noret, J. (2010). *Deuil et funérailles dans le Bénin méridional.* Enterrer à tout prix: Éditions de l'Université de Bruxelles.

Nugent, P. (2021). Lomé and Aflao: ambivalent affinity at the Ghana-Togo border. In: *Twin Cities: Borders, Urban Communities and Relationships over Time* (ed. J. Garrard and E. Mikhailova). Routledge.

Nyuur, R. and Sobiesuo, P. (2016). The history and development of brewing and the beer industry in Africa. In: *Brewing, Beer and Pubs* (ed. I. Cabras, D. Higgins and D. Preece), 145–161. London: Palgrave Macmillan.

OECD/UNECA/AfDB (2022). *Africa's Urbanisation Dynamics 2022: The Economic Power of Africa's Cities, West African Studies.* OECD Publishing. Paris. https://doi.org/10.1787/3834ed5b-en.

Obeng-Odoom, F. (2015). Informal real estate brokerage as a socially-embedded market for economic development in Africa. In: *Real Estate, Construction and Economic Development in Emerging Market Economies* (ed. R.T. Abdulai, F. Obeng-Odoom, E. Ochieng and V. Maliene). London.: Routledge.

Okorafor, N. (2014). *Lagoon.* London: Hodder.

Osmont, A. (1995). *La Banque mondiale et les villes: Du développement à l'ajustement.* Paris: Karthala.

Ouma, S. (2020). 'Africapitalism' and the limits of any variant of capitalism. *Review of African Political Economy,* https://roape.net/2020/07/16/africapitalism-and-the-limits-of-any-variant-of-capitalism.

Page, B. and Mercer, C. (2012). Why do people do stuff? Reconceptualizing remittance behaviour in diaspora-development research and policy. *Progress in Development Studies* 12 (1): 1–18.

Page, B. and Sunjo, E. (2017). Africa's middle class: building houses and constructing identities in the small town of Buea, Cameroon. *Urban Geography* 39 (1): 75–103.

Parnell, S., Robinson, J. (2012). (Re)theorizing Cities from the Global South: Looking Beyond Neoliberalism. *Urban Geography* 33 (4): 593–617.

Parnell, S. and Pieterse, E. (2014). *Africa's Urban Revolution.* London: Zed Books.

Parnell, S., Pieterse, E., and Watson, V. (2009). Planning for cities in the global south: an African research agenda for sustainable human settlements. *Progress in Planning* 72: 233–241.

Peck, J. and Theodore, N. (2015). *Fast Policy: Experimental Statecraft at the Thresholds of Neoliberalism*. University of Minnesota Press http://data.rero.ch/01-R008167689/html?view=GE_V1.

Peck, J. and Tickell, A. (2002). Neoliberalizing space. *Antipode* 34 (3): 380–404. https://doi.org/10.1111/1467-8330.00247.

Péclard, D., Kernen, A., and Khan-Mohammad, G. (2020). États d'émergence. Le gouvernement de la croissance et du développement en Afrique. *Critique internationale* 4 (4): 9–27. https://doi.org/10.3917/crii.089.0012.

Peduzzi, P. (2014). Sand, Rare than one thinks, UNEP Global environmental Alert Service, www.heros.nl › dbdocs › file_60.

Pellow, D.N. (2007). *Resisting Global Toxics: Transnational Movements for Environmental Justice*. MIT Press.

Perec, G. (1997). *Species of Spaces and Other Pieces*. Penguin Classics.

Pilo', F. (2020). Material politics: utility documents, claims-making and construction of the "deserving citizen" in Rio de Janeiro. *City & Society* 32 (1): 71–92. https://doi.org/10.1111/ciso.12244.

Pilo', F. and Jaffe, R. (2020). Introduction: the political materiality of cities. *City & Society* 32 (1): 8–22. https://doi.org/10.1111/ciso.12252.

Pinard, E. (2016). From compound houses to villas: the incremental transformation of Dakar's urban landscape. *Open House International* 41 (2): 15–22.

Pinson, G., Morel Journel, C. (2017). *Debating the Neoliberal City*. Routledge. https://halshs.archives-ouvertes.fr/halshs-01586747.

Piot, C. (1999). *Remotely Global: Village Modernity in West Africa*. Chicago: University of Chicago Press.

Pitcher, A. (2012). Lions, tigers, and emerging markets: Africa's development dilemmas. *Current History* 111 (745): 163–168.

Pitcher, A. (2017). Entrepreneurial governance and the expansion of public investment funds in Africa. In: *Africa in World Politics: Constructing Political and Economic Order*, 6e (ed. J.W. Harbeson and D. Rothchild), 45–68. Boulder, CO: Westview Press.

Pliez, O. (2007). Des Jeans chinois dans les rues du Caire, ou les espaces discrets de la mondialisation. *Mappemonde* 88 (4): 14.

Pollio, A., Cirolia, L.R., and Pieterse, E. (2022). *Infrastructure Financing in Africa: Overview, Research Gaps, and Urban Research Agenda*. Cape Town: African Centre for Cities & Alfred Herrhausen Gesellschaft.

Prahalad, C.K. and Hammond, A. (2002). Serving the World's poor, profitably. *Harvard Business Review* 80 (9): 48–59.

Quayson, A. (2014). *Oxford Street, Accra: City Life and the Itineraries of Transnationalism*. Durham: Duke University Press.

Rams, D. (2021). *Scrap-worlds in Ghana: assembling migrant livelihoods, metal markets and international intervention* PhD University of Lausanne.

Rateau, M. and Choplin, A. (2021). Electrifying urban Africa: energy access, city-making and globalisation in Nigeria and Benin. *International Development Planning Review* https://doi.org/10.3828/idpr.2021.4.

Ravelli, Q. (2017). *Les briques rouges. Dette, logement et luttes sociales en Espagne.* Paris: Éditions Amsterdam.

Ricciotti, R. (2020). *Le béton en garde à vue : Manifeste architectural et théâtral.* Edition Textuel.

Robinson, J. (2002). Global and world cities: a view from off the map. *International Journal of Urban and Regional Research* 26 (3): 531–554.

Robinson, J. (2006). *Ordinary Cities: Between Modernity and Development.* London: Routledge.

Robinson, J. (2013). The urban now: Theorising cities beyond the new. *European Journal of Cultural Studies* 16: 659–677.

Robinson, J. (2016). Thinking cities through elsewhere: Comparative tactics for a more global urban studies. *Progress in Human Geography* 40 (1): 3–29.

Robinson, J. and Roy, A. (2016). Debate on global urbanisms and the nature of urban theory. *International Journal of Urban and Regional Research* 40 (1): 181–186.

Rohat, G., Flacke, J., Dosio, A. et al. (2019). Projections of human exposure to dangerous heat in African cities under multiple socioeconomic and climate scenarios. *Earth's Future* 7 (5): 528–546. https://doi.org/10.1029/2018EF001020.

Rosenfeld, M. (2017). *Car connection : La filière euro-africaine de véhicules d'occasion.* Paris: Karthala.

Roy, A. (2005). Urban informality: toward an epistemology of planning. *Journal of the American Planning Association* 71 (2): 147–158. https://doi.org/10.1080/01944360508976689.

Roy, A. (2009). The 21st-century Metropolis: new geographies of theory. *Regional Studies* 43 (6): 819–830. https://doi.org/10.1080/00343400701809665.

Roy, A. (2011). Slumdog cities: rethinking subaltern urbanism. *International Journal of Urban and Regional Research* 35 (2): 223–238. https://doi.org/10.1111/j.1468-2427.2011.01051.x.

Roy, A. and Ong, A. (ed.) (2011). *Worlding Cities: Asian Experiments and the Art of Being Global.* Wiley-Blackwell https://doi.org/10.1002/9781444346800.

Rubbers, B. (2019). Mining Boom, Labour Market Segmentation and ocial inequality in the Congolese Copperbelt. Development and Change. https://onlinelibrary.wiley.com/doi/abs/10.1111/dech.12531.

Sahakian, M. (2014). *Keeping Cool in Southeast Asia : Energy Consumption and Urban Air-Conditioning.* Palgrave Macmillan UK. https://doi.org/10.1057/9781137308832

Sarr, F. (2020). *Afrotopia.* Minneapolis: University of Minnesota Press.

Sawyer, L. (2016). *PLOTTING the prevalent but undertheorised residential areas of Lagos. Conceptualising a process of urbanisation through grounded theory and comparison,* ETH Zürich PhD dissertation, https://doi.org/10.3929/ethz-a-010898517.

Sawyer, L., Schmid, C., Streule, M., and Kallenberger, P. (2021). Bypass urbanism: re-ordering center-periphery relations in Kolkata, Lagos and Mexico City. *Environment and Planning A: Economy and Space* https://doi.org/10.1177/0308518X20983818.

Schmidt, W., Otieno, M., Olonade, K. et al. (2020). Innovation potentials for construction materials with specific focus on the challenges in Africa. *RILEM Technical Letters* 5: 63–74.

Schorch, P., Saxer, M., and Elders, M. (ed.) (2020). *Exploring Materiality and Connectivity in Anthropology and beyond*. London: UCL Press https://doi.org/10.14324/111.9781787357488.

Schubert, J., Engel, U., and Macamo, E.S. (ed.) (2018). *Extractive Industries and Changing State Dynamics in Africa: Beyond the Resource Curse*. London, UK: Routledge.

Seignobos, C. (2018). *Des mondes oubliés: Carnets d'Afrique*. Paris: IRD Éditions.

Sémond, P., Gauzin-Müller, D., Doat, P. et al. (2016). *Architecture en terre d'aujourd'hui: les techniques de la terre crue*, 10. Grenoble: AE&CC-ENSAG.

Sennett, R. (2018). *Building and Dwelling: Ethics for the City*. Straus and Giroux: Farrar.

Shatkin, G. (2008). The City and the bottom line: urban megaprojects and the privatization of planning in Southeast Asia. *Environment and Planning A: Economy and Space* 40 (2): 383–401. https://doi.org/10.1068/a38439.

Sheppard, E., Leitner, H., and Maringanti, A. (2014). Provincializing Global Urbanism: A Manifesto. *Urban Geography* 34 (7): 893–900.

Silver, J. (2014). Incremental infrastructures: material improvisation and social collaboration across post-colonial Accra. *Urban Geography* 35 (6): 788–804. https://doi.org/10.1080/02723638.2014.933605.

Simay, P. (2006). *Capitales de la modernité, Walter Benjamin et la ville*. Paris: Edition de l'éclat.

Simmel, G. (2005). *Les grandes villes et la vie de l'esprit. In Philosophie de la modernité*. Paris: Payot.

Simone, A.M. (2004). People as infrastructure, intersecting fragments in Johannesburg. *Public Culture* 16 (3): 407–429.

Simone, A.M. and Pieterse, E. (2017). *New Urban Worlds: Inhabiting Dissonant Times*. London: Polity.

Simonetti, C. and Ingold, T. (2018). Ice and concrete: solid fluids of environmental change. *Journal of Contemporary Archaeology* 5 (1): 19–31.

Simonneau C. (2017). « Stratégies citadines d'accès au sol et réforme foncière au Bénin. La pluralité comme enjeu? », *Métropolitiques*, URL: https://www.metropolitiques.eu/Strategies-citadines-d-acces-au.html.

Simonnet, C. (2005). *Le béton: Histoire d'un matériau. Économie, technique, architecture*. Marseille: Éd. Parenthèses.

Sinou, A. (2011). *L'architecture afro-brésilienne de la côte du Golfe du Bénin, Un genre imparfait, entre ignorance et oubli*, 107–195. Riveneuve éditions: In Caroline gaultier. patrimoines oubliés de l'Afrique.

Sinou, A. and Agbo, B. (1995). *Le comptoir de Ouidah : Une ville africaine singulière*. Paris: Karthala.

Sinou, A. and Oloudé, B. (1988). *Porto-Novo, ville d'Afrique noire*. Parenthèses.

Sklair, L. (2017). *The Icon Project: Architecture, Cities, and Capitalist Globalization*. Oxford University Press.

Smith, C. (2020). Collapse. Fake buildings and gray development in Nairobi. *Focaal* 2020 (86): 11–23. https://doi.org/10.3167/fcl.2020.860102.

Smith, C. and Woodcraft, S. (2020). Introduction: tower block "failures"? High-rise anthropology. *Focaal* 2020 (86): 1–10.

Soares de Oliveira, R. (2007). *Oil and Politics in the Gulf of Guinea*. London: Hurst.

Soares de Oliveira, R. (2021) "Researching Africa and the Offshore World", Oxford Martin School working paper, 10 June 2021.

Söderström, O. (2014). *Cities in Relations: Trajectories of Urban Development in Hanoi and Ouagadougou*. John Wiley & Sons.

Sotindjo, S.D. (2010). *Cotonou l'explosion d'une capitale économique (1945–1985)*. Paris: L'Harmattan.

Spire, A. (2011). *L'Etranger et la ville en Afrique de l'Ouest*. Paris: Karthala.

Spire, A. and Choplin, A. (2018). Street vendors facing urban beautification in Accra (Ghana): eviction, relocation and formalization. *Articulo - Journal of Urban Research* 17–18. https://doi.org/10.4000/articulo.3443.

Spire, A. and Pilo', F. (2021). The politics of urban resettlement. Spatial governmentality, "soft constraints," and everyday life in Lomé, Togo. In: *Urban Resettlements in the Global South: Lived Experiences of Housing and Infrastructure between Displacement and Relocation* (ed. R. Beier, A. Spire and M. Bridonneau). London; New York: Routledge/Taylor & Francis Group.

Steck, J.-F. (2005). Abidjan et le Plateau: quels modèles urbains pour la vitrine du « miracle » ivoirien? *Géocarrefour* 80-3 (2005): 215–226.

Steel, G., Van Noorloos, F., and Otsuki, K. (2019). Urban land grabs in Africa? *Built Environment* 44 (4): 389–396.

Stocking, G. (1987). *Victorian Anthropology*. New York: The Free Press.

Storper, M. and Scott, A.J. (2016). Current debates in urban theory: a critical assessment. *Urban Studies* 53 (6): 1114–1136. https://doi.org/10.1177/0042098016634002.

Streule, M., Karaman, O., Sawyer, L., and Schmid, C. (2020). Popular urbanization: conceptualizing urbanization processes beyond informality. *International Journal of Urban and Regional Research* 44 (4): 652–672. https://doi.org/10.1111/1468-2427.12872.

Swyngedouw, E. (2004). *Social Power and the Urbanization of Water: Flows of Power*. Oxford, UK: Oxford University Press.

Swyngedouw, E. and Heynen, N.C. (2003). Urban political ecology, justice and the politics of scale. *Antipode* 35 (5): 898–918. https://doi.org/10.1111/j.1467-8330.2003.00364.x.

Sylvanus, N. (2016). *Patterns in Circulation: Cloth, Gender, and Materiality in West Africa*. Chicago; London: The University of Chicago Press.

Táíwò, O.O. (2022). *Reconsidering Reparations: Worldmaking in the Case of Climate Crisis*. New York: Oxford University Press.

Tall, M. (2009). *Investir dans la ville Africaine. Les émigrés et l'habitat à Dakar*. Paris: Karthala.

Tassi, S. (2019). *Du dedans au dehors Connexions à partir d'un espace public d'une ville multiple: Ajace, Xogbonú, Porto-Novo (Sud-Bénin)*, Thèse de doctorat, Université libre de Bruxelles.

Taussig, M. (2004). *My Coicaine Museaum*. Chicago, London: The University of Chicago Press.

Terrefe, B. (2020). Urban layers of political rupture : the 'new' politics of Addis Ababa's megaprojects. *Journal of Eastern Africa Studies* 14 (3): 375–395. https://doi.org/10.1080/17531055.2020.1774705.

The World Bank. (2009). *World Development Report 2009 : Reshaping Economic Geography*. World Bank. https://openknowledge.worldbank.org/handle/10986/5991

The World Bank. (2016). *Breaking down barriers : unlocking Africa's potential through vigorous competition policy*. The World Bank. Retrieved March 18, 2020, from http://documents.worldbank.org/curated/en/243171467232051787/Breaking-down-barriers-unlocking-Africas-potential-through-vigorous-competition-policy.

Theunynck, S. (1994). *Economie de l'habitat et de la construction au Sahel*. Paris: L'Harmattan.

Tirado, R., Aublet, A., Laurenceau, S., and Habert, G. (2022). Challenges and opportunities for circular economy promotion in the building sector. *Sustainability* 14 (3): 1569.

Tsing, A.L. (2015). *The Mushroom at the End of the World: On the Possibility of Life in Capitalist Ruins*. Princeton, NJ: Princeton University Press.

Turner, J.F.C. (1976). *Housing by People: Towards Autonomy in Building Environments*. London: Marion Boyars.

UNEP (2019). *Sand and Sustainability: Finding New Solutions for Environmental Governance of Global Sand Resources*. GRID-Geneva: United Nations Environment Programme, Geneva, Switzerland.

UNEP (2022). *Sand and Sustainability: 10 Strategic Recommendations to Avert a Crisis*, GRID-Geneva: United NationsEnvironment Programme (UNEP). https://wedocs.unep.org/20.500.11822/38362.

UN-Habitat (2003). *The Challenge of Slums: Global Report on Human Settlements, 2003*. Earthscan Publications.

UN-Habitat (2012). *State of the World's Cities Report 2012/2013: Prosperity of Cities*. United Nations Human Settlements Programme (UN-Habitat).

Van Beemen, O. (2019). *Heineken in Africa. A Multinational Unleashed*. Hurst.

Van Damme, H. (2018). Concrete material science : past, present, and future innovations. *Cement and Concrete Research* 112: 5–24. https://doi.org/10.1016/j.cemconres.2018.05.002.

Van Damme, H. and Houben, H. (2018). Earth concrete. Stabilization revisited. *Cement and Concrete Research* 114: 90–102. https://doi.org/10.1016/j.cemconres.2017.02.035.

Van Noorloos, F. and Kloosterboer, M. (2018). Africa's new cities. The contested future of urbanisation. *Urban Studies* 55 (6): 1223–1241. https://doi.org/10.1177/0042098017700574.

Van Noorloos, F., Cirolia, L.R., Friendly, A. et al. (2020). Incremental housing as a node for intersecting flows of city-making: rethinking the housing shortage in the global south. *Environment and Urbanization* 32 (1): 37–54. https://doi.org/10.1177/0956247819887679.

Vandermeeren, O. (2020). *Construire en terre au Sahel aujourd'hui*. Museo.

Vellinga, M., Oliver, P., and Bridge, A. (2007). *Atlas of Vernacular Architecture of the World*. Abingdon, Oxon; New York: Routledge.

Verdeil, E. (2014). The energy of revolts in Arab cities: the case of Jordan and Tunisia. *Built Environment* 40 (1): 128–139. https://doi.org/10.2148/benv.40.1.128.

Walls, R.S., Maseland, J., Rochell, K., and Spaliviero, M. (2018). *The State of African Cities 2018. The Geography of African Investment (No. HS/053/18E)*. Nairobi: UN-Habitat.

Walther, O. (2015). Business, brokers and Borders: the structure of west African trade networks. *The Journal of Development Studies* 51 (5): 603–620.

Warnier, J.P. (1999). *Construire la culture matérielle*. Paris: PUF.

Watson, V. (2014). African urban fantasies: dreams or nightmares? *Environment and Urbanization* 26 (1): 215–231. https://doi.org/10.1177/0956247813513705.

Watson, V. (2020). Digital visualisation as a new driver of urban change in Africa. *Urban Planning* 5 (2): https://doi.org/10.17645/up.v5i2.2989.

Watts J. (2019). Concrete: the most destructive material on Earth. *The Guardian*, https://www.theguardian.com/cities/2019/feb/25/concrete-the-most-destructive-material-on-earth.

White L (2015). The case of cement. In McNamee T, Pearson M and Boer W, *African Investing in Africa: Understanding Business and Trade, Sector by Sector*. Hampshire: Palgrave Macmillan.

Wiegratz J. (2018). The Great Lacuna: Capitalism in Africa. *Review of African Political Economy*, http://roape.net/2018/10/19/the-great-lacuna-capitalism-in-africa.

Windapo, A.O. and Rotimi, J.O. (2012). Contemporary issues in building collapse and its implications for sustainable development. *Buildings* 2 (3): 283–299.

Yates, D. (2012). *The Scramble for African Oil: Oppression, Corruption and War for Control of Africa's Natural Resources*. London: Pluto Press.

Zola., E. (2006). *The fat and the thin: the Belly of Paris*. Project Gutenberg. *[1st edition 1873]*

Index

Concrete City: Material Flows and Urbanization in West Africa, First Edition. Armelle Choplin.
© 2023 John Wiley & Sons Ltd. Published 2023 by John Wiley & Sons Ltd.